FOUR COMEDIES BY
CHARLES MACKLIN

PORTRAIT OF MACKLIN (*aet. sua* 93) by OPIE

(*By courtesy of the Garrick Club*)

Four Comedies by Charles Macklin

LOVE À LA MODE   THE TRUE-BORN IRISHMAN

THE SCHOOL FOR HUSBANDS   THE MAN OF THE WORLD

Edited, and with a
Biographical and Critical Sketch
of Macklin, by

J. O. BARTLEY
M.A., D.LIT.
Senior Lecturer in English
at the University College of Swansea

SIDGWICK & JACKSON · LONDON
in association with
ARCHON BOOKS · HAMDEN, CONNECTICUT

To
AMÉLIE AND DIXON
BOYD

Acknowledgements

I acknowledge, with dutiful thanks, permission from the Henry E. Huntington Library to print, from the Larpent MS., *The School for Husbands* for the first time; but regretfully note that permission even to quote shortly from the other MSS. of Macklin's comedies in the Larpent Collection has not been obtainable.

My very special thanks are due to the National Library of Ireland for generous and never-failing help over a long period; and I am also grateful to the British Museum Reading Room and Department of Prints and Drawings, to the Gabrielle Enthoven Collection at the Victoria and Albert Museum, to the Library of the University College of Swansea, and to those libraries which have made books available under the Inter-Library Loan Scheme.

I am deeply indebted to the Garrick Club who have allowed me full use of their MS. of *Love à la Mode*, and have also given permission to reproduce two portraits from their collection and a page of the MS. The other illustrations are thanks to the courtesy of the British Museum and the Gabrielle Enthoven Collection.

I am grateful for the privilege of reading an unpublished (1952) thesis by Professor Denis Donoghue, and to Messrs. Sidgwick and Jackson for the interest and care which have made this edition possible.

Last but not least, I most gladly acknowledge assistance of various kinds from the following, and thank them for the trouble they have taken: Miss K. Barker, Miss J. H. Berrow, Mr. R. Bevis, Mrs. I. Bisson, Professor D. Greene, Dr. R. B. McDowell, Maelseachlainn (C. F. MacLoughlin), Dr. E. MacLysaght, Professor C. J. L. Price, Dr. J. G. Simms, and the Directors of the Bristol Old Vic and Pitlochry Festival Theatres.

J. O. B.

Contents

Illustrations

Editor's Note

The following writings are directly relevant, as sources or commentary, to the present work. When an abbreviated reference is given in parentheses, it is used throughout the footnotes.

W. W. Appleton: *Charles Macklin, An Actor's Life*, Harvard University Press, Cambridge, Mass., and Oxford University Press, London, 1961.
(Cited as *Appleton*)

J. O. Bartley: *Teague, Shenkin, and Sawney*, Cork University Press, Cork, 1954. (Cited as *TSS*.)
'Macklin', in *Enciclopedia dello Spettacolo*, Rome, 1962.

F. Congreve: *Authentic Memoirs of Mr. Charles Macklin, Comedian*, Barker, London, 1798.

W. Cooke: *Memoirs of Charles Macklin*, Asperne, London, 1804.

J. T. Kirkman: *Memoirs of the Life of Charles Macklin*, Lackington, Allen, London, 1799.

D. MacMillan: 'The Censorship in the Case of Macklin's *Man of the World*', *Huntington Library Bulletin*, October, 1936.

W. Matthews: 'The Piracies of Macklin's *Love à la Mode*', *Review of English Studies*, Vol. X, 1934.

E. A. Parry: *Charles Macklin*, Kegan Paul, London, 1891.
(Cited as *Parry*.)

The MSS. of all Macklin's extant plays (except *Love à la Mode*), as submitted to the Lord Chamberlain for licensing, are in the Larpent Collection in the Henry E. Huntington Library, San Marino, California.

Part One

CHARLES MACKLIN

A Biographical and Critical Sketch

Introduction

Charles Macklin was one of the most notable theatrical figures of the eighteenth century. Difficult as it is to recapture the quality of any actor after his death, even with modern technical facilities, something can be got from contemporary records, incomplete though they may be; but in any attempt to do so after more than a century and a half some use of imagination is unavoidable. There is a better chance of success in the case of such an unusually individual and forceful character, powerful in controversy, and a highly successful practitioner in more than one branch of the dramatic art. One might place Macklin as second only to Garrick in an age of great British acting, and his career was much longer and his experience much more varied than that of the English Roscius, who, theatrically, was born with silver in his mouth. Macklin anticipated Garrick in opposing the declamatory style in vogue early in the century, and he was an outstanding teacher of acting. Also, though his dramatic writing falls short of the best work of his compatriots, Farquhar, Goldsmith and Sheridan, he was the author of the best of eighteenth-century farces and of an outstanding comedy: some of his other work is far from negligible.

He has, in fact, been surprisingly neglected. A short biography by Francis Congreve, and longer ones by James Kirkman and William Cooke appeared soon after his death: these—of which Congreve's is the best—tend to be gossipy and unreliable, but for some things they are all we have to depend on. Edward Parry made some corrections, but added little, in the *Life* which he wrote for William Archer's 'Eminent Actors' series, nearly a century later. The present writer wrote the article in *Enciclopedia dello Spettacolo* and has lectured on him to the Society for Theatre Research; but the first full and scholarly biography was William Appleton's *Charles Macklin* in 1961.[1] Since then, more interest has been shown.

Macklin was of old Irish native stock. His early years were spent under the rigour of the penal laws at a time when it was with difficulty that any native and especially Catholic Irishman—except for a few

[1] General matter to be found in the biographies is not referenced in these notes.

privileged persons—who had ambitions outside commerce (or even within it) could achieve the smallest part of them without emigration. Many Irishmen sought openings overseas, many of them in Continental military service; many also in England and not a few in the theatre, then, as always, very much a community of its own. No successful Irish dramatist showed himself before George Farquhar—unless we count Congreve who was Irish only in education: no important Irish actor appeared on the English stage before William Bowen, who flourished up to 1715: but many followed them. It was the cream of Ireland which tended to emigrate. Writing of diet in *The Wealth of Nations* in 1776,[1] Adam Smith says: 'The common people of Scotland, who are fed with oatmeal, are in general neither so strong or so handsome as the same rank of people in England who are fed with wheaten bread. . . . But it seems to be otherwise with potatoes. The chairmen, porters, and coal heavers in London, and those unfortunate women who live by prostitution, the strongest men and the most beautiful women perhaps in the British dominions, are said to be, the greater part of them, from the lowest rank of people in Ireland, who are generally fed with this root'. Although Adam Smith's dietetic deduction may not hold water, it speaks to the facts: just as the strongest and most beautiful emigrated, so did the best equipped and most gifted in other ways. And the actor's profession calls for both physical and mental talent. In addition to Macklin—himself of very powerful physique—London audiences during the century saw such Irish stars as Bowen, James Quin, Spranger Barry and his wife, Laurence Clinch, Peg Woffington, John Moody, John Johnstone, Anthony Rock and Elizabeth Younge, as well as many lesser lights.

Origins

The conflicting accounts given by his first biographers leave Macklin's parentage and early life largely matters of speculation and probability. Not much is known for certain about him before he settled in London in 1733. That, within a month or two of his birth in 1690, he was rushed away from the Battle of the Boyne, where his father was fighting on the losing Jacobite side, in a turf-creel carried by a donkey, is altogether too good to be true. It is true that, as the

[1] I, pp. 201–2.

MacLOUGHLIN
(*Tirconnell*)

MacLOUGHLIN
(*formerly O'Melaghlin*)

THE COATS OF ARMS OF THE TWO FAMILIES
MacLAUGHLIN *or* MacLOUGHLIN

The Tirconnell motto *Cuimhnigh ar do gheallamhnacha* may be
translated 'Be mindful of your promises'

report of his mother's death at Cloncurry in 1759 gave her age as ninety-nine, he could have been born in 1690; but 1699 is to be accepted. His memorial in St. Paul's, Covent Garden, says he was 107 when he died; but his coffin-plate gave ninety-seven, and he himself agreed with the coffin's plate. Did he, over the years, represent himself as ten years younger than he was? It seems unlikely. Nevertheless, there is probably a basis of truth in the quasi-legendary accounts of his ancestry and youth, and they could be dismissed too easily.

Kirkman and Cooke both assert—however inconsistent and confusing they may otherwise be—that his father was a landowner and one of the real unmixed old Irish; but Appleton,[1] who is not at his best when he is concerned with Irish matters, accepts the suggestion that he was of humble parentage, and implies that he so regarded himself. By the time he appears in English theatrical records, he had altered his name to Mechlin and later Macklin, presumably because the English found it difficult to get Cathal MacLaughlin right. There were two families of Milesian-descended MacLaughlins in Ireland.[2] One, whose original name was Ó Maoilsheachlainn,[3] later O'Melaghlin, produced kings of Meath, notably Malachy II, who 'wore the collar of gold which he won from her proud invader'. The other, originally MacLocháinn, had special connections with the Inishowen peninsula in north-east Donegal, where the name is only less frequent than O'Dogherty, under whose chiefry the MacLochláinns held their land.

It is doubtful to which of these families Macklin belonged. His statement, late in life, that had he been able to prove himself his father's son he would have been entitled to an estate in Ireland, would incline to the O'Melaghlins rather than the MacLochláinns, as the latter had suffered more from internal wars and outside aggression. Moreover, the family tree of the O'Melaghlins would not exclude his possible descent from one of them, and the name Cathal (Charles) is not infrequent. On the other hand, Charles Macklin was most probably

---

[1] Cf. *Appleton*, p. 2, etc.

[2] For Irish names, here and elsewhere, cf. E. MacLysaght, *Irish Families* (1957) and *More Irish Families* (1960).

[3] In a personal communication, the present head of this family confirms the old Irish aristocratic status of both; affirms the relation between such a background and Macklin's character and behaviour; considers that Appleton has been too ready to reject the implications of Cooke and Kirkman because of inconsistency of detail; and believes that Macklin could not well, when young, have escaped hearing much about family history and Irish tradition.

born at Culdaff in Inishowen. After Cahir O'Dogherty's abortive rebellion in 1608, James I granted Inishowen to Sir Arthur Chichester as part of the plantation of Ulster: a very few rebels were pardoned, but they included MacLochláinns, and fifty years later, according to the records, several of the name, described as gentlemen, held land in Inishowen. So, while much of the biographer's embroidery may be dismissed, and no matter from which family he came, there is good reason to accept that after the Boyne Macklin's father did suffer under the penal laws, and did belong to the old Irish gentry to whom the English were *parvenus*. Irish memories are long, and as late as the 1840s it was not uncommon for Irishmen in the depths of poverty to bequeath land from which their ancestors, euphemistically speaking, had been expropriated. No Irishman with such a background would have considered himself of low origin, quite the contrary: and it fits in with and helps understanding of the facts of his character and behaviour.

It is said that his widowed mother (*née* O'Flanagan—an ancient family, once hereditary stewards to the kings of Connacht) married a Protestant, Luke O'Meally,[1] who kept the Eagle tavern in Werburgh Street, near Dublin Castle, and that he was sent to a school kept by a Scot called Nicolson. Kirkman's suggestion that Macklin's antipathy to the Scots arose from his master's harshness does not tally with his own friendly reference to Nicolson in his commonplace book. If he played Monimia in a school performance of Otway's *Orphan*—and played it well—it was an odd choice of part for one of his physique, unless he was a small boy at the time. It is certainly unlikely that in later life he succeeded in impersonating a woman so well that he was admitted to share his elderly landlady's bed. But, on the other hand, Kirkman's story of how Macklin's uncle, Captain O'Flanagan of the Prussian service, was arranging for him to take up a commission in that army, but on their way left him alone in London which gave him the opportunity to run off with a troupe of strollers, though uncorroborated, does carry some conviction. A good many of the Irish Catholic gentry were officers in various European armies, and it is very likely that he did have some such relative, and no less likely that such employment seemed the right outlet for a strong and spirited young Irish-

[1] A Mayo family, noted for Gráine ni Mháille (Grace O'Malley), sixteenth-century pirate and rebel. In the form Granuaile, her name became one of the symbolic names of Ireland.

man—had he not been stage-struck. It is not fanciful to think that the very pleasant portrait of Sir Callaghan O'Brallaghan in *Love à la Mode* might be a reminiscence of Captain O'Flanagan, perhaps stirred by the meeting with an Irish Prussian officer which Cooke suggests as the genesis of Sir Callaghan.

Kirkman also rings true when he says, in effect, that Mrs. Mac-Laughlin's second marriage was a happy one, disturbed only by her strong Catholic beliefs (which she impressed on her son, who seems to have remained a Catholic till about 1740) as against Mr. O'Meally's Protestantism. Nor is there anything really inherently improbable about Macklin's having been disappointed, by the death of a wealthy relative, of the higher education promised him; so that, already being friendly with students of Trinity College whom he had hoped to join, he took the menial job of badgeman—i.e. licensed College messenger —in order to acquire some learning by, as it were, subjecting himself to 'the strong contagion of the gown'. Certainly he always showed strong intellectual tastes, devoted a great deal of effort to self-education—e.g. learning French—and came to have, in Dr. Johnson's phrase, considerable literature.

Early Career and Character

The stories of his early theatrical career include much that is obviously apocryphal. He must, however, have taken pains to overcome his Irish accent before he could succeed in the great variety of parts he was to play; that he had to do so may have helped to give him his obviously capable ear for dialect. Apparently, his Scottish accent was not quite perfect, but there is no suggestion that his English fell short. Irish could well have been his first language: presumably he was bilingual from an early age. We need not doubt that as a schoolboy he was noted for his physical prowess, diving from the masts of ships into the Liffey, and became, as an adult actor, 'a great fives player, a hard drinker, a great bruiser, and a general lover'.

In 1733 Macklin begot an illegitimate daughter—Maria, who was to become an actress of some repute—upon Ann Grace, who continued to act with him and whom he married in 1739. Their son John was born about 1750, and Ann died in 1758. Before long Macklin was living with Elizabeth Jones (who may have been his housekeeper), but did not marry her till 1778. The relationship was happy. Maria died in 1781 because, in her frequent breeches parts, she buckled her garter too tightly and brought on a fatal tumour 'which, from motives of delicacy, she would not suffer to be examined, till it had increased to an alarming size'! John Macklin was wild and irresponsible, and a continual drain on his father's resources. He was sent to India in 1769, but returned in disgrace in 1773. He idled, gambled, became a law student and gave it up, went to America as a soldier, and again returned in disgrace. His father suffered much sorrow and distress until, in 1790, John died of his excesses.

In spite of the uncertainties about his birth and early life, a coherent and psychologically convincing character emerges. His virtues and vices were largely those of the stock from which he came, with its traditional social outlook, 'aristocratic, regional, and personal, and all three to an extreme degree',[1] in spite of his having lost his social position and missed the education to which it and his abilities entitled him. He has been called litigious, and it is true he often went to law, but never frivolously. Cooke stresses that his obsession with legal rights 'arose more from a self-abhorrence of doing wrong, than any sinister or disputatious views'. He respected his own rights and those of others: when he had recourse to the law it was to defend his rights as actor and author, and he succeeded in establishing them: his Irish sense of logical justice would not allow him to seek solution in compromise. He was impatient, arrogant, violent, and proud; but he was also fair-minded, generous, benevolent, and honourable.

In the Theatre

The regular theatres in which Macklin performed and for which he wrote were very different from today's.[2] Even the largest of them were small, holding perhaps 600 early in the century, and reaching something like double that size by his last appearance in 1789. An actor facing the audience from the centre of the slightly raked stage, directly under the proscenium, would have before him a forestage extending twelve feet or more, with a small orchestra-pit beyond it, and

---

[1] Cf. Seán Ó Faoláin, *The Irish* (1947), p. 37.
[2] Cf. Allardyce Nicoll, *The Development of the Theatre* (1949) and Richard Southern, *The Georgian Playhouse* (1948).

8

on either hand a pair of doors (used for entrances and exits, internal or external according as the scene was indoor or outdoor) with openings above them at which characters could appear. Next he would see a pair of boxes abutting directly on the forestage, on the rail of which, if he wished, he could lean his elbow and chat to the occupants. From these, surrounding the benched pit on three sides, a tier of boxes would continue round the auditorium with another tier along each side above, and a gallery at the back. Behind him there would be a back-stage about equal to the forestage in depth, with rows of masking flats standing in the wings. But the most remarkable feature of this kind of stage was a series of four or more pairs of flats (or shutters), painted to represent various scenes, and sliding in grooves across the backstage, which could be run in from the wings at either side to meet in the middle. As well as using the doors, the actor could make an entrance or exit through the wings, or step backwards and have the shutters close to hide him, or be discovered by their opening. Such scene-changes were made in full view of the audience, for the proscenium curtain was rarely used except at the beginning and end of a piece. The forestage and auditorium were lit by hanging chandeliers, and there was some provision for lighting the scenery behind the proscen-ium from above or from the sides. Footlights were a late innovation (attributed to Garrick); and of course there was no question of altering the house-lights or of controlling any lighting more than a very little.

The audiences[1] were often rowdy, shouting, catcalling, or hissing: not infrequently there was fighting, and rioting on occasion. Drunk-en and even indecent incidents were far from unknown. Claques could ensure that a play would not be heard, and an actor who dis-pleased might be shouted down or rudely compelled to apologise on his knees. The actor's task was by no means easy: he had his occupa-tional risks. Macklin met with his fair share of them.

It seems likely that by about 1717 he had become a professional actor and before long was a regular member of the company playing the Bath-Bristol circuit. His first appearance in London may have been as early as 1725. He joined the Drury Lane company in 1733, left it for a short time, but within a year of rejoining it in 1734 had become one of its most important personalities.

---

[1] Cf. Allardyce Nicoll, *Early Eighteenth Century Drama* (1952), pp. 11–19, and *Late Eighteenth Century Drama* (1952), pp. 5–10.

Certain events in his life are illustrative. On 10 May 1735, in the greenroom at Drury Lane, Macklin was made up and ready to play Sancho in Fabian's *Trick for Trick*, only to find that Hallam had appropriated his wig. High words passed, and in a rage he struck out with the cane he carried for the part, and pierced Hallam's left eye. Charged with murder, he defended himself, and part of his statement throws a curious light on the customs of the time. 'His left side was towards me; but he turned about unluckily and my stick went into his eye. "Good God", said I, "what have I done?" and I threw the stick into the chimney. He sat down and said to Mr. Arne's son (who was dressed in woman's clothes) "Whip up your clothes, you little b—h, and urine in mine eye". But he could not, so I did.' Macklin was much distressed and solicitous about Hallam's welfare; but after his death the following day he concealed himself: one newspaper carried a story of his climbing out secretly by the theatre roof to avoid immediate arrest. He surrendered himself after the coroner's verdict of murder; was released on bail and so had time to prepare his defence, which he conducted very ably; was found guilty of manslaughter and sentenced to branding in the hand—a cold iron was probably used, as there is never any suggestion that he bore a scar. James Quin was among those actors who testified to the accused's 'quiet and peaceable disposition'—stretching a little in favour of a colleague: Quin himself, in 1718, had suffered the same verdict and punishment, having killed his compatriot, William Bowen, *se defendendo*. Then, about January 1738, Macklin annoyed the leading actor by the success of his clever comic business when he was playing Jerry Blackacre to Quin's Manly in Wycherley's *Plain Dealer*. Quin raged; Macklin was recalcitrant; Quin threw a piece of chewed apple into Macklin's face: Macklin gave him such a bashing that he only just managed to complete the play. This is the story as Macklin told it: the sequel is given in an unfathered anecdote[1] of how, after some ten years of estrangement, they found themselves, in the small hours, alone together at a tavern—the last of the party to remain above the surface. Macklin accepted Quin's gesture of reconciliation, called for another bottle, and at dawn took his unconscious colleague—a very heavy man—on his back and carried him home.

[1] Cf. *Parry*, pp. 40–1.

Relations with Garrick

Then there was the actors' strike of 1743. In the previous two years Garrick had risen to the top of the tree and at Drury Lane was at least equal in status to the older actor. Nevertheless, they were on very friendly terms, and had been for several years, Garrick being an exemplar of the more natural acting which Macklin had introduced against the traditional declamatory style represented by Quin. Fleetwood's incompetence as manager and patentee threatened the company's livelihood: they met at Garrick's instance and agreed to try, if possible, to set up together elsewhere, and to accept no terms from the patentee unless they all agreed. Kirkman says that Macklin wished to try a final discussion with Fleetwood before taking so desperate a step as secession, but was overruled by the others for fear their application for a licence at another theatre might be stymied. But the licence was refused, and they had to negotiate. Fleetwood's situation had not improved and his substitute company was weak. He was forced to yield much, but refused to reinstate Macklin on any conditions. Macklin called for adherence to the all-or-none agreement, but Garrick refused. We need not accept the evil motives which Kirkman ascribes to Garrick: but he did get and accept improved terms for himself and the others, and Macklin suffered. So, one surmises, did Garrick's conscience, for he offered to give Macklin a weekly gratuity out of his own pocket, and to get Mrs. Macklin £3 a week at Covent Garden with Rich. Macklin's Irish pride and strong sense of justice were outraged: a pamphlet war started; and there were partisan demonstrations in the theatre. Garrick (who, Cooke says, 'like a true politician, neither loved nor hated in the way of business') could of course claim that he had acted for the greatest good of the greatest number—but Macklin was in the right, and knew it, for Garrick had broken his 'solemn engagement'.

The British Inquisition

In 1754 Macklin entered upon an extraordinary project. He bade farewell to the stage, and set up a tavern-cum-lecture-room in Hart Street, Covent Garden, which he called 'The British Inquisition'. Twice a week, after the table-d'hôte, he proposed to lecture upon a theatrical or literary subject, with a debate to follow. His was, indeed, the first series of public lectures on Shakespeare ever given. Debating societies were popular. He was a noted public figure. The idea was new. At first, all went very well; but although Macklin was well-read, intelligent, and better qualified for the task than many with the formal education he lacked, his arrogance laid him open to ridicule and was no help on the one side, while his ignorance of business was damaging on the other. Foote's ungrateful (for he owed something to Macklin who had coached him when he commenced acting) witty heckling at the lectures and burlesque of them on the stage were the last straw. The enterprise was bankrupt in less than a year.

A score of years later, at Covent Garden, George Colman engaged Macklin to take over the parts of Macbeth and Richard III from 'Gentleman' Smith,[1] who had resigned: but Smith failed to make new arrangements for himself, and it was agreed that they should alternate the parts—a situation inevitably tense and productive of jealousy. A journalistic campaign, emanating from partisans of Smith and Garrick, anticipated Macklin's appearance as Macbeth on 23 October 1773, at which, though it was finally applauded, there was an undercurrent of sibilant hostility. At the second performance, a week later, he publicly accused the actors Reddish and Sparks of having hissed him personally. Denials were bandied to and fro; very public statements were made; and the father and mother of a row boiled up. The following week he just managed to carry the play through in spite of the organised claque, but at the fourth performance the theatre was the scene of riot and confusion, and little of the play was heard. For the time being Macklin's Macbeth was out. He charged Smith with procuring the hissers: Smith with his friend the notorious Henry Bate (Dudley)[2] called on him, raged, threatened violence, and proposed a duel. Macklin was not the man to refuse a challenge, even at his age, and Smith drew in his horns. He stated his position ironically and very characteristically in a letter dated 16 November: 'I declared that if Mr. Smith had asked a civil or reasonable account of the matter, I should have given it him with pleasure, for that I was really a great coward and hated fighting more than any one thing besides, in human

---

[1] William Smith (1730?–1819): the original and the best Charles Surface; a good comedian; competent in serious parts, but belonging to the declamatory school.

[2] The Rev. Henry Bate, later Sir Henry Bate Dudley, Bart. (1745–1824), 'the fighting parson'; in his younger days a scurrilous journalist, ready to answer for himself with fisticuffs.

dealings, yet that I still must confirm that I did write the account in question; nor unsay it, but on the contrary would defend it, and so I say still.'[1]   When he was to appear as Shylock on 18 November, his enemies had organised so successfully that, even in his greatest and most popular part, he was shouted down and called on to kneel and apologise, which he would not.   The play could not continue: some rioters began to break up the furnishings: Colman was compelled to announce his dismissal.   After some legal delays, he succeeded in bringing a King's Bench action against five persons for conspiracy 'to deprive him of his bread'.   Macklin was awarded his costs and accepted much less than he might have claimed as damages; namely that the defendants should take £100 of tickets for each of his own and his daughter's benefits, and another £100 on some night of his acting as a kind of compensation to the management.   Lord Mansfield, L.C.J., praised his honest, honourable, and handsome conduct, saying, 'You have met with great applause today: you never acted better.'   Lord Mansfield's statement of the law was important for the acting profession: applauding and hissing in the theatre is an unalterable right in expressing the natural sensations as they arise on what is seen and heard, but it is a crime to pervert this right in a preconceived design to drive an actor from the stage.   In 1780 Lord Mansfield gave judgment for Macklin against Colman for breach of contract: the settlement was for £500.

Macklin also was of some service to his fellow-authors by his firm and repeated insistence on the principle of a writer's exclusive right and property in his own works, a matter about which there was some legal uncertainty during the second half of the eighteenth century. Not only did he guard the script of *Love à la Mode* very jealously,[2] taking it into his own custody after rehearsals, and preventing copies from being made, but he also took forcible steps against unauthorised publication or performance.   When, in 1766, the first act was printed in the *Court Miscellany*,[3] Macklin took the publishers to law and was granted a perpetual injunction against their repeating the offence. Garrick and Tate Wilkinson were among those whom he threatened

---

[1] Autograph letter from Macklin to Smith: cf. R. J. Smith, *Collection . . . towards a History of the Stage*, in the British Museum.   The end of this letter is reproduced opposite p. 36.
[2] Cf. John O'Keeffe, *Recollections* (1826), II, pp. 314–16.
[3] Cf. W. Matthews, *The Piracies of Macklin's 'Love à la Mode'* (*Review of English Studies*, Vol. X, 1934).

with legal action for performing his work without permission, and he obtained injunctions against provincial and Irish managers for playing at the same game.

Variety of Roles

His acting career was remarkable for variety as well as length. The records show him to have played well over 200 parts between 1733 and 1789, and they are far from complete.   Of his first professional years Kirkman says: 'sometimes he was an architect, and knocked up the stage and seats in a barn; sometimes he wrote an opening prologue or a parting epilogue, for the company: at others he wrote a song, complimentary and adulatory of the village they happened to play in, which he always adapted to some sprightly popular air, and sung himself; and he often was champion, and stood forward to repress the persons who were accustomed to intrude upon, and be rude to the actors.   His circle of acting was more enlarged than Garrick's; for, in one night, he played *Antonio* and *Belvidera*, in *Venice Preserved*—Harlequin, in the entertainment—sung three humorous songs between the acts, and indulged the audience with an Irish jig between the play and the entertainment'—exaggerated, no doubt, but such was the life of the strolling Thespian.

Amid these exhibitions of divers talents, his eye must have been on the metropolis: he seems to have appeared at Lincoln's Inn Fields as early as 1725, and in a booth theatre at Southwark Fair in 1730, before he settled in London in 1733.   From this time, except for periods in Ireland, he worked in the London theatres, though he did occasionally pay short visits to the provinces.

Descriptions, portraits, and caricatures—all after he was middle-aged—show what he looked like: tall, very upright in carriage and powerful in build, with aquiline nose, jutting chin, and strongly marked features.   'I don't know about lines', said Quin, 'but there is a deal of cordage in his face', and again, when they were on bad terms, 'If God Almighty writes a legible hand, that man must be a villain'.[1]   His voice was somewhat harsh, but resonant, flexible, and expressive, and his personality forcefully projected.   'I wish, Your Majesty,' said Walpole, 'it were possible to find a recipe for frightening the House of

---

[1] Cf. *Parry*, p. 37.

Commons'. 'What do you think', George II replied, 'of sending them to the theatre to see the Irishman play Shylock?'[1]

Inevitably an actor of such singular appearance, powerful and individual personality, advancing years and great reputation tended to become typed. After his return in 1773 from Ireland, where he had spent much time for the previous twelve years, he limited himself to a few parts. Up to 1777 they were: Sir Archy in his own *Love à la Mode*; Shylock, Macbeth, Iago, and Richard III; Ben (with song) and Sir Paul Pliant in Congreve's *Love for Love* and *Double Dealer*; Sir Gilbert Wrangle and Sir Francis Wronghead in Cibber's *Refusal* and *Provoked Husband*; Lovegold in Fielding's *Miser*, and Sir John Brute in Vanbrugh's *Provoked Wife*. Thereafter he played Sir Francis Wronghead once, and otherwise only Shylock, Sir Archy, and Sir Pertinax in his own *Man of the World*. This process of limitation had begun during the fifties, by which time his reputation was established and he could begin to pick and choose. It is clear that he was most successful in parts which demanded strong and even harsh acting, and character if not caricature.

Earlier, however, his roles were extraordinarily varied. Coming up the hard way, unlike Garrick most of whose parts were leads, he had to begin by being an actor-of-all-work. Here are a few of the more important, picked out not quite at random: the first gravedigger, Osric, and Polonius; the first witch, Touchstone, and Mercutio; Foigard and Teague in Farquhar's *Beaux' Stratagem* and *Twin Rivals*; Jerry Blackacre in Wycherley's *Plain Dealer*; Petulant and Sir Wilful Witwoud, and Lord Froth, in Congreve's *Way of the World* and *Double Dealer*; Lord Foppington and Sir Novelty Fashion in Cibber's *Careless Husband* and *Love's Last Shift*, and Peachum in Gay's *Beggar's Opera*. Most of these were quite often repeated, so he must have done pretty well in them. The number of light, foppish, or weak characters—which one would have thought *a priori* foreign to his style—is surprising: but they are all character parts, and it is hard to imagine him in any part without a strong element of character.

Francis Gentleman, in 1770, had some interesting things to say about Macklin's acting.[2] His Polonius was 'far the best of many we have seen; he showed oddity, grafted upon the man of sense, and

---

[1] Cf. John Bernard, *Retrospections of the Stage* (1830), II, pp. 121–2.
[2] Cf. *The Dramatic Censor* (1770).

retained most of that scene at the beginning of the second act, which good sense and Shakespeare's friends, must lament the general omission of . . .'. (This speaks well for Macklin's perception; he must have seen how important this scene, showing how closely the Polonius family is bound together, is to the whole movement of *Hamlet*.) As Peachum, he was superior to any competitors for his 'general dryness, and a just, cynical turn of humour'. His Touchstone marked the meaning of the character very strongly, but wanted volubility. In Mercutio he was extremely well received, although miscast—'a saturnine cast of countenance, sententious utterance, hollow-toned voice, ill-suited to the whimsical Mercutio, who was metamorphosed into a mere cynic—but the author's sense was critically preserved'. As Don Lewis in Cibber's *Love Makes a Man*: 'Don Lewis is a very extraordinary creature; he seems to have a good nature, but then it appears to be merely founded on the spirit of opposition; he is perverse and positive, more of a humorist than an object of esteem; many of his expressions, though gross, are laughable; the mode of performing the part is a cynic dryness of expression which we are apt to think Mr. Macklin hit off better than any other performer'. As Faddle, in Moore's *Foundling*: 'he never had, in voice, figure, or features, much capability for the fop cast, yet struck out some things in Faddle, which we have not seen any body equal; particularly marking the obsequious knave all through'. As Sir Francis Wronghead: 'Beyond all doubt, he filled the author's ideas of the part, and conveyed them to the audience admirably; consequential stupidity sat well painted in his countenance, and brought laughable effects without the paltry resource of a grimace: when he affected to be very wise, a laborious emphatic slyness marked the endeavour humorously; while the puzzles between political and domestic concerns occasioned much food for merriment'. And in Iago, he showed 'pre-eminence for understanding the part and expressing it through the whole with equal and suitable merit . . . he has got the indisputable, involuntary applause of as many curses in Iago, as in Shylock'.

The Jew that Shakespeare Drew

Shylock was Macklin's greatest part, first played at Drury Lane on 14 February 1741, and repeated again and again throughout his career with immense success. As is well known, he restored Shakespeare's play to the theatre, ousting Lord Lansdowne's perversion, *The Jew of Venice*, which had held the stage since the beginning of the century; in it Shylock was a villainous buffoon, played by such leading broad comedians as Dogget. He may well have been offered the part because, up to this time, he had been more of a comedian than anything else; but—perhaps wisely—he concealed his reading of the part; at rehearsals he merely went through the moves and repeated the lines with little or no expression. When the first night came he played Shylock seriously; as a villain, but also as a human being, with all the force and power which he could bring to bear. After a quiet start, the applause became tumultuous and his triumph was complete. Alexander Pope is apocryphally alleged to have exclaimed, 'This is the Jew that Shakespeare drew'. He had established a new tradition for Shylock, amid the enthusiasm of the critics and his fellow-actors, and brought himself to the very top rank of his profession. Francis Gentleman was to write: 'he looks the part of Shylock as much better than any other actor as he plays it; in the level scenes his voice is most happily suited to that sententious gloominess of expression the author intended; which, with a sullen solemnity of deportment, marks the character strongly; in his malevolence, there is a forcible and terrifying ferocity: in the third act scene, where alternate passions reign, he breaks the tone of utterance and varies his countenance admirably; in the dumb action of the trial scene he is amazingly descriptive; and through the whole displays unequalled merit'. Towards the end of his life, when he had played Shylock for the last and well over the hundredth time, he recalled that first night of triumph in touching words: 'No money, no title could purchase what I felt. And let no man tell me what Fame will not inspire a man to do, and how far the attainment of it will not inspire his greatest labours. By God, Sir, though I was not worth £50 in the world at that time, let me tell you, I was Charles the Great for that night'.

Scottish Roles

In Macbeth, as already mentioned, circumstances were against him, yet he achieved more than a little; and, like his Shylock, it was a breach with the accepted. He made some sort of approximation to

Scottish dress, for himself at least, and did not wear a periwig. Contemporary illustrations show him in a court dress (presumably in certain scenes) and—caricatured—in a kind of tunic, with tartan stockings, a plaid hanging from his shoulders, a Scots bonnet, a claymore, and footwear nearer to brogues than boots. It was certainly far from authentic Scottish costume, but it was probably nearer the real thing than anything that had been seen on the stage since before the interregnum. Critics praised his understanding of the character, his intelligent reading, his judicious emphasis, and the coherent propriety of the whole conception—in spite of his age, which was beginning to show a little. He played the part again in 1775 and 1776 at Covent Garden. His other greatest parts were the two Scotsmen, Sir Archy and Sir Pertinax, in his own plays—strong characterisations, much more than caricatures, of Scottish pride, careerism, avarice, and cunning, which lent themselves readily to his *persona*: but of these more later.

Actor

It is not hard to imagine what sort of actor Macklin was. His Shylock preceded Garrick's famous début as Richard III by six months. Some years earlier he had established himself as the effective director at Drury Lane, where he had the opportunity of stressing the belief in natural acting, in which Garrick was to follow him, as against the formal and declamatory method of the Quin school. John Hill[1] summed it up: 'It was his manner to check all the cant and cadence of tragedy: he would bid his pupil first speak the passage as he would in common life, if he had occasion to pronounce the same words; and then giving them more force, but preserving the same accent, to deliver them on the stage'.

The comparison with Garrick is inevitable. Great actor as Garrick was, Macklin had qualities, and important ones, that Garrick lacked. He did not have Garrick's extreme flexibility, showmanship, extraordinary gift for mimicry, or instinctive capacity for theatrical interpretation, and though he did succeed in so many various parts, he no doubt had to struggle against his idiosyncrasies in order to do so. His approach to his art was much more thoughtful and intellectual than Garrick's, whose natural gifts were greater, but whose brains were less.

[1] Cf. John Hill, *The Actor* (1755), pp. 239-40.

What always comes out in accounts of Macklin's acting is his intelligence and understanding, even in parts that did not suit him. Boaden[1] says: 'He abhorred all tricks, all start and ingenious attitude', and his attacks on Garrick's acting were always directed against 'the restless abundance of action and gesture, by which, rather than by the fair business for character, the great little man caught and detained all attention to himself'.

Producer

That he was an outstanding teacher of acting is attested on all sides. When, after the actors' strike in 1743, he opened the Haymarket (evading the licensing act by employing musicians and announcing the plays as concerts) he surrounded himself with raw recruits, including Foote, whose first appearance was as Othello to Macklin's Iago. This was no success, but considering the material he had to work with, it was something of an achievement. Some years later he coached the stage-struck Sir Francis Delaval, with his amateur company of persons of quality, in *Othello*; this was a very successful performance (attended by Royalty) at Drury Lane.

Foote parodied his teaching in *The Diversions of the Morning* (1758),[2] in a scene between Puzzle and Bounce (played by Foote and Tate Wilkinson):

Puzzle: Advance, Bounce . . . begin at 'Othello's occupation's gone'. Now catch at me, as you would tear the very strings and all—keep your voice low—loudness is no mark of passion—mind your attitude.
Bounce: Villain.
Puzzle: Very well.
Bounce: Be sure you prove my love a whore.
Puzzle: Admirable.
Bounce: Be sure on't.
Puzzle: Bravo!
Bounce: Give me the ocular proof.
Puzzle: Lay your emphasis a little stronger upon oc—oc—oc.
Bounce: Oc—oc—ocular proof.

[1] Cf. James Boaden, *Memoirs of J. P. Kemble* (1825), I, p. 442.
[2] Cf. W. Cooke, *Memoirs of Samuel Foote* (1805), III, 121–5.

Puzzle: That's right.

Bounce: Or by the worth of my eternal soul, thou had'st better been born a dog. (*sic*)

Puzzle: Grind *dog* a little more—do-o-g, Iago.

Bounce: A d-o-g, Iago, then answer my waked wrath.

Puzzle: Charming!   Now quick.

Bounce: Make me to see it, or at least so prove it, that the probation bears no hinge or loop to hang a doubt on—woe.

Puzzle: A little more terror upon *woe*—wo-o-e, like a mastiff in a tanner's yard—wo-o-e.   (*they answer each other—wo-o-e, etc.*)

Bounce: Upon thy life, if thou dost slander her and torture me.

Puzzle: (*pushing him away*)   Oh! go about your business—'twon't do—go—go—go—I am sorry I have given you this trouble.

Bounce: Why, Sir, I——

Puzzle: (*imitating Macklin*) Sir, do you consider the mode of the mind—that a man's soul is tossed and lost, and crossed, and his entrails boiling on a gridiron—bring it from the bottom of your stomach, Sir—with a grind, as T–O–R–R——

Bounce: Tor—r—torture me.

Puzzle: That's my meaning.

Bounce: Never pray more—abandon all remorse.

Puzzle: Now—out with your arm and show your chest—there's a figure.

Bounce: On horror's head—

Puzzle: Now out with your voice.

Bounce: Horrors accumulate.

Puzzle: Now tender.

Bounce: Do deeds to make heaven weep.

Puzzle: Now terror.

Bounce: All earth amaz'd! for nothing canst thou to damna——

Puzzle: Grind na—na—na—tion.

Bounce: Na—na—nation add, greater than that.

Puzzle: Now throw me from you and I'll yield—very well!—keep that attitude—your eye fixed—there's a figure! there's a contrast! His majestic rage—and my timorous droop—um—Are you a man —have you a soul or sense?—Stay—stay—this will never do—we must think of some mechanical means to keep your fire alive—such as whispering to yourself—oh!—hah!—bitch! hell! &c. &c.

Bounce: (*repeats after him*) Oh! ah! bitch! hell! &c.

Puzzle: That's the mode of the mind: for if you observe the physical operations of nature, and the moral agency of the passions—when the soul is so far analysed, as the corporeal is entirely swallowed by the intellectual—why then the organical powers are as it were stagnated—for stagnation I define to be a total absence or secession—so that the—I am amazed (*in imitation of Macklin*)—how—do you like him?

Freeman: Under so able an instructor he cannot fail.

John O'Keeffe gives an amusing account of him in 1765 when in Dublin:[1] 'In Macklin's garden there were three long parallel walks, and his method of exercising their voices was thus: his two young pupils with backboards walked firmly, slow, and well, up and down the two side walks: Macklin himself paraded the centre walk. At the end of every twelve paces he made them stop; and turning gracefully, the young actor called across the walk, "How do you do, Miss Ambrose?" She answered, "Very well, I thank you, Mr. Glenville." Then they took a few more paces, and the next question was, "Do you not think it a fine day, Mr. Glenville?" "A very fine day indeed, Miss Ambrose", was the answer.... And this exercise continued for an hour or so.... Such was Macklin's method of training the management of the voice; if too high, too low, a wrong accent, or a faulty inflection, he immediately noticed it, and made them repeat the words twenty times till all was right. Soon after this Mr. Glenville played Antonio to his Shylock, and Miss Ambrose Charlotte in his own *Love à la Mode.*' Both the parody and the friendly humorous description show what Macklin was trying to do, and John Hill gives a similar picture: 'A too lofty and sonorous delivery ... ought, as the excellent instructor just mentioned used eternally to be inculcating into his pupils, to be always avoided when the simple recital of facts was the substance of what was to be spoken or when pure and cool reasoning was the sole meaning of the scene: but though he banished noise and vehemence on these occasions, he allowed that on many others, the pompous and sounding delivery was just'.[2]

All this supports what reading between the lines suggests; that he came nearer to being a producer in the modern sense—a director who

[1] Cf. O'Keeffe, *Recollections*, I, pp. 284–6.
[2] Cf. John Hill, *The Actor* (1750), pp. 194–5.

sets out to control the performance of a play and see it as a whole—than any worker in the British theatre before the advent of Boucicault, Robertson, and Gilbert in the later nineteenth century. Yet he was a star actor naturally tempted to put personal success before artistic unity.

Playwright

There have been many British actor-dramatists, most of whom, if they were any good at it, were writers first and actors second. Shakespeare was the greatest of dramatists, but probably no more than a fairly competent character-actor. Garrick was a very great actor, but his plays are worth very little. Macklin alone, though no doubt greater as actor than writer, can claim real distinction in both fields.

The first play of his writing was *King Henry VII, or The Popish Impostor* (Drury Lane, 18 January 1746; printed 1746). He apologises in both prologue and preface for the haste with which it had been scrambled together. Possibly he may have hoped to exploit the feeling roused by the Jacobite invasion of the previous year. This very poor play deserved its immediate failure. The verse, often hardly distinguishable from prose, is feeble in the extreme; the play wholly lacks the passion and psychological perception of its source, Ford's *Perkin Warbeck*: its only merit is to show some satiric force.

His second effort followed hard upon. *A Will and no Will, or A Bone for the Lawyers* (Drury Lane, 23 April 1746; not printed; Larpent MS.) is based on Regnard's *Le Légataire Universel* (1708), on which he improves by leaving his miser unreconciled at the end—a touch of nature which he was to echo in *The Man of the World*. This vigorous, satiric, and somewhat Jonsonian farce is a considerable advance on the former play, but of no outstanding merit. It ran for only two nights, but was occasionally revived.

The New Play Criticized, or The Plague of Envy (Drury Lane, 23 March 1747; not printed; Larpent MS.) is a slight entertainment of one act, which, taking advantage of the controversial popularity of Benjamin Hoadly's *Suspicious Husband* (first presented at Covent Garden a month earlier) satirises the theatrical *cognoscenti*; it has little sparkle but has some interest as a *pièce d'occasion*, and contains quite an amiably amusing stage Irishman. Citing Plautus, Terence, Molière and Ben Jonson as examples, Macklin's spokesman stresses propriety, character, and humour, rather than wit, as the important things in comedy, and accepts the audience as the final judge of dramatic values.

The Club of Fortune-Hunters, or The Widow Bewitched, a farce, was acted at Drury Lane on 28 April 1748; *The Fortune-Hunters . . . as it was acted at MacL—n's Amphitheatre* was printed in London in 1750: the same farce was printed in Dublin the same year, leaving 'MacL—n's Amphitheatre' off the title-page and giving the authorship to J. Carlisle. These can hardly be the same: the printed farce is very thin and rather silly, has none of Macklin's characteristic vigour, contains no part suitable for him, and has nothing to do with any widow. The former, which was not printed and of which no MS. exists, was presumably his work.

Covent Garden Theatre, or Pasquin turned Drawcansir[1] (Covent Garden, 8 April 1752; facsimile, Augustan Reprints, 1965: Larpent MS.) is a short satirical afterpiece of little merit, with some forceful but ephemeral criticism of contemporary life and theatre: the tone reflects Henry Fielding's satiric quality, and the title obviously refers to him.

The Whim, a 'Christmas Gambol', was performed at Crow Street, Dublin, on 26 December 1764. It seems to have made fun of strolling players. No more is known of it.

Success, and Failure

The two acts of *Love à la Mode* (Drury Lane, 12 December 1759) gave Macklin his first real success as a dramatist, and it was a great one; perhaps the most popular and often revived farce of the later eighteenth century, the author's performance in it was one of his most celebrated, and it held the stage for long after his retirement. A piracy of the first act was printed in 1766, and pirated versions of the whole play in Edinburgh in 1782, in London in 1784, and in Dublin in 1785 and 1786. The first authorised publication was by Murphy in 1793, and it continued to appear in collections of plays up to well on in the nineteenth century. After Macklin's retirement G. F. Cooke made some

---

[1] Pasquin—nickname for a satiric lampooner; Drawcansir—a blustering braggart in Buckingham's *Rehearsal* (1671).

Pasquin was the title of Henry Fielding's 'Dramatic Satire' performed in 1736; 'Sir Alexander Drawcansir' was the pseudonym under which he wrote his *Covent Garden Journal* (1752).

of his most distinguished appearances in it. It is a simple piece, actually nearer to comedy than farce, on the old theme of rival suitors and the success of the one who is ready to marry the girl when he believes she has lost her fortune. A hostile Scottish contemporary[1] suggested plagiarism from Thomas Sheridan's *Brave Irishman*[2] (1737: based on Molière's *Monsieur de Pourceaugnac*) in which, in a similar situation, the Irishman is also the successful suitor—the plagiarism is possible, but most unlikely. In any case Macklin produced something very much better than the broad shallow amusement of Captain O'Blunder, if we can judge from the mutilated version of *The Brave Irishman* printed. The success of *Love à la Mode* depends on the skilful construction, the lively dialogue, in general humorous rather than witty, and the very vigorous characterisation, caricature only up to a point, which gives splendid opportunities for comic impersonation. The flat characters of Sir Theodore the uncle-guardian and the heroine Charlotte have a little more individual life than many of their kind. Groom is a very well presented specimen of the stock rural squire with no interests beyond horses and drink; and the other three suitors are brilliantly done. Sir Callaghan, like Sir Lucius O'Trigger later, transcends the conventional stage Irishman,[3] only retaining enough of that figure to tickle the audience's conditioned reflexes without losing humanity or degenerating into mere absurdity. These characters are heightened, of course, but they are firmly based on fact and observation. Sir Callaghan is an attractive and lovable personality. Beau Mordecai, the Jewish cit with macaronic pretensions, is an original and most entertaining conception. But the most notable is Macklin's own part, Sir Archy Macsarcasm,[4] a novel and idiosyncratic presentation of Scottish character, founded on current English reactions to the Scots infiltration then going on and the facts about it. It uses something of the convention[5]—in so far as there was an established stage Scotsman—but it is not conventional. These characters have a degree of individuality unusual in farce. Macklin had originally intended to play the Irishman, but failed to find a Sir Archy to satisfy him: it was for the best, since his own success led on to Sir Pertinax, and his strongest

---

[1] Cf. *A Scotsman's Remarks on . . . 'Love à la Mode'* (1760).
[2] Cf. *TSS*, pp. 113–15.
[3] Cf. *TSS*, Chaps. VI, X, XI, XV, and *passim*.
[4] Cf. *TSS*, pp. 220–1.
[5] Cf. *TSS*, Chaps. VIII, XIII, XV, and *passim*.

support came from John Moody[1] whose brilliant Sir Callaghan started off his career as an extremely popular and successful actor of Irish parts. King and Blakes shone as Mordecai and Groom. Macklin's original draft was in five acts, but on Arthur Murphy's advice he concentrated it into two. Garrick—a touch of jealousy can hardly be excluded, since he was too experienced a judge not to see its possibilities —was reluctant to put it on, but it turned out a well-deserved and continuant success. George II asked for a script, which was read to him, it is said, by an old Hanoverian gentleman deficient in English and humour—but the king liked the comedy. This is the only existing MS. and is now in the library of the Garrick Club.

The School for Husbands, or The Married Libertine (Covent Garden, 28 January 1761; Larpent MS.; here printed for the first time) is a five-act comedy, on the whole farcical in tone, but not without elements of genuine characterisation and intelligent thinking. The audience was hostile, and included a group of Scotsmen offended by Sir Archy: others objected because Lord Belville was taken to be a hit at a notorious nobleman. In fact, it is not a particularly good play. It is slow in getting under way, and the plot is too thin to support the action. For subsequent performances it was altered and cut, and went better, but it failed to grip and its ninth night was its last. Unfortunately, since all we have is the MS. submitted to the Lord Chamberlain, we have no means of knowing what cuts and alterations were made: but, looking at what we have, we can see some merit in it. Once the *longueurs* of the first two acts are over, there is much fertility of comic and farcical invention, and one sometimes wonders whether the author has run dry, only to find that he has not. The dialogue is only occasionally witty, but then Macklin did not stress wit: it is, much of it, trenchant, humorous, and well-balanced. The satirical element which was never far away when Macklin was writing is in evidence, but not strongly—most in the presentation of Lord Belville, and in Angelica's impersonation of a military officer: indeed, one is sometimes tempted to suspect that the playwright had a little bit of his tongue in his cheek during sentimental passages. Even if the conception of a complementary degree of sexual freedom for men and women—'Because the husband is vile—should the wife be vile also?' asked Lady Windermere— is in terms of the place of women in eighteenth-century society, it is

[1] Cf. *TSS*, pp. 245–7, 312.

not inhumanly treated. Harriet, and especially Angelica—an energetic breeches-part which suited Maria Macklin—are lively and amusing; Lord Belville has his moments, though he does not offer enough for an actor of Macklin's force to work with; and there is a real woman inside Lady Belville, trying to get out. Among the minor characters the Serjeant and Lucy have theatrical life at least. The tempo of the dialogue, ranging from not ineffectual rhetoric to stichomythic snip-snap, shows the ear skilled in stage speech. Many worse comedies had more contemporary success. Perhaps the play hovers too much between broad and sentimental comedy: satire, one of Macklin's strengths, is weak here; the sentiment and the sentimental pronouncements, never things he was very good at, are, superficially at least, less related to genuine human feeling than, say, in *The Man of the World*. No eighteenth-century theatrical professional, of course, could help being affected by the sentimental style. Goldsmith wasn't because he wasn't professional: Sheridan was because he was.

An Irish Play

The True-born Irishman (Crow Street, Dublin, 14 May 1762; printed in Jones's *British Theatre*, 1793) is a two-act comedy which was very popular in Ireland, but failed completely in an altered version, *The Irish Fine Lady* (Covent Garden, 28 November 1767; not printed in this form: Larpent MS.), when performed in London. For London, there was a prologue protesting against the conventional stage Irishman as the product of Dulness, and pointing to O'Dogherty as an Irish character presented according to Nature. An added opening scene begins with newspaper-sellers, off, crying the news and the three chief Dublin journals. It appears that Mrs. Diggerty has returned from England in the same ship as the Lord-Lieutenant, whose arrival is part of the news. Then O'Dogherty is sarcastic about the imitation of French fashions, rather than of English. Thereafter there are minor changes and additions which, on the whole, tend to weaken the play. The alterations were designed to make it palatable to the English, but the play is so Irish in attitude, theme, and allusions, that the attempt was hopeless. It is a lively and stageable comedy, both farcical and satirical, by no means as good as *Love à la Mode*, but a better work of art than *The School for Husbands*. As such it speaks

for itself; but its Irishness gives it special interest. The play is satiri-
cally anti-English, and its inner sentiment and appeal reach beyond
the 'West British' element in the Dublin audience to touch a deeper
nationalist feeling. The implications, though more superficial, are
wider than those of Swift's nationalist writings, for they hint at Irish
unity as well as touching Irish prosperity; and though subordinate to
the plot, and emerging as part of the presentation of character, they
are real and revealing. The main theme, of which Mrs. Diggerty is
the focus, is to make fun of the pretentious aping of English manners
and behaviour by Irish people.

The conventional stage Irishman, imported from England, so long as
not grossly offensive to Irish sensibilities, was quite popular in Dublin.
But Murrough O'Dogherty is much further from that figure than Sir
Callaghan, who also breaks away from it, and is essentially an attempt
at a realistic portrait of a definite and representative type of Irishman,
presented without perversion or caricature, and appealing to Irishmen
as such. Macklin wrote the part for himself and played it to great
applause, and here only, among his parts in his major plays, seems to be
his own mouthpiece. His own strong views on corruption in politics
appear clearly for the first time, but Ireland is the important thing.
His views about Ireland do not find expression elsewhere, except
vaguely in the extracts from his commonplace book published in the
Monthly Mirror[1] after his death, and though he settled down in
England well enough, he was probably nationalist in his younger days,
and, had it been possible, would probably have retired to Ireland.

The Irish in the eighteenth century fell into several main groups:
the O's and the Macs of old Irish descent; those deriving from the
Anglo-Norman settlers (*Hiberniores Hibernis ipsis*); those of English
blood from the Elizabethan plantation; those from the Scots of James
I's plantation of Ulster; some from the Cromwellian soldiery; and
scattered later arrivals. Many of the native Irish Catholic gentry
had become Protestant in self-preservation against the penal laws:
O'Dogherty is probably the descendant of such a family: his brother-
in-law is a Hamilton of the Ulster plantation, a name usually Protestant, but found among both Williamites and Jacobites. His and Mrs.
O'Dogherty's mother—who had 'a thick brogue' and 'not two of
whose ancestors could even speak three words of English to be under-

---

[1] Cf. *The Monthly Mirror* (1797–9).

stood'—was an O'Gallagher, descended from a seventh-century king of Ireland. The O'Dohertys were also a Donegal family, and, like the MacLaughlins whose overlords they were, associated with the Inishowen peninsula. The choice of names is hardly likely to have been accidental when made by a MacLaughlin. There must be some self-identification here. Macklin, had circumstances been different, might well have found himself in a position like O'Doherty's, from which to object to English manners and influences, and taxes, to dislike and distrust politicians, and to praise Irish traditions and the names symbolising them. And we should remember that Macklin acted in various country towns as well as Dublin, and that he could speak Irish. It would be wrong to press this theme too far, but it is part of the whole picture of the man.

Broad and entertaining characterisation, vigorous and expressive dialogue, pointed satire, lively comic invention, and the professional awareness of what is theatrically effective, are found in *The True-born Irishman*, as in all Macklin's best work.

Last and Best

The Man of the World was Macklin's last play, and in many ways a great one. It was first performed (in three acts) as *The True-born Scotsman* (Crow Street, Dublin, 10 June 1764) with great success. The licensing act of 1737, though also directed against blasphemy, obscenity, personal libel, and slander, gave powers to prohibit matter seditious or offensive to the Government: it had in fact been introduced mainly to suppress Fielding's savage satirical attacks on the Walpole administration. The Lord Chamberlain's writ did not run in Ireland, but when a five-act version (the first *Man of the World*) was submitted for his licence in 1770, it was turned down.[1] A considerably altered script was submitted again in 1779 and again refused a licence. A third version, only slightly altered from the second, was licensed in 1781. (These three scripts are among the Larpent MSS.) The last *Man of the World* (Covent Garden, 10 May 1781) was received with great enthusiasm. Somewhat tightened up after the first performance, it was presented again and again with never-failing success during the

[1] Cf. D. MacMillan, *The Censorship . . . of Macklin's 'Man of the World'* (*Huntington Library Bulletin*, October 1936).

next eight years: after Macklin's retirement Cooke took it over, as he had *Love à la Mode*, and gained great applause in it. It held the stage for a long time.

Pirated texts were published in London and Dublin in 1785, 1786, and 1791. The first authorised printing was the subscription edition, with *Love à la Mode*, published by Arthur Murphy in 1793, and there-after it appeared in various collections of plays. Murphy's text was facsimilied in *Augustan Reprints* in 1951.

In the last version, *The Man of the World* is a much-improved play. Alterations to the plot were negligible, but in addition to trying to meet the Lord Chamberlain's objections, Macklin tightened up both action and dialogue to good effect; indeed, the toning down of the political satire was an artistic advantage in stressing the genuine human comedy rather than topical matters.

Dr. Johnson was not alone in his hostility to the Scots, but shared it with a great many other Englishmen, especially from about 1750 when Lord Bute began to gain influence at court and in politics: this hostility reached a peak when George III appointed Bute Secretary of State almost immediately upon his accession in 1760, and promoted him First Lord of the Treasury two years later. Bute had been notorious for favouring his compatriots, and his increased power, controlling the civil list, pensions, and patronage, was not exercised to their disadvantage: the influx of Scots and their prosperity in England increased. Macklin's commonplace book makes very evident his mistrustful hostility to the Scots, his detestation of Bute, and the tenacity of his political beliefs.

Moreover Bute was both head and figurehead of the corrupt administration of which Wilkes was the chief opponent, and Macklin was Wilkesite in politics; and if not personally associated with Wilkes at this time, was intimate with some of his leading supporters. Political feeling ran very high during these years, and it is in no way surprising that a licence was refused to the 1770 version, which might well have produced cheers and countercheers, if not rioting, in the theatre. Feeling had become less strong by 1779, when the play was again submitted, but was still inflamed by opposition to the Catholic Relief Act and the activities of Lord George Gordon, and the much milder second version was refused. But by early in 1781 reform was in the air, and the younger Pitt had begun to make his mark in

Parliament: the atmosphere was now easier, and the third version of *The Man of the World* was approved.

It is certainly one of the best of eighteenth-century comedies, and indeed the outstanding one not from Macklin's compatriots, Farquhar, Goldsmith, and Sheridan. Though it belongs to its time, it is as marked with the playwright's individuality as *The Beaux' Stratagem*, *The School for Scandal*, or *She Stoops to Conquer*, and it is superior to the best of Cibber, Colman, Cumberland, Kelly, or Murphy. It stands on its strength and solidity, for Macklin had little of Farquhar's gaiety, Goldsmith's gentle and easy grace and good humour, or Sheridan's sharpness and quickness of wit. Some characters in *The Man of the World* are near enough to being sentimental clichés: the chaste, moral, and maligned Constantia; the precise, dignified, altruistic Sidney; the devious, self-seeking lawyers; the wooden Melville. Betty Hint rises above the mere type in her selfish malice, mainly because Macklin has given her a personal style of speech. Lady Macsycophant, though unelaborated, is neither conventional nor sentimental; her feelings are real. Lord Lumbercourt, for all his faults, is a gentleman, if a disreputable one. The solemn, high-principled, sententious Egerton is, in a way, the 'angry young man' of the time—and the fact that it is political venality, rather than vague general morality, that he is solemn, high-principled and sententious about, lifts him out of the sentimental rut. When he rings false, it is because he is too good to be true, like some of Wesker's young idealists—but the delightfully funny scene with Lady Rodolpha, taken with the generally satirical tone latent at least in all Macklin's writing, suggests that there may perhaps be a touch of irony in the way he is treated. And Lady Rodolpha herself is great fun. There is nothing very original about the good-hearted romp and tease, but Lady Rodolpha is something more, and indeed her perceptive humour is a little reminiscent of Barbara Grant in *Catriona*. Partly by imposing Scottish dialect upon her, and so strengthening her marked personal quality, Macklin has created a character of vivid individuality.

But everything else in the play is secondary to the dominating personality of Sir Pertinax Macsycophant[1]—a much better name for the character than the Sir Hector MacCrafty of the original version. No doubt, in the conception of the character, the humours of Scottish

[1] Cf. *TSS*, pp. 227–9.

self-regard, arrogance, venality, and careerism joined to make up a satirical caricature. But Sir Pertinax is a good deal more than this. Just as Jonson, starting from the notion of a humour-type, could build up so individual a character as Volpone or Sir Epicure Mammon, so Macklin moved from the general conception to the particular man. There is something of Massinger's Sir Giles Overreach—Edmund Kean, who was tremendous as Sir Giles, also played Sir Pertinax—in the power and force of Sir Pertinax's ruling passions, which find vent in a manner of speech peculiar to himself and reinforced by the rhythm and accent of his dialect, nowhere heard better than in the famous 'boowing' scene. We feel that he does feel: the strength of his feeling is the one redeeming and humanising feature in his passionate careerism. And he is one of the earlier presentations of the self-made man. In him Macklin made no gesture to current sentimentality; against the practice of sentimental comedy, he allows no character to reform: Lord Lumbercourt and Sir Pertinax go their ways as before. The savage storming final exit of Sir Pertinax, thwarted and furious with rage and disappointment—even though his scheme has not really failed—at his family's rebellion, coming so near as it does to the happy ending, is an extremely powerful dramatic moment.

There is only one location, and the time is three hours, but this observation of the unities leads to no awkwardness—like his others, the play is very well constructed. There is no secondary plot, no secondary pair of lovers, no 'Charles's friend', no confidante. Lady Rodolpha's lover is incidental to her involvement in the central theme; and he never appears. The whole effect is of great concentration, and it is a pity that opportunities to see it are very rare, for it is most impressive on the stage, as a recent revival at the Pitlochry Festival has shown.[1]

Allardyce Nicoll, with certain reservations, places *The Man of the World* in the class of sentimental comedy.[2] There are some sentimental elements in Macklin's plays, which is perhaps only to be expected from an actor-dramatist with professional perception of what his

[1] Charles A. Read, who included the scene between Sidney and Betty in Act I and the opening of Act III from *The Man of the World*, and Mordecai's first scene from *Love à la Mode* in *A Cabinet of Irish Literature* (1880), remarked: 'there is scarcely a character in these two plays but is worthy of careful study and first-class acting'.
[2] Cf. Nicoll, *Late Eighteenth Century Drama*, p. 140.

audiences like and expect, writing at a time when almost all comedy that was not broad farce was tainted with sentimentality: but Macklin's comedy is basically far from the sentimental, genteel, or *larmoyante*, in spite of Hamilton's mild sententiousness and Mrs. Diggerty's reformation in *The True-born Irishman*, the triumph of the good-hearted in *Love à la Mode*, the reconciliation of Lord and Lady Belville in *The School for Husbands*, and the moral pronouncements of Egerton and Sidney in *The Man of the World*: indeed, these last are to some extent saved from sentimentality by the way in which their moralisings are related to what is being satirised in Sir Pertinax. What Cumberland called 'sentiments that deserve applause'[1]—the sententious tag rounding off act, or scene, or long speech, and designed to draw a round of applause to itself—are comparatively rare. Effectively broad and farcical scenes are found in all Macklin's plays—though less in *The Man of the World*. Strong characterisation and vigorous dialogue are always evident. He is to be regarded especially as a follower of Ben Jonson, adapting his master's approach and method to the times, just as Goldsmith looks back to Shakespearian comedy and Sheridan to Congreve's comedy of manners. The satiric quality which he shares with Jonson is the seasoning of the dish.

Declining Years

In 1777 Macklin and his wife took new lodgings in Tavistock Row, Covent Garden, where they remained till his death. Even though he was now at least seventy-seven, and though he had some thoughts of retiring—which he could not afford to do—and had reduced his parts to the three, and was performing much less often than before, he retained much of his old energy. Indeed, from 1777 till 1789, he played Shylock, Sir Archy, and Sir Pertinax well over fifty times each, and managed in 1785 to play them in both Dublin and Manchester as well as London. All are parts imposing a heavy strain upon the performer: and they are of substantial length, Shylock approaching 4,000 words, Sir Archy, in a short play, over 3,000, and Sir Pertinax about 9,000!—and he usually followed one of the others with Sir Archy on the same night. He must have seemed indestructible.

In these later years, though not financially comfortable, and sad-

[1] Cf. R. Cumberland, *Memoirs* (1807), I, p. 276.

dened by the deaths of many old friends and colleagues, and by his son's behaviour, he led a fairly active social life, seeing his intimates, and visited by younger people keen to hear his anecdotes and comments; and he often went to the theatre.

In January 1788 he broke down in Shylock, and appealed to the audience to forgive him for his loss of memory: but he was able to pull himself together enough to complete the performance, and he continued to act occasionally. In November his memory failed him again, this time in Sir Pertinax, and he had to give up. He appeared for the last time, as Shylock, on 7 May 1789, almost exactly eight years after the first production of *The Man of the World*. Before the performance he was bewildered and confused: he did go on stage and make an effort, but to little effect. He was obliged to yield, and leave his understudy, Ryder, to carry on. Cooke concludes his account of the event thus: 'the audience accepted his apology with a mixed applause of indulgence and commiseration, and he retired from the stage for ever'. This was the beginning of the end, but he had eight more years to live.

They were rather sad years, at least to the looker-on, for he does not seem to have been depressed in his senility, with his mind more often clouded than lucid. The death of his son in 1790, though it ended, too late, the financial drain that had been going on for years, hardly affected him. In 1793, to relieve his poverty, his friend and compatriot, Arthur Murphy, published by subscription a finely produced edition of the two major plays, realising over £1,500 and providing him with an annuity of £200, and one of £75 for his widow. He often visited taverns and the theatres, and sometimes was able to talk and reminisce with a little of his old fire for a short time, but such moments were few and far between. He died peacefully in his sleep on 11 July 1797, and on the 16th was buried in St. Paul's, Covent Garden. So ended the longest and one of the most distinguished of British theatrical careers.

He was a great actor and a notable playwright, who did much to strengthen the arts he practised, and a strong and singular character whose every action and speech was stamped with the force of his personality. He was loved and hated: he was never negligible.

33

Part Two

FOUR COMEDIES

to me. that, Sir, wou'd have produced a very civil & a very
explicit Answer from me; wou'd have saved you a great deal
of Intemperance in your impetuous Visit; & have prevented me
from troubling you with long Epistles. that Favour, Sir, I now
request of you; which I think is not too late for me to ask
or you to grant, to which, Sir, I shall return you a speedy &

29 MA 55

explicite Answer. I am, Sir,

James Street   Sincerely
Covent Garden   Your humble Servant to Command
16th November 1773   Chas Macklin
Eleven in the Morning   Sent to Mr Smith the Actor —
                                 about the Riots when Macklin play'd Macb

EXTRACT FROM AUTOGRAPH LETTER
FROM MACKLIN TO SMITH

(*By courtesy of the British Museum*)

THE FIRST PAGE OF THE MS. OF
LOVE À LA MODE

(*By courtesy of the Garrick Club*)

Preface to the Plays

The aim has been to produce, without modernisation, easily and pleasantly readable texts of the four plays, which take speech rhythms into account and would be convenient as acting versions. The texts are therefore approximately standardised to the conventions of good play-printing in the last decade of the eighteenth century, a procedure to some extent necessarily arbitrary. There can be no question here of establishing an authentic author's text, except that the Garrick Club MS. of *Love à la Mode* (and the alterations marked on it) did have Macklin's approval, but more likely than not in general rather than in detail.

Each play presents its own problems. *The School for Husbands* is simplest, because the only source is the Larpent MS., which, however, is not that of the author but that of theatre scribes. It was written by several different hands, using different conventions of spelling, punctuation, use of capitals, and stage direction. There can be no question of authority where detail is concerned: all we can assume is that the author was content that this script should be submitted to the licenser. Had the play been printed, it would certainly not have been printed as it stands in the MS. Apart from regularising the whole, as explained above, the indications of West Country dialect in Harriet's speeches have been made consistent: that is, no indications have been added from outside the MS., but those already present in some places inserted in others where they had been carelessly and inconsistently omitted. The very few indications of Irish speech have been left as they stand, for the reason given below.

The True-born Irishman is also fairly simple. The basic text here is the authorised Dublin printing of 1793. The Larpent MS. of the version adapted for London performance differs from this almost entirely in respect of certain modifications made to accommodate the play to English knowledge, tastes, and prejudice. These are of some interest, but of little relevance to textual detail. Here again the conventions have been approximately standardised. There is next to no dialect here. O'Dogherty is naturalistically presented with some

Irish interjections and turns of phrase, and Macklin has put his own observation to good use in pointing Mrs. Diggerty's overcorrections of her own Irish speech in her attempt to acquire an English accent. These have not been changed.

As regards the other two plays, the same approximate standardisation has been applied; but they raise further and more difficult problems. A minor one is that of Sir Callaghan O'Brallaghan in *Love à la Mode*: only occasionally, but especially when he is reading out a letter he has written, is his Irish pronunciation indicated. There is no consistency, and the few indications given him are conventional and to be found in most contemporary stage Irishmen. In respect of this, no alterations have been made. Because, at this time, the conventional stage Irishman was firmly established and had hardened into a mould, only a few marks of dialect are usually shown: it was left to the reader or actor, both of whom were very familiar with the conventional figure, to fill in the gaps.

It was very different with Scottish characters. No firm convention for them established itself before the nineteenth century, and therefore during the eighteenth century we find their speech-idiosyncrasies much more fully indicated, whether accurately or not, than those of the Irish or Welsh. The main character in *Love à la Mode*, Sir Archy Macsarcasm, and the two leads in *The Man of the World*, Sir Pertinax Macsycophant and Lady Rodolpha Lumbercourt, use a dialect which is unquestionably based on South-west Scots, probably Ayrshire, at which Macklin has not made a bad effort.

The pirated printings, and the versions in various play-collections published after Macklin's death, cannot be regarded as having any authority: they have been examined, and may be dismissed. We are left with, for *Love à la Mode*, the Garrick Club MS. and Murphy's subscription edition of 1793. For *The Man of the World*, there are the three Larpent MSS. of the three successive versions submitted to the licenser; but these are scribal, vary much in their indications of dialect, and cannot have any authority in regard to this kind of detail. For the Scottish dialect, then, we are finally left with the Garrick Club MS. and Murphy's edition of the two plays, the basic text here. The MS. and Murphy's versions of *Love à la Mode* are in fairly close agreement, though internally there is much inconsistency in both: but both are much fuller in their indications of dialect than is *The Man of the World* in Murphy or in MS. The present writer can claim some special knowledge of the way in which dialect is presented in English drama, and finds these irregular indications irritating, troublesome, and sometimes misleading. Sir Archy, Sir Pertinax, and Lady Rodolpha could, of course, have been made consistent by being translated into such standard eighteenth-century literary Scots as Allan Ramsay used, but this would have meant an unwarrantable amount of alteration, and would have sacrificed the peculiar flavour of speech given us by Macklin's own ear for a South-western Scottish dialect. No wholly satisfactory solution is possible: but to print any single text as it stands, no matter how elaborate the *apparatus criticus*, could only serve to obnubilate the playwright's intentions and the reader's pleasure. Collation of all the versions shows that such an attempt would be a waste of scholarly effort.

The solution adopted here as most likely to get near achieving the ends in view has been to take those indications of Scottish speech, and no others, which occur in the Garrick Club MS. and Murphy's subscription volume, and to apply these, and these only, consistently throughout the Scottish parts. Inconsistencies remain; some inherent in the uncertainty of the originals, some because a number of obviously parallel Scottish pronunciations are not indicated in them at all. Certain special points receive attention in footnotes.

Love à la Mode

A FARCE

in Two Acts

Theatrical Note

Love à la Mode retained its popularity well into the nineteenth century. At Drury Lane in 1794, King played Sir Archy, Palmer Sir Callaghan, the younger Bannister Groom, and Suett Mordecai; in 1800 at Drury Lane there were G. F. Cooke, the very popular Irish actor Johnstone, Lewis, and Simmons; at Bath in 1814 Mathews, imitating Cooke, appeared as Sir Archy; and at Covent Garden the same year Mathews again imitated Cooke, supported by Johnstone, Jones, and Simmons.

Love à la Mode

DRURY LANE   12 DECEMBER 1759

Dramatis Personae

Sir Theodore Goodchild	Mr. Burton
Sir Archy Macsarcasm	Mr. Macklin
Sir Callaghan O'Brallaghan	Mr. Moody
Squire Groom	Mr. King
Beau Mordecai	Mr. Blakes
Charlotte	Miss Macklin

Time: from an hour before dinner till an hour after.
Scene: London, in a Room in Sir Theodore's House.

Love à la Mode

ACT I

Enter SIR THEODORE *and* CHARLOTTE

CHARLOTTE: Nay, there can be no harm in a little mirth, guardian; even those who happen to be the objects must approve the justice of it.

SIR THEODORE: But consider, Charlotte, what will the world say of me? Will it not be in every mouth, that Sir Theodore Goodchild was a very imprudent man, in combining with his ward to turn her lovers into ridicule?

CHARLOTTE: Not at all, sir: the world will applaud the mirth, especially when they know what kind of lovers they are; and that the sole motive of their addresses was the lady's fortune. Well, sure, since the days of giants and enchanted castles, no poor damsel has been besieged by such a group of odd mortals. Let me review my equipage of lovers! The first upon the list is a beau Jew,[1] who, in spite of nature and education, sets up for a wit, a gentleman, and a man of taste.

SIR THEODORE: Aye, laugh at him as much as you will.

CHARLOTTE: The next is a downright English, Newmarket, stable-bred, gentleman jockey, who, having ruined his finances by dogs, grooms, cocks, horses, and such polite company, now thinks to retrieve his affairs by a matrimonial match with a city fortune.

SIR THEODORE: Ha, ha, ha! I find, madam, you have perused the squire with great exactness.

CHARLOTTE: Pretty well, sir. To this Newmarket wight succeeds a proud, haughty, Caledonian knight; whose tongue, like the dart of death, spares neither sex nor age, it leaves none unvisited. All dread, and all feel it.

[1] At Drury Lane, 1738–42, one of Macklin's regular parts was Beau Mordecai in T. Cibber's *Harlot's Progress* (first performed, 1733; based on Hogarth; mime and song only): it may have suggested the name, but nothing more.

SIR THEODORE: Yes, yes, his insolence of family, and licentiousness of wit, have gained him the contempt and general toleration[1] of mankind. But we must not look upon his spleen and ill nature, my dear, as a national, but a personal vice.

CHARLOTTE: As such, sir, I always understand and laugh at him. Well, of all my swains, he is the most whimsical; his passion is to turn every mortal into ridicule; even I, the object of his flame, cannot escape, for while his avarice courts my fortune, his pride despises, and sneers at my birth.

SIR THEODORE: That, Charlotte, is only to shew his wit.

CHARLOTTE: True, sir. The next in Cupid's train is your nephew, guardian, a wild Irish, Prussian, hard-headed soldier, whose military humour, and fondness for his profession, make me fancy sometimes that he was not only born in a siege, but that Bellona had been his nurse, Mars his schoolmaster, and the furies his play-fellows—ha, ha, ha!

SIR THEODORE: Ha, ha, ha! O fye, Charlotte, how can you be so severe upon my poor nephew?

CHARLOTTE: Upon my honour, Sir Theodore, I don't mean to be severe, for I like his character extremely—ha, ha, ha!

SIR THEODORE: Well, well, notwithstanding your mirth, madam, I assure you, he has gained the highest esteem in his profession. But what can you expect, my dear, from a soldier, a mere rough-hewn soldier, who, at the age of fifteen, would leave Ireland, his friends, and every other pursuit, to go a volunteer into the Prussian service—and there he has lived seventeen years; so that I don't suppose he has six ideas out of his own profession—garrisons and camps have been the courts and academies that have formed him. But he ever had, from a child, a kind of military madness.

CHARLOTTE: O, I am in love with his warlike humour—I think it highly entertaining.

SIR THEODORE: As he has not made any direct addresses to you, Charlotte, let me inform him how improper such a step would be, and even let us leave him out of our scheme to-night.

CHARLOTTE: O, sir, impossible! our day's sport, our plot, our every thing, would be imperfect without him; why, I intend him to be the leading instrument in the concert. One cannot possibly do

[1] Mankind contemns, but reluctantly puts up with him.

without Sir Callaghan Brall—Bra—Brall.   Pray, guardian, teach me to pronounce my lover's name.

SIR THEODORE: Thou art a mad creature!   Well, madam, I will indulge your wicked mirth.   His name is Callaghan O'Brallaghan.[1]

CHARLOTTE: O shocking!   Calligan O'Bralligan![2]—why, it is enough to choak one; and is as difficult to be uttered as a Welsh pedigree.[3] Why, if the fates should bring us together, I shall be obliged to hire an Irish interpreter to go about with me, to teach the people to pronounce my name—ha, ha, ha!

SIR THEODORE: You may laugh, madam, but he is as proud of that name as any of your lovers are of their titles.   I suppose they all dine here.

CHARLOTTE: Certainly—all but Squire Groom.

SIR THEODORE: Oh! you must not expect him; he is at York, he was to ride his great match there, yesterday.   He will not be here, you may be sure.   Let me see; what is't o'clock?—almost three—who's there?

Enter SERVANT

SERVANT: 'Tis ready, sir.   (*Exit*)

SIR THEODORE: I will but just step to Lincoln's Inn Hall, and see what they are doing in your cause; it is to be ended to-day.   By the time I return, I suppose, your company will be come.   A good morning to you, Charlotte.

CHARLOTTE: Sir, a good morning.   (*Exit* SIR THEODORE)

MORDECAI: (*Sings Italian without*) Sir Theodore, your humble servant.

SIR THEODORE: (*Without*) Mr. Mordecai, your most obedient.

Enter SERVANT

SERVANT: Mr. Mordecai, madam.

CHARLOTTE: Shew him in.   (*Exit* SERVANT)

MORDECAI: (*Without*) I see your coach is at the door.   Sir Theodore, you dine with us, I hope.

SIR THEODORE: (*Without*) Certainly.   You'll find Miss Charlotte within.   Your servant.

---

[1] Ó Ceallacháin, a Co. Cork family, descended from a king of Munster: Ó Brolláchain, a Co. Tyrone family, one branch of which settled in Cork.   Macklin has given Sir Callaghan some conventional Hibernicisms and indicated a very few pronunciations: he makes a few bulls, but they are witty, not absurd.   Cf. *TSS* pp. 116–17.

[2] Thus in MS., Callaghan O'Brallaghan in Murphy.

[3] A frequent joke against the Welsh.   Cf. *TSS* pp. 62, 63, 69, 143, 214.

MORDECAI: (*Without*) Yours, Sir Theodore.

    Enter MORDECAI *singing an Italian air,*[1] *and addressing*
                    CHARLOTTE *fantastically*

CHARLOTTE: *O caro, caro, carissimo!*

MORDECAI: *Voi sete molto cortese! anima mia!* Here let me kneel, and pay my softest adoration; and thus, and thus, in amorous transport breathe my last. (*Kisses her hand*)

CHARLOTTE: Ha, ha, ha! softly, softly! You would not sure breathe your last yet, Mr. Mordecai.

MORDECAI: Why no, madam, I would live a little longer for your sake. (*Bowing very low*)

CHARLOTTE: Ha, ha, ha! you are infinitely polite—but a truce with your gallantry—why you are as gay as the sun!—I think I never saw any thing better fancied than that suit of yours, Mr. Mordecai.

MORDECAI: Ha, ha!—a—well enough—just as my taylor fancied—ha, ha, ha! Do you like it, madam?

CHARLOTTE: Quite elegant: I don't know any one about town deserves the title of beau, better than Mr. Mordecai.

MORDECAI: O dear madam, you are very obliging.

CHARLOTTE: I think you are called Beau Mordecai by every body.

MORDECAI: Yes, madam, they do distinguish me by that title, but I don't think I merit the honour.

CHARLOTTE: No body more: for I think you are always by far the finest man in town. But do you know that I have heard of your extraordinary court the other night, at the opera, to Miss Sprightly.

MORDECAI: O heavens, madam, how can you be so severe? that the woman has designs, I steadfastly believe; but as to me—Oh!—

CHARLOTTE: Ha, ha, ha! nay, nay, you must not deny it—for my intelligence is from very good hands.

MORDECAI: Pray, who may that be?

CHARLOTTE: Sir Archy Macsarcasm.

[1] In a letter (printed in *Monthly Mirror*, 1798) to Quick, the creator of Tony Lumpkin, who had failed to satisfy him as Mordecai, Macklin wrote; 'The character is an egregious coxcomb, who is striving to be witty; at the top of dress, with an awkward fancy of his own, so as to be ridiculous and as badly matched or sorted as such a fellow ignorant of propriety can be. His manner is very lively —singing, conceited, dancing—throwing himself out, body, voice and mind, as much as conceit and impudence and ignorance can effect'.

Act I

MORDECAI: O shocking! the common Pasquin[1] of the town; besides, madam, you know he's my rival, and not very remarkable for veracity in his narrations.

CHARLOTTE: Ha, ha, ha! I cannot say he's a religious observer of truth, but his humour always makes amends for his invention. You must allow he has humour, Mr. Mordecai.

MORDECAI: *O cuor mio!* how can you think so?—bating his scandal, dull; dull as an alderman after six pounds of turtle, four bottles of port, and twelve pipes of tobacco.

CHARLOTTE: Ha, ha, ha! O surfeiting, surfeiting!

MORDECAI: The man indeed has something droll—something ridiculous in him: his abominable Scots accent, his grotesque visage, almost buried in snuff, the roll of his eyes, and twist of his mouth, his strange inhuman laugh, his tremendous periwig, and his manners altogether, indeed, has something so caricaturely risible in it, that—ha, ha, ha! may I die, madam, if I don't always take him for a mountebank doctor at a Dutch fair.

CHARLOTTE: Oh, oh! what a picture has he drawn! why, you're as severe in your portraits as Sir Archy himself.

Enter SERVANT

SERVANT: Sir Archy Macsarcasm is below, madam.

CHARLOTTE: Shew him up. (*Exit* SERVANT)

MORDECAI: Don't you think, madam, he is a horrid, foul-mouthed, uncouth fellow? he is worse to me, madam, than assafoetida, or a tallow chandler's shop in the dog days; his filthy high dried[2] poisons me, and his scandal is grosser than a hackney news writer's. Madam, he is as much despised by his own countrymen, as by the rest of the world. The better sort of Scotland never keep him company; but that is *entre nous, entre nous.*

SIR ARCHY: (*Without*) Randol, bid Sawney be here wi' the chariot at eight o'clock axactly.

Enter SIR ARCHY—MORDECAI *runs up to embrace him*

SIR ARCHY: Ha, ha, ha! my cheeld of circumcision, gi' us a wag of thy loof;[3] hoo dun ye do, my bonny Girgishite?[4]

---

[1] Cf. p. 23, n. 1, above.
[2] A kind of snuff: Scottish addiction to snuff is often made a joke of. Cf. *TSS* p. 237.
[3] Hand: Scots dialect.
[4] Girgasite (*Genesis*, X, 16) or Girgashite (*Genesis*, XV, 21), a Canaanite tribe.

MORDECAI: Always at your service, Sir Archy.   He stinks worse than a Scotch snuff-shop.   (*Aside*)

SIR ARCHY: Weel, Mordecai, I see ye are as deelegent in the service of yeer mistress, as in the service of yeer leuking glass, for yeer face and yeer thoughts are awways turned upon the yean or the aither.

MORDECAI: And I see your wit, Sir Archy, like a lawyer's tongue, will ever retain its usual politeness and good nature.

CHARLOTTE: (*Coming forward*) Ha, ha, ha! civil and witty on both sides.   Sir Archy, your most obedient.   (*Curtsies*)

SIR ARCHY: Tan thoosand pardons, madam, I did na[1] observe ye; I hope I see yeer ladyship weel.   Ah! ye leuk like a deveenety. (*Bowing awkwardly and low*)

CHARLOTTE: Sir Archy, this is immensely gallant.

SIR ARCHY: Weel, madam, I see my friend Mordecai here is determined to bear awa the prize frai us aw!   Ha, ha, ha! he is tricked oot in aw the colours of the rainbow.

CHARLOTTE: Mr. Mordecai is always well dressed, Sir Archy.

SIR ARCHY: Upon honour he is as fine as a jay.   Turn aboot, mon, turn aboot, lat us view yeer finery—step along, and lat us see yeer shapes! he has a bonny march wi' him: vary weel, vary ailegant. Ha, ha, ha! guid traith, I think I never saw a tooth-drawer[2] better dressed in aw my life.   (*Viewing and admiring his dress*)

CHARLOTTE: Ha, ah, ha!

MORDECAI: You are very polite, sir.

CHARLOTTE: But, Sir Archy, what is become of my Irish lover, your friend Sir Callaghan?   I hope he dines here.

SIR ARCHY: Ah, ha! guid faith, wull he!   I hai brought him along wi' me.

CHARLOTTE: What, is he in the house?

SIR ARCHY: Aye, in this vary mansion, madam; for ye mun ken that like the monarchs of auld, I never travel noo withoot my feul.

CHARLOTTE: Then pray, Sir Archy, exhibit your fool.

MORDECAI: Let's have a slice of him.

SIR ARCHY: Jauntly, jauntly, nai so fast! he is na in reeght order yat.

CHARLOTTE: How do you mean, Sir Archy?

[1] It is evident that Macklin had observed Scottish negative usages, but they are confusedly and inconsistently given in MS. and Murphy.   Here they are settled as: 'na'＝not (unstressed); 'nai'＝ not (stressed), and no.

[2] Tooth-pullers at fairs were gaily dressed.

Act I

SIR ARCHY: Madam, as we came heether, I coonselled him till wreete a loove epestle till ye, by way of introduction till his courtship: he is noo aboot it below stairs, and in tan meenutes ye mun leuk till see an amorous beellet, sic as has na been penned sin the days of Don Quixote—ha, ha, ha!

OMNES: Ha, ha, ha!

CHARLOTTE: O charming! I shall be impatient till I see his passion upon paper.

SIR ARCHY: Guid faith, madam, he has done that awready; for he has composed a jargon, that he caws a sonnet, upon his bewitching Charlotte, as he tarms ye. Mordecai, ye hai heard him sing it.

MORDECAI: I beg your pardon, Sir Archy, I have heard him roar it. Madam, we had him last night at the tavern, and made him give it to us in an Irish howl[1] that might be heard from here to West Chester.

SIR ARCHY: Ha, ha, ha! why ye hai a deevelish deal of wit, Mordecai.

CHARLOTTE: Ha, ha, ha! I must hear this song.

MORDECAI: Madam, your servant—I will leave Sir Archy to entertain you for a few minutes.

CHARLOTTE: You are not going, Mr. Mordecai?

MORDECAI: Madam, I am only going down stairs, to see if Sir Callaghan is disengaged; and, if he be, to have a laugh at him before dinner, by way of a whet—that's all, madam, only by way of a whet. (Going)

SIR ARCHY: But, hark'ee, Mordecai, nai a seelable o' the latter.

MORDECAI: O never fear me, Sir Archy, I am as secret as a spy. (Exit)

SIR ARCHY: What a fantastical baboon this Eesrelite maks o' himsel. The fallow is the mockery of the whole nation.

CHARLOTTE: Why to say the truth, he is entertaining, Sir Archy.

SIR ARCHY: O yas, he is redeeculous, therefore vary useful in society, for wherever he comes there mun be laughter. But noo, madam, guin ye please, a word or twa of oor ain maiters; ye see I do na paster ye wi' flames, and darts, and seeghings, and lamentations, and freevolous protestations, like yeer silly loovers in a romance; for ye ken, I awways speak my thoughts wi' a blunt integrity— madam, I loove ye, and guin I did na, I would scorn to say it.

[1] The 'Irish howl' is an old and frequent association. Cf. *TSS* pp. 31, 106, 120.

51

CHARLOTTE: O, Sir Archy, all the world allows you sincerity, which is the most valuable quality a friend or a lover can possess.

SIR ARCHY: Vary true, madam, therefore I canna help gi'ing ye a hint, by way of a leetle fore knowledge concerning these things that are aboot ye, wha caw themsels yeer loovers. Squeere Groom, doubtless, is a mon of honour, and my vary guid freend, but he is a baggar, a baggar; and, touching this Mordecai, the fallow is wealthy, 'tis true—yas, yas, he is wealthy, but he is a reptile, a mere reptile! and as till the Irishman, Sir Callaghan O'Brallaghan, the fallow is weel enough till laugh at, but I would hai ye leuk aboot ye there, for ye ken that yeer guardian is his uncle—and till my certain knowledge there is a deseegn upon yeer fortune in that quarter, depend upon it.

CHARLOTTE: Very possible, Sir Archy, very possible; for a woman's fortune, I believe, is the principal object of every lover's wish.

SIR ARCHY: Madam, yeer observation is vary orthodox—vary orthodox in truth, as till Mordecai, Sir Callaghan, Squeere Groom, and sic like fallows; but men of honour—men of honour, madam, hai aither preenciples. I assure ye, lady, the tanure of my affaction is na for yeer pecuniar, but for the mental graces of yeer soul, and the deevene perfactions of yeer body, which are indeed till me a Peru and a Mexico.

CHARLOTTE: O, Sir Archy, you overwhelm me.

SIR ARCHY: Madam, I speak upon the varity of mine honour: beside, madam, guin ye marry me, ye wull marry a mon of sobreeity and oeconomy;[1] 'tis true I am na in the high day of blood, yat, as the poet sings, far frai the vale of years; nai like yeer young flashy whupsters, that gang off like a squib or a cracker on a rejoicing neeght, in a noise and a stanch, and are never heard of after.

CHARLOTTE: You are certainly right, Sir Archy, the young fellows of fashion are mere trifles.

SIR ARCHY: They are baubles, madam, absolute baubles and prodigals, therefore ye should preponderate the maiter weel, before ye mak yeer elaction. Conseeder, madam, there is nai scant of wealth or honour in oor faimily. Lady, we hai in the hoose of Macsarcasm twa Barons, three Viscoonts, sax Earls, yean Marqueesate, and twa Dukes—besides Baronets and Lairds oot of aw reckoning.

---

[1] This is the first dramatic reference to Scottish thrift and parsimony. Cf. *TSS* pp. 234-5.

CHARLOTTE: Ha, ha, ha!

SIR ARCHY: What gars ye laugh, madam?

CHARLOTTE: I beg your pardon, sir; but—ha, ha, ha! I am laughing—ha, ha, ha! to think what a—ha, ha!—a number of noble relations I shall have.

SIR ARCHY: Faith wull ye, madam! and aither guess faimilies than ye hai in this part of the world—Odzwuns, madam, there is as muckle deeference betwixt oor nobeelety of the North, and yeers o' th' Sooth, as there is betwixt a hound of blood and a mungrel.

CHARLOTTE: Ha, ha, ha! pray how do you make that out, Sir Archy?

SIR ARCHY: Why, madam, in Scotland, aw oor Nobeelety are sprung frai Monarchs, Warriors, Heroes, and glorious achievements: noo here i' th' Sooth, ye are aw sprung frai sugar hogsheads, rum puncheons, wool packs, hop sacks, iron bars, and tar jackets—in short, ye are a composeetion of Jews, Turks, and refugees, and of aw the commercial vagrants of the land and sea—a sort of ampheebious breed ye are.

CHARLOTTE: Ha, ha, ha! we are a strange mixture indeed, nothing like so pure and noble as you are in the North.

SIR ARCHY: O, naithing like it, madam, naithing like it; we are of anaither kidney—quite of anaither kidney. Noo, madam, as ye yeersel are na weel propagated, as ye hai the misfortune till be a cheeld o' commerce, ye should endeavour till mak yeer espousals intill yean of oor auncient noble faimilies of the North; for ye mun ken, madam, that sic an alliance wull purify yeer blood, and gi' ye a rank and consequence in the world, that aw yeer palf, were it as muckle as the bank of Edinburgh, could na purchase for ye.

CHARLOTTE: Very true, Sir Archy, very true; upon my word, your advice is friendly and impartial, and I will think of it.

Enter MORDECAI

MORDECAI: Here he is! he is coming, madam! he is but just giving some orders to his servant about his baggage and post horses.

CHARLOTTE: I hope he is not going away.

SIR ARCHY: Traith is he, madam! he is impatient [till return till the army—he is quite oot of his element here, he says. But this vary morning he tauld me that naithing kept him but till seek an opportunity till break his affaction till ye, madam.

CHARLOTTE: O pray, Sir Archy, don't let him go to-day; at least not till he has given us some account of his battles and transactions in Germany.

SIR ARCHY: Dear madam, ye need yeersel but ask him till favour ye wi' a sleeght narration of them, and guin ye aince set his tongue a wagging, I'll engage he wull fight ye as many battles as Quintus Curtius, and aw in as guid meeletary Irish as ever came frai the banks of the Shannon, or the bogs of Tipperary.

MORDECAI: Aye, aye, madam, never fear, we will shew him off, I warrant you no man shews a monster better than I do upon these occasions.][1]

SIR CALLAGHAN: (*Within*) Is Sir Archy Macsarcasm and the lady this way, young man?

SERVANT: (*Within*) Yes, sir.

SIR CALLAGHAN: Then I'll trouble you with no further ceremony.

Enter SIR CALLAGHAN

SIR CALLAGHAN: Madam, I am your most devoted and most obedient humble servant, and am proud to have the honour of kissing your fair hand this morning.   (*Salutes her*)

CHARLOTTE: Sir Callaghan, your humble servant—I am sorry to hear we are likely to lose you.   I was in hopes the campaign had been quite over in Germany, for this winter.

SIR CALLAGHAN: Yes, madam, it was quite over, but it began again: a true genius never loves to quit the field till he has left himself nothing to do; for then, you know, madam, he can keep it with more safety.

OMNES: Ha, ha, ha!

SIR ARCHY: Vary true, sir, vary true.   But, Sir Callaghan, just as ye entered the apartment, the lady was urging she should like it meeghtily, guin ye would favour her wi' a sleeght narrative of the late transactions and battles in Germany.

CHARLOTTE: If Sir Callaghan would be so obliging.

SIR CALLAGHAN: O dear, madam, don't ax me.

CHARLOTTE: Sir, I beg pardon, I would not press any thing that I thought might be disagreeable to you.

---

[1] This passage, replaced by 'to be with the army in Germany', was cut from the MS. It seemed worth including.   The cuts all help to tighten up the play: there is no reason to suppose that any of them were made at George II's instance.

SIR CALLAGHAN: O, dear madam, it is not for that; but it rebutes[1] a man of honour to be talking to ladies of battles and sieges and skirmages—it looks like gasconading and making the fanfaron. Besides, madam, I give you my honour, there is no such thing in nature as making a true description of a battle.

CHARLOTTE: How so, sir?

SIR CALLAGHAN: Why, madam, there is so much doing every where, there is no knowing what is done any where; for every man has his own part to look after, which is as much as he can do, without minding what other people are about. Then, madam, there is such drumming and trumpeting, firing and smoking, fighting and rattling every where—and such an uproar of courage and slaughter in every man's mind—and such a delightful confusion altogether, that you can no more give an account of it than you can of the stars in the sky.

SIR ARCHY: As I shall answer it, I think it a vary descriptive accoont that he gi'es of a battle.

CHARLOTTE: Admirable! and very entertaining.

MORDECAI: O, delightful!

SIR ARCHY: Mordecai, ask him some questions—till him, till him mon—hai a leetle fun wi' him—smoke him, smoke him; rally him, mon, rally him. (*Whispering* MORDECAI *apart*)

MORDECAI: I'll do it, I'll do it: yes, I will smoke the captain. Well—and pray, Sir Callaghan, how many might you kill in a battle?

SIR CALLAGHAN: Sir!

MORDECAI: I say, sir, how many might you have killed in any one battle?

SIR CALLAGHAN: Kill?—Um—why, I generally kill more in a battle than a coward would choose to look upon, or than an impertinent fellow would be able to eat. Ha!—are you answered, Mr. Mordecai?

MORDECAI: Yes, yes, sir, I am answered. He is a devilish droll fellow—vastly queer.

SIR ARCHY: Yas, he is vary queer—but ye were vary sharp upon him. Odzwuns, at him again—hai anaither cut at him.

MORDECAI: Yes, I will have another cut at him.

---

[1] An obsolete and northern form of 'rebut', of which the nearest sense to the use here is the obsolete one of 'reproach'.

SIR ARCHY: Do, do. He wull bring himsel intill a damned scrape presently. (*Aside*)

MORDECAI: (*Going up to* SIR CALLAGHAN *and sneering at him*) He, he, he! but hark'ee, Sir Callaghan—he, he, he!—give me leave to tell you now, if I was a general—

SIR CALLAGHAN: You a general! faith, then, you would make a very pretty general! (*Turns* MORDECAI *about*) Pray, madam, look at the general—ha, ha, ha![1]

OMNES: Ha, ha, ha!

SIR CALLAGHAN: O my dear Mr. Mordecai, be advised, and don't prate about generals; it is a very hard trade to learn, and requires being in the field late and early, a great many frosty nights and scorching days—to be able to eat and drink, and laugh and rejoice, with danger on one side of you, and death on the other—and a hundred things beside, that you know no more of than I do of being a high priest of a synagogue: so hold your tongue about generals, Mr. Mordecai, and go and mind your lottery-tickets, and your cent per cent, in 'Change-Alley.

OMNES: Ha, ha, ha!

SIR ARCHY: Ha, ha, ha! he has tickled up the Eesrelite—he has gi'en it the Moabite on baith sides of his lugs.

CHARLOTTE: But, Sir Callaghan, sure you must have been in imminent danger in the variety of actions you have gone through.

SIR CALLAGHAN: Ho! to be sure, madam, who would be a soldier without danger? Danger, madam, is a soldier's greatest glory, and death his best reward.

MORDECAI: Ha, ha, ha! that is an excellent bull! death a reward! Pray, Sir Callaghan, no offence, I hope—how do you make out death being a reward?

SIR CALLAGHAN: How? Why, don't you know that?

MORDECAI: Not I, upon honour.

SIR CALLAGHAN: Why, a soldier's death in the field of battle, is a monument of fame, that makes him as much alive as Caesar, or Alexander, or any dead hero of them all.

OMNES: Ha, ha, ha!

CHARLOTTE: Very well explained, Sir Callaghan.

---

[1] A caricature (1802) of Mordecai at this point is reproduced opposite page 69: the actor is almost certainly Samuel Simmons (1777?–1819) whose best part it was.

SIR ARCHY: Axcellently weel! vary logically, and like a true hero.

SIR CALLAGHAN: Why, madam, when the history of the English campaigns in America comes to be written, there is your own brave young general, that died the other day in the field of battle before Quebec, will be alive to the end of the world.

CHARLOTTE: You are right, Sir Callaghan, his virtues, and those of his fellow soldiers in that action—aye, and of those that planned it too—will be remembered by their country, while Britain or British gratitude has a being.

SIR ARCHY: Oh! the Highlanders did guid service in that action—they cut them, and slashed them, and whupt them aboot, and played the vary deevil wi' them, sir. There is nai siccan a thing as standing a Highlander's Andrew Ferrara[1]—they wull slaughie[2] off a fallow's heed at yean dash, slap; it was they that did the business at Quebec.

SIR CALLAGHAN: I dare say they were not idle, for they are tight fellows. Give me your hand, Sir Archy; I assure you your countrymen are good soldiers—aye, and so are ours too.

CHARLOTTE: Well, Sir Callaghan, I assure you, I am charmed with your heroism, and greatly obliged to you for your account. Come, Mr. Mordecai, we will go down to Sir Theodore, if you please, for I think I heard his coach stop.

MORDECAI: Madam, I attend you with pleasure. Will you honour me with the tip of your ladyship's wedding finger? Sir Callaghan, your servant; yours, yours—look here, look here. (*Leads* CHARLOTTE *off, singing in great exultation*)

SIR CALLAGHAN: I find he is a very impertinent coxcomb, this same Beau Mordecai.

SIR ARCHY: Yas, sir, he is a damned impudent rascal.

SIR CALLAGHAN: I assure you, I had a great mind to be upon the *qui vive* with him for his jokes and his mockeries, but that the lady was by.

SIR ARCHY: Yas, he is a cursed impudent fallow—because he is suffered till speak till a mon of fashion, at Bath and Tunbridge and aither public places, the rascal awways obtrudes himsel upon ye. But, Sir Callaghan, hai ye wreeten the latter till the lady?

---

[1] Cf. W. F. Sullivan, *The Test of Union and Loyalty* (1797): 'The brawny Scot...whose Andrea-Ferrara and his kirk alike be dear to Caledonian mind...'

[2] Meaning obvious, but not in Scottish Dialect Dictionary.

SIR CALLAGHAN: I have not.

SIR ARCHY: Hoo happened that, mon?

SIR CALLAGHAN, Why, upon reflecting, I found it would not be consisting with the decorums of a man of honour to write to a lady in the way of matrimonial advances, before I had first made my affections known to her guardian, who is, you know, my uncle; so I have indited the letter to him, instead of the lady, which is the same thing you know.

SIR ARCHY: Ha, ha! axactly, axactly, for so ye do but wreet aboot it, ye ken, it maiters not till whom.

SIR CALLAGHAN: Aye, that is what I thought myself: so here it is. (*Takes out a letter, and reads*) 'To Sir Theodore Goodchild'—

SIR ARCHY: Aye, lat's hai it—I warrant 'tis a bonny epestle.

SIR CALLAGHAN: 'Sir, as I have the honour to bear the character of a soldier, and to call Sir Theodore Goodchild uncle, I do not think it would be conshisting vid a man of honour to behave like a scoundrel'—

SIR ARCHY: That is an axcellent remark, Sir Callaghan—an axcellent remark, and vary new.

SIR CALLAGHAN: Yes, I think it is a good remark. 'Therefore I thought proper, before I proceeded any farther (for I have done nothing as yet), to break my mind to you, before I engage the affections of the young lady'—you see, Sir Archy, I intend to carry the place like a soldier, *à la militaire*, as we say abroad; for I make my approaches regularly to the breast work, before I attempt the covered way.

SIR ARCHY: Axcellent! that's axcellent.

SIR CALLAGHAN: Yes, I think it will do. 'For as you are a gentleman, and one that knows my family, by my fader's side, which you are shensible is as ould as any in the three kingdoms, and oulder too—so I thought it would be foolish to stand shilli shalli any longer, but come to the point at once'. You see, Sir Archy, I give him a rub; but by way of a hint about my family: because why, do you see, Sir Theodore is my uncle only by my moder's side, which is a little upstart family that came in vid one Strongbow[1] but t'other day—lord, not above six or seven hundred years ago: whereas my

---

[1] The nickname of Richard de Clare, Earl of Pembroke, leader of the Anglo-Norman invasion of Ireland, 1169–70.

family, by my fader's side, are all the true old Milesians,[1] and related to the O'Flahertys, and O'Shocknesses, and the Mac-Laughlins, the O'Donnegans, O'Callaghans, O'Geogaghans,[2] and all the tick blood of the nation—and I myself, you know, am an O'Brallaghan, which is the ouldest of them all.

SIR ARCHY: Ha, ha, ha! aye, aye! I believe ye are of an auncient faimily, Sir Callaghan, but ye are oot in yean point.

SIR CALLAGHAN: What is that, Sir Archy?

SIR ARCHY: When ye said ye were as auncient as ainy family in the three kingdoms.

SIR CALLAGHAN: Faith, den, I said nothing but truth.

SIR ARCHY: Hut[3], hut, hut awa, mon, hut awa, ye mun na say that; what the deevil, conseeder oor faimilies i'th'North; why ye of Ireland, sir, are but a colony frai us, an oot cast! a mere oot cast, and as sic ye remain till this 'oor.

SIR CALLAGHAN: I beg your pardon, Sir Archy, that is the Scotch account, which, you know, never speaks truth, because it is always partial—but the Irish history, which must be the best, because it was written by an Irish poet of my own family, one Shemus Thurlough Shannaghan O'Brallaghan[4]; and he says, in his chapter of genealogy, that the Scots are all Irishmen's bastards.

SIR ARCHY: Hoo, sir! baistards! do ye mak us illegeetemate, illegeetemate, sir?

SIR CALLAGHAN: Faith, I do—for the youngest branch of our family, one Mac Fergus[5] O'Brallaghan, was the very man that went from Carrickfergus, and peopled all Scotland with his own hands; so

---

[1] The followers of Miled, the leader of the quasi-legendary last pre-Christian invasion of Ireland. Originally Scythian, like Aeneas and his Trojans they wandered in search of a promised land—Inis Fail, the Island of Destiny—and after a long sojourn in Spain, found it in Ireland. From them descend the O's and the Macs.

[2] Ó Flaithbhertaigh—a leading family of S.W. Connacht and the Aran Islands: Ó Seachnasaigh—chiefly from the Kiltartan area of Galway, descended from the last pagan king of Ireland and chiefs in Connacht in the late sixteenth century: MacLochláinn—Macklin's own name, cf. p. 5 above: Ó Donegáin, a widely spread Milesian name: Ó Ceallacháin—cf. p. 47, n. 1 above: O'Geogaghan, commonly MacEochagáin, an important Westmeath family.

[3] Other playwrights spell 'hoot': Macklin was possibly trying to indicate the narrow rounded Scots *u*-sound.

[4] James Turlough—King Brian's grandson who died heroically at the Battle of Clontarf, aged fifteen: Ó Seancháin—a Clare family.

[5] In A.D. 503, Fergus MacErc led an invasion and established himself as ruler of a large territory in Western Scotland.

that, my dear Sir Archy, you must be bastards of course, you know.

SIR ARCHY: Hark'ee, Sir Callaghan, though yeer ignorance and vanity would mak conquerors and ravishers of yeer auncestors, and harlots and Sabines of oor maithers—yat, ye shall prove, sir, that their issue are aw the cheeldren of honour.

SIR CALLAGHAN: Hark'ee, hark'ee, Sir Archy, what is that you mentioned aboot ignorance and vanity?

SIR ARCHY: Sir, I denoonce ye baith ignorant and vain, and mak yeer maist of it.

SIR CALLAGHAN: Faith, sir, I can make nothing of it; for they are words I don't understand, because they are what no gentleman is used to: and therefore, you must unsay them.

SIR ARCHY: Hoo, sir! eat my words? a North Briton eat his words?

SIR CALLAGHAN: Indeed you must, and this instant eat them.

SIR ARCHY: Ye shall first eat a piece of this weapon. (*Draws his sword*)

SIR CALLAGHAN: Pooh, pooh, Sir Archy, put up, put up—this is no proper place for such work; consider, drawing a sword is a very serious piece of business, and ought always to be done in private—we may be prevented here; but if you are for a little of that fun, come your ways to the right spot, my dear.

SIR ARCHY: Nai equeevocation, sir, donna ye think ye hai gotten Beau Mordecai till cope wi'. Defend yeersel, for by the sacred honour of Saint Andrew, ye shall be responsible for making us illegeetemate, sir, illegeetemate.

SIR CALLAGHAN: Then, by the sacred crook of Saint Patrick, you are a very foolish man to quarrel about such a trifle. But since you have a mind for a tilt, have at you, my dear, for the honour of the sod. Oho! my jewel, never fear us; you are as welcome as the flowers in May. (*They fight*)

Enter CHARLOTTE

CHARLOTTE: Oh! bless me, gentlemen! what are you doing? what is all this about?

SIR CALLAGHAN: Madam, it is about Sir Archy's great grandmother.

CHARLOTTE: His great grandmother?

SIR CALLAGHAN: Yes, madam, he is angry that I said my ancestor, Fergus O'Brallaghan, was a gallant of hers.

CHARLOTTE: Grandmother! pray, Sir Archy, what is the meaning of all this?

SIR ARCHY: Madam, he has cast an affront upon a whole nation.

SIR CALLAGHAN: I am sure if I did, it was more than I intended; I only argued out of the history of Ireland, to prove the antiquity of the O'Brallaghans.

SIR ARCHY: Weel, sir, sin ye say ye didna intend the affront, I am satisfied. (*Puts up his sword*)

SIR CALLAGHAN: Not I upon my honour—there are two things I am always afraid of; the one is of being affronted myself, and the other of affronting any man.

CHARLOTTE: That is a prudent and a very generous maxim, Sir Callaghan. Sir Archy, pray let me beg that this business may end here. I desire you will embrace, and be the friends you were before this mistake happened.

SIR ARCHY: Madam, yeer commands are absolute.

CHARLOTTE: Sir Callaghan—

SIR CALLAGHAN: Madam, with all my heart and soul, I assure you, Sir Archy, I had not the least intention of affronting or quarrelling with you. (*He offers to embrace* SIR ARCHY, *who starts from him with contempt*)

SIR ARCHY: Vary weel, sir, vary weel.

SIR CALLAGHAN: Oh! the curse of Cromwell[1] upon your proud Scotch stomach.

CHARLOTTE: Well, gentlemen, I am glad to see you are come to a right understanding—I hope 'tis all over.

SIR ARCHY: I am satisfied, madam, there is an end on't. But noo, Sir Callaghan, lat me tell ye as a freend, ye should never enter intill a dispute aboot leeterature, history, or the anteequety of faimilies, for ye hai gotten sic a wecked, awkward, cursed jargon upon yeer tongue, that ye are never intelligible in yeer language.

SIR CALLAGHAN: Ha, ha, ha! I beg your pardon, Sir Archy, it is you that have got such a cursed twist of a fat Scotch brogue about the middle of your own tongue, that you can't understand good English when I speak it to you.

[1] A common Irish imprecation: Irishmen naturally regard Cromwell as an incarnation of evil and cruelty.

SIR ARCHY: Ha, ha, ha! weel, that is droll enough, upon honour—ye are as guid as a farce or a comedy; but ye are oot again, Sir Callaghan, it is ye that hai the brogue, and nai me; for aw the world kens I speak the Sooth Country so well, that wherever I gang, I am awways taken for an Englishman: but we wull mak judgment by the lady, which of us twa has the brogue.

SIR CALLAGHAN: O, with all my heart. Pray, madam, have I the brogue?

CHARLOTTE: Ha, ha, ha! not in the least, Sir Callaghan, not in the least.

SIR CALLAGHAN: I am sure I could never perceive it.

CHARLOTTE: Pray, Sir Archy, drop this contention, or we may chance to have another quarrel—you both speak most elegant English; neither of you have the brogue, neither. Ha, ha, ha!

Enter SERVANT

SERVANT: The ladies are come, madam, and Sir Theodore desires to speak with you.

CHARLOTTE: I will wait on him. (*Exit* SERVANT) Gentlemen, your servant—you will come to us? (*Exit*)

SIR ARCHY: Instantly, madam. Weel, Sir Callaghan, donna lat us drop the deseegn of the latter, notwithstanding what has happened.

SIR CALLAGHAN: Are we friends, Sir Archy?

SIR ARCHY: Pooh! upon honour am I; it was aw a mistake.

SIR CALLAGHAN: Then give me your hand; I assure you, Sir Archy, I always love a man when I quarrel with him, after I am friends.

Enter SERVANT

SERVANT: Dinner is served, gentlemen.

SIR ARCHY: Come along then, Sir Callaghan—I wull bring ye and the lady together after dinner, and then we shall see hoo ye wull mak yeer advances in loove.

SIR CALLAGHAN: O never fear me, Sir Archy—I will not stay to make a regular siege of it, but will take her at once with a *coup de main*, or die upon the spot: for, as the old song says, Sir Archy— (*Sings to an Irish tune*)

You never did hear of an Irishman's fear,
In love or in battle, in love or in battle,
We are always on duty, and ready for beauty,

62

Though cannons do rattle, though cannons do rattle:
By day and by night, we love and we fight,
We're honour's defender, we're honour's defender;
The foe and the fair—we always take care,
To make them surrender, to make them surrender. (*Exeunt*)

END OF THE FIRST ACT

ACT II

Enter SIR ARCHY *and* CHARLOTTE

SIR ARCHY: Odzwuns, madam, step intill us for a moment—ye wull crack yeersel wi' laughter; we hai gotten anaither feul come till divert us unexpactedly, which I think is the highest finished feul the age has produced.

CHARLOTTE: Whom do you mean, Sir Archy?

SIR ARCHY: Squeere Groom, madam; but such a feegure, the finest ye ever beheld: his leetle half beuts, black cap, jockey dress, and aw his pontificalibus[1]—just as he rid the match yesterday at York. Anteequety, in aw its records of Greek and Roman folly, never produced a senator veeseting his mistress in so compleat a feul's garb.

CHARLOTTE: Ha, ha, ha! ridiculous!   I thought I had done wondering at the mirror of folly; but he is one of those geniuses that never appear without surprising the world with some new stroke.

Enter MORDECAI

MORDECAI: O madam! ha, ha, ha! I am expiring—such a scene betwixt your two lovers, Squire Groom and Sir Callaghan: they have challenged each other.

CHARLOTTE: O heavens, I hope not.

SIR ARCHY: Ha, ha, ha! that's guid!   I thought it would come till action; ha, ha, ha! that's clever—noo we shall hai yean of them penked, ha, ha, ha!

CHARLOTTE: How can you laugh, Sir Archy, at such a shocking circumstance?

MORDECAI: Don't be frightened, madam—ha, ha, ha! don't be frightened; neither of them will be killed, take my word for it—unless it be with claret, for that's their weapon.

CHARLOTTE: O Mr. Mordecai, how could you startle one so?

SIR ARCHY: O, I am sorry for that—guid traith, I was in hopes they had a mind till shew their prowess before their mistress, and that we

---

[1] Cf. illustration opposite page 68, which gives some indication of the dress.

64

should hai a leetle Irish, or Newmarket blood spilt. But what was the cause of challenge, Mordecai?

MORDECAI: Their passion for this lady, sir. Squire Groom challenged Sir Callaghan to drink your ladyship's health in a pint bumper—which the knight gallantly accepted in an instant, and returned the challenge in a quart—which was as gallantly received and swallowed by the Squire, ha, ha, ha! and out-braved by a fresh daring of three pints; upon which I thought proper to decamp, not thinking it altogether safe to be near the champions, lest I should be deluged by a cascade of claret.

OMNES: Ha, ha, ha!

CHARLOTTE: O monstrous! they will kill themselves.

MORDECAI: Never fear, madam.

GROOM: (*Within, hallooing*) Come along, Sir Caligaligan Bragligan,[1] haux, haux! hark forward, my honies.

Enter SQUIRE GROOM, *drunk*

MORDECAI: Here your champion comes, madam.

GROOM: Madam, I beg a million of pardons for not being with you at dinner—it was not my fault, upon my honour—for I sat up all night, on purpose to set out betimes; but about one o'clock last night, at York, as we were all damned jolly, that fool, Sir Roger Bumper, borrowed my watch to set his by it—there it is—look at it, madam, it corrects the sun—they all stop by it at Newmarket—and so, madam, as I was telling you, the drunken blockhead put mine back two hours, on purpose to deceive me—otherwise I would have held fifty to one I should have been here to a second.

CHARLOTTE: O sir, there needs no apology; but how came you to travel in that extraordinary dress?

GROOM: A bet, a bet, madam, a bet—I rid my match in this very dress, yesterday: so Jack Buck, Sir Roger Bumper, and some more of them, layed me a hundred each that I would not ride to London and visit you in it, madam—ha, ha! don't you think I have touched them, madam, ha? I have taken them all in—ha? ha'n't I, madam.

OMNES: Ha, ha, ha!

CHARLOTTE: You have, indeed, sir; pray what time do you allow yourself to come from York to London?

[1] Thus in MS. Sir Callaghan Brallaghan in Murphy.

GROOM: Ha! time! why, bar a neck, a leg, or an arm, sixteen hours, seven minutes, and thirty-three seconds—sometimes three or four seconds under:[1] that is, to the stones' end,[2] not to my own house.

SIR ARCHY: Nai, nai! nai till yeer ain hoose, that would be too muckle.

GROOM: No, no, only to the stones' end: but then, I have my own hacks, steel to the bottom, all blood—stickers and lappers[3] every inch, my dear—that will come through if they have but one leg out of the four. I never keep any thing, madam, that is not bottom—game,[4] game to the last—aye, aye, you will find every thing that belongs to me game, madam.

SIR ARCHY: Ha, ha, ha! weel said, squeere—yas, yas, he is game, game till the bottom. There, walk aboot, and lat us see yeer shapes—ha! what a fine feegure—why ye are so fine a feegure, and hai so guid an understanding for it, it is a peety ye should ever do ainy thing aw yeer life, but ride horse-races—donna ye think he is a cursed eediot, Mordecai? (*Whispering to* MORDECAI)

MORDECAI: Um! he is well enough for a squire—ha, ha!

GROOM: Madam, I am come to pay my respects to you, according to promise. Well, which of us is to be the happy man? you know I love you—may I never win a match if I don't.

OMNES: Ha, ha, ha!

CHARLOTTE: O sir, I am convinced of your passion; I see it in your eyes.

SIR ARCHY: Weel, but, squeere, ye hai gi'en us nai accoont hoo the match went.

CHARLOTTE: Pray, what was the match, sir?

GROOM: Our contribution, madam. There are seven of us—Jack Buck, Lord Brainless, Bob Rattle—you know Bob, madam; Bob's a damned honest fellow—Sir Harry Idle, Dick Riot, Sir Roger Bumper; and myself. We put in five hundred apiece, all to ride ourselves, and all to carry my weight—there I had the pull. The odds at starting were six and seven to four against me, the field round; and the field, ten, fifteen, and twenty to one—for you

---

[1] York to London is about 190 miles: Groom claims to have averaged nearly 12 m.p.h., outdoing Dick Turpin.

[2] i.e. to the last milestone.

[3] Stickers—having endurance: lappers = leapers ('lap', dial. and obsolete for leap).

[4] Bottom, game—with staying power and spirit.

must know, madam, the thing I was to have rid was let down—do you mind?—was let down, madam, in his exercise.[1]

SIR ARCHY: That was unlucky.

GROOM: O damned unlucky! however, we started—off score,[2] by Jupiter—and for the first half mile, madam, you might have covered us with your under pettycoat. But your friend Bob, madam—ha, ha, ha! I shall never forget it—poor Bob went out of the course, and ran over two attornies, an exciseman, and a little beau Jew—Mordecai's friend, madam, that you used to laugh at so immoderately at Bath—a little, fine, dirty thing, with a chocolate coloured phiz, just like Mordecai's. Ha, ha, ha! the people were in hopes he had killed the lawyers, but were damnably disappointed, when they found he had only broke the leg of one, and the back of the other.

OMNES: Ha, ha, ha!

SIR ARCHY: And hoo did it end, squeere? Wha won the subscription?

GROOM: It lay between Dick Riot and me. We were neck and neck, madam, for three mile, as hard as we could lay leg to ground—made running every inch—but at the first loose I felt for him, found I had the foot—knew my bottom—pulled up—pretended to dig and cut—all fudge, all fudge, my dear—gave the signal to pond, to lay it on thick—had the whip hand all the way—lay with my nose in his flank, under the wind—thus, (*Here* SQUIRE GROOM *imitates all the postures and motions of a rider in a severe struggle to win his match*) snug, snug, my dear, quite in hand—while Riot was digging and lapping, right and left—but it would not do, my dear, against foot, bottom, and head; so within a hundred yards of the distance post, poor Dick knocked up as stiff as a turnpike,[3] and left me to canter in by myself, madam, and to touch them all round—for I took all the odds, split me! Ha? wasn't I right? ha? took the odds! Aye, aye, took all the odds, my dear.

---

[1] This seems to mean that the original odds lengthened when it became known that his horse had been let down—i.e. had trouble with a sinew.

[2] Making a sudden dash at full speed.

[3] This seems to mean: at the first opportunity to loose the reins I weighed up my opponent and found I had more speed; knowing my horse's reliability, I slowed down and pretended to use spur and whip—urged my mount to pound on and do his best, and had the advantage all the way—stayed a little behind Dick Riot on the sheltered side, in easy control, while he was spurring his horse which was jumping from side to side: but he could not succeed against my speed and endurance, and so had to give up when his horse could do no more.

OMNES: Ha, ha, ha!

SIR ARCHY: Weel, it is wonderful till think till what a pitch of axcellence oor nobeelety are arrived at in the art of sporting—I believe we axcel aw the nobeelety in Europe in that science, especially in jockeyship.

GROOM: Sir Archy, I'll tell you what I will do—I will start a horse, fight a main, hunt a pack of hounds, ride a match or a fox-chase, drive a set of horses, or hold a toast, with any nobleman in Europe for a thousand each—and I say done first, damn me!

OMNES: Ha, ha, ha!

SIR ARCHY: Why, I ken ye wull, and I wull gang yeer halves. Why madam, the squeere is the keenest sportsman in aw Europe: madam, there is naithing comes amiss till him; he wull fish, or fowl, or hunt—he hunts every thing—every thing, frai the flea in the blanket till the elephant in the forest. He is at aw—a perfect Nimrod; are ye nai, squeere?

OMNES: Ha, ha, ha!

GROOM: Yes, damn me, I am a Nimrod, madam—at all, at all—any thing, any thing! why, I ran a snail with his grace, the other day, for five hundred—nothing in it—won it hollow, above half a horn's length.

SIR ARCHY: By above half a horn's length! that was hollow indeed, Squeere.

GROOM: O, devilish hollow.

SIR ARCHY: But where is Sir Callaghan aw this time?

GROOM: Oh! he's with Sir Theodore, who is joking him about his drinking bumpers with me—and his passion for you, madam.

SIR ARCHY: Ye mun ken, gentlemen, this lady and I hai laid a scheme till hai a leetle sport wi' Sir Callaghan—noo, if ye will step behind that screen, and promise till be silent, I'll gang and fetch him, and ye shall hear him mak loove as fierce as ainy hero in a tragedy.

GROOM: Sir Archy, I'll be as silent as a hound at fault.

SIR ARCHY: Then do ye retire, madam, and come in till him, as guin ye came on purpose—I'll fetch him in an instant.

CHARLOTTE: I shall be ready, Sir Archy   (*Exit*)

SIR ARCHY: Get ye behind, get ye behind, gentlemen.   (*Exit*)

GROOM: Aye, aye, we'll squat, never fear, Sir Archy—an Irishman make love! I should be glad to hear what an Irishman can say

ENGRAVING AND BALLAD OF *LOVE A LA MODE*

(By courtesy of the British Museum)

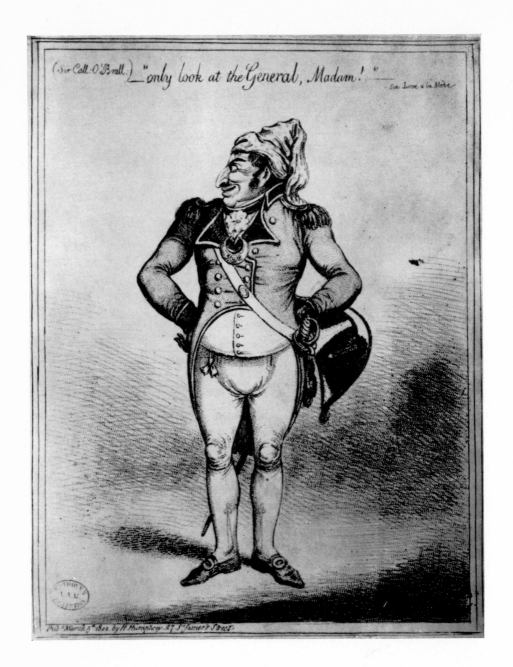

CARICATURE OF SIMMONS AS MORDECAI

(*By courtesy of the Gabrielle Enthoven Collection*)

when he makes love. What do you think he'll say, little Shadrach? Do you think he'll make love in Irish?

MORDECAI: Something very like it, I dare say, squire. Let us retire, here they come. (*They retire*)

Enter SIR ARCHY *and* SIR CALLAGHAN

SIR ARCHY: Speak bawldly, mon; ye ken the auld proverb, "Faint heart"—

SIR CALLAGHAN: That is true—"never won fair lady". Yes, I think now I have got a bumper or two, I may tell her my passion, and bring the point to an *eclaircissement*.

SIR ARCHY: Aye, that's reeght, mon! stick to that, she wull be wi' ye in a twankling. Yeer servant—I wish ye guid success. (*Exit*)

SIR CALLAGHAN: Sir Archy, your servant. Well now, what am I to do in this business?—I know it is a great scandal for a soldier to be in love in time of war—I strive to keep her out of my mind, but can't; the more I strive to do it, the more she comes in. I am upon the forlorn hope here, so must e'en make my push with vigour at once.

Enter CHARLOTTE

CHARLOTTE: Sir Callaghan, your servant.

SIR CALLAGHAN: Madam, I humbly beg your pardon for not seeing of you sooner; but I was spaking a soliloquy to myself, about your ladyship, and that kept me from observing you.

CHARLOTTE: Sir Theodore told me you wanted to speak to me upon some particular business.

SIR CALLAGHAN: Why, look you, madam, for my part, I was never born or bred in a school of compliments, where they learn fine bows, and fine speeches; but in an academy where heads, and legs, and arms, and bullets dance country dances without the owner's leave —just as the fortune of war directs. Therefore, madam, all that I can say to you is, that your eyes have made me a prisoner of war, that Cupid has made a garrison of my heart, and keeps me to devilish hard duty; and if you don't relieve me, I shall be a dead man before I come to action.

OMNES: Ha, ha, ha!

SIR ARCHY: He begins vary weel; he has got intill the heat of the action awready. (*Aside*)

CHARLOTTE: But, Sir Callaghan, among all your symptoms of love, you have forgot to mention one that I am told is very elegant and very powerful.

SIR CALLAGHAN: Pray, what is that, madam?

CHARLOTTE: A song that I hear you have made, and set yourself in the true Irish taste.

SIR CALLAGHAN: Madam, I own I have been guilty of torturing the Muses in the shape of a song, and I hope you will pardon my putting your ladyship's name to it.

CHARLOTTE: Upon one condition I will, which is, that you will do me the favour to let me hear you sing it.

SIR CALLAGHAN: O, dear madam, don't ax me; it is a foolish song, a mere bagatelle.

CHARLOTTE: Nay, I must insist upon hearing it, as you expect or value the smiles, or fear the frowns of your mistress; for by your poetry I shall judge of your passion.

SIR CALLAGHAN: Then, madam, you shall have it, if it was ten times worse—hem, hem! fal, lal, la—ha! I don't know how I shall come about the right side of my voice.

SIR ARCHY: Aye, aye, noo for it—noo ye shall hear sic a song as has na been penned sin they first clepped the wings and tails of the wild Irish. (*Aside*)

SIR CALLAGHAN: Now, madam, I tell you before hand, you must not expect such fine singing from me, as you hear at the Opera—for, you know, we Irishmen are not cut out for it, like the Italians. (*Sings*)

> Let other men sing of their goddesses bright,
> That darken the day and enlighten the night;
> I sing of a woman—but such flesh and blood,
> A touch of her finger would do your heart good.
> > With my fal, lal, lal, etc.
> Ten times in each day to my charmer I come,
> To tell her my passion—but can't, I'm struck dumb;
> For Cupid he seizes my heart with surprise,
> And my tongue falls asleep at the sight of her eyes.
>
> Her little dog Pompey's my rival, I see;
> She kisses and hugs him, but frowns upon me:
> Then prithee, dear Charlotte, abuse not your charms
> Instead of a lap-dog, take me to your arms.

SIR ARCHY: Come, noo the song is over, lat us steal off. (*Aside*)

GROOM: He is a damned droll fellow!—Instead of a lap-dog, take me to your arms. (*Aside*)

SIR ARCHY: Hush! saftly, donna lat him see us; steal off, steal off—he is an excellent droll fallow; a deevelish comical cheeld. (*Aside: exeunt* SIR ARCHY, GROOM, *and* MORDECAI)

CHARLOTTE: Well, Sir Callaghan, your poetry is excellent; nothing can surpass it but your singing.

SIR CALLAGHAN: Look'ee, madam, to come to the point: I know I can't talk fine courtship, and love, and nonsense, like other men; for I don't speak from my tongue, but my heart: so that if you can take up your quarters for life with a man of honour, a sincere lover, and an honest Prussian soldier, now is your time, I am your man— what do you say, madam? Come, speak the word boldly, and take me to your arms.

CHARLOTTE: Ha, ha, ha! don't be so violent, Sir Callaghan—but say a lady were inclined to do herself the honour of going before a priest with you, I suppose you would have so much complaisance for your mistress as to quit your trade of war, and live at home with her, were she to request it of you.

SIR CALLAGHAN: Why look you, madam, I will deal with you like a man of honour in that point too, and let you into a secret. I have received the king[1] my master's money (and a brave king he is, I assure you) for above seventeen years, when I had none of my own; and now I am come to a title and fortune, and that he has need of my service, I think it would look like a poltroon to leave him—no, madam, it is a rule with me, never to desert my king, or my friend in distress.

CHARLOTTE: Your sentiment is great, I confess; I like your principles; they are noble, and most heroic, but a little too military for me. Ha, ha, ha! (*Exit*)

SIR CALLAGHAN: What, does she decline the battle? Well, then, I'll not quit the field yet, though; I'll reconnoitre her once more, and if I can't bring her to action, why then I'll break up the camp at once, ride post to Germany to-morrow morning, and so take my leave in a passion, without saying a word. (*Exit*)

Enter SIR ARCHY *and* MORDECAI

---

[1] Frederick the Great.

MORDECAI: Prithee, what is the meaning of all this, Sir Archy? The house seems to be in the possession of bailiffs, and Sir Theodore looks and speaks as if an earthquake had just happened.

SIR ARCHY: Yeer conjacture is vary reeght, Mr. Mordecai; 'tis aw over wi' him—he is undone—a baggar, and so is the girl.

MORDECAI: You astonish me.

SIR ARCHY: It is an unaxpacted business; but 'tis a fact, I assure ye: here he is himsel; poor deevil, hoo dismal he leuks.

Enter SIR THEODORE *and an* ATTORNEY

SIR THEODORE: You are the attorney concerned for the creditors, Mr. Atkins?

ATTORNEY: I am, Sir Theodore, and am extremely sorry for the accident.

SIR THEODORE: I am obliged to you, sir; you do but your duty: the young lady is that way, sir; if you will step to her, I'll follow you. (*Exit* ATTORNEY) I hope you will excuse me, Sir Archy—this is a sudden and unhappy affair. I am unfit for company; I must go and open it myself to poor Charlotte. (*Exit*)

MORDECAI: But pray, Sir Archy, what has occasioned all this?

SIR ARCHY: Faith, Mordecai, I do na ken the parteeculars—but it seems, by the word of Sir Theodore himsel, that he and a rich merchant in Holland, his partner, and joint guardian over this girl, are baith bankrupt; and as the lawyer that is wi'oot there confirms, hai failed for above a hundred thoosand pounds mair than they can answer.

MORDECAI: But how is this to affect the young lady?

SIR ARCHY: Why, sir, the greatest part of her fortune was in trade, it seems, wi' Sir Theodore and his partner; besides, the suit in Chancery that she had wi' the company for above forty thoosand pounds, has been determined against her this vary day, so that they are aw undone. Baggars! baggars!

MORDECAI: I understood that the affair was clearly in her favour.

SIR ARCHY: O, sir, ye do na ken the law—the law is a sort of hocus-pocus science, that smiles in yeer face while it pecks yeer pocket: and the glorious uncertainty of it is of mair use till the professors than the justice of it. Here the parties come, and seemingly in great affliction.

Enter SIR THEODORE *and* CHARLOTTE

CHARLOTTE: Dear sir, be patient, moderate your sorrow; it may not be so terrible as your apprehensions make it; pray, bear up.

SIR THEODORE: For myself I care not. But that you should be involved in my ruin, left fortuneless, your fair expectation of a noble alliance blasted! your dignity and affluence fallen to scorn and penury—

CHARLOTTE: It cannot prove so bad, sir; I will not despair, nor shall you—for though the law has been so hard against me, yet in spite of all its wiles and treachery, a competency will still remain, which shall be devoted to mitigate your misfortunes. Besides, Sir Archy Macsarcasm is a man of honour, and on his promise and assistance I will rely.

SIR ARCHY: Wull ye! ye may as weel rely upon the assistance of the philosopher's stone—what the deevil, would she marry me till mak me tinker up the fortunes of broken ceetezens? But I wull speak till them, and end the affair at aince. I am concerned till see ye in this disorder, Sir Theodore.

CHARLOTTE: O, Sir Archy, if all the vows of friendship, honour, and eternal love, which you have so often made me, were not composed of idle breath, and deceitful ceremony, now let their truth be seen.

SIR ARCHY: Madam, I am sorry till be the messenger of ill tidings, but aw oor connection is at an end; oor hoose has heard of my addresses till ye; and I hai had letters frai the dukes, the marquis, and aw the deegnetaries of the faimily remonstrating—nay, axpressly pro-heebeting my contaminating the blood of Macsarcasm wi' ainy thing sprung frai a hogsheed, or a coonting hoose. I assure ye my passion for ye is meeghty strong, madam, but I cannot bring disgrace upon an honourable faimily.

CHARLOTTE: No more—your apology is baser than your perfidy; there is no truth, no virtue in man!

SIR ARCHY: Guid traith, nor in woman neither that has nai fortune. But here is Mordecai—noo, madam—a wandering Eesrelite, a casualty—a mere casualty, sprung frai annuities, bulls, bubbles, bears, and lottery tickets—and can hai nai faimily objections—he is passionately fond of ye, and till this offspring of accident and mammon I reseegn my interest in ye.

MORDECAI: Sir, I am infinitely obliged to you; but—a—matrimony is a subject I have never thoroughly considered, and I must take some time to deliberate, before I determine upon that inextricable business. Besides, madam, I assure you, my affairs are not in a matrimonial situation.

CHARLOTTE: No apology, sir. Begone! I despise them and you.
(*Enter* SQUIRE GROOM)

GROOM: Haux! haux! what's the matter here? What is all this? What, are we all at fault? Is this true, Sir Theodore? I hear that you and the filly have both run on the wrong side of the post.

SIR THEODORE: It is too true; but, I hope, sir, that will make no alteration in your affections.

GROOM: Hark'ee, Sir Theodore, I always make my match according to the weight my thing can carry. When I offered to take her into my stable, she was sound, and in good case; but I hear her wind is touched—if so, I would not back her for a shilling. I'll take her into my stud, if you will—she has a good fore hand,[1] sets both her ends well, has good paces, a good deal of fashion, some blood, and will do well enough to breed out of—but she cannot carry weight sufficient to come through. Matrimony, Sir Theodore, is a cursed long course, devilish heavy, and sharp turnings; it won't do—can't come through, my dear, can't come through.

SIR ARCHY: I think, squeere, ye judge vary nicely. Noo, in my thoughts, the best thing the lady can do is to snap the Irishman.

MORDECAI: Well observed, Sir Archy.

GROOM: Macsarcasm has an excellent nose, and hits off a fault as well as any hound I ever followed.

SIR ARCHY: It would be a deevelish lucky match for her—the fallow has a guid fortune, is a great blockheed, and looves her vehemently; three as guid qualities for a matrimonial bubble,[2] as a lady in her circumstances would wish. Snap him, snap, him, madam.

MORDECAI: Hush! he's here.

Enter SIR CALLAGHAN

SIR ARCHY: Ha! my guid friend; Sir Callaghan, I kiss yeer hond; I hai been speaking till the lady in yeer behalf, wi' aw the ailoquence I hai: she is enamoured o' yeer person, and ye are just come i' the nick till receive her heart and her hond.

[1] All the horse in front of the saddle.
[2] Deceit, from South Sea Bubble.

SIR CALLAGHAN: By the honour of a soldier, madam, I shall think that a greater happiness than any that fortune can bestow upon me.

SIR ARCHY: Come, come, madam, true loove is impatient, and despises ceremony; gi' him yeer hond at aince.

CHARLOTTE: No, sir, I scorn to deceive a man who offers me his heart: though my fortune is ruined, my mind is untainted; even poverty shall not pervert it to principles of baseness.

SIR CALLAGHAN: Fortune ruined! Pray, Sir Theodore, what does the importance of all this language mean?

SIR THEODORE: The sad meaning is, Sir Callaghan, that, in the circuit of fortune's wheel, the lady's station is reversed; she, who some hours since was on the highest round, is now degraded to the lowest: this, sir, has turned the passion these gentlemen professed for her into scorn and ridicule; and I suppose will cool the fervency of yours.

SIR CALLAGHAN: Sir Theodore, I assure you, I am heartily glad of her distress.

SIR THEODORE: Sir!

SIR CALLAGHAN: When she was computed to have a hundred thousand pounds, I loved her, 'tis true, but it was with fear and trembling, like a man that loves to be a soldier, yet is afraid of a gun; because I looked upon myself as an unequal match to her—but now she is poor, and that it is in my power to serve her, I find something warm about my heart here, that tells me I love her better than when she was rich, and makes me beg she will take my life this instant, and all I have, into her service.

SIR THEODORE: Generous indeed, Sir Callaghan.

SIR CALLAGHAN: Madam, my fortune is not much, but it is enough to maintain a couple of honest hearts, and have something to spare for the necessities of a friend; which is all we want, and all that fortune is good for.

SIR THEODORE: Here, take her, sir—she is yours; and, what you first thought her, mistress of a noble fortune.

GROOM: What! (*Aside*)

MORDECAI: How's this?

SIR ARCHY: Jauntly! hush! saftly! he is ainly taking him in—he is taking him in—the bubble's[1] bit.

---

[1] Here: gull, sucker.

SIR THEODORE: And had she millions, your principles deserve her—she has a heart loving and generous as your own, which your manly virtue has subdued, and tempered to your warmest wishes.

SIR CALLAGHAN: Pray, Sir Theodore, what does all this mean? are you in jest or in earnest? By my honour, I don't know how to believe one word you say. First she has a fortune, then she has no fortune—and then she has a great fortune again! this is just what the little jackanapes about town call humbugging a man.

SIR THEODORE: Sir, I am serious.

SIR CALLAGHAN: And pray, what are you, madam? are you in serious too, or in joke?

CHARLOTTE: Such as I am, sir, if you dare venture upon me for life, I am yours.

SIR CALLAGHAN: By the integrity of my honour, madam, I will venture upon you not only for life, but for death too—which is a great deal longer than life, you know.

SIR THEODORE: I hope, nephew, you will excuse the deceit of my feigned bankruptcy, and the pretended ruin of the lady's fortune. It was a scheme devised to detect the illiberal, selfish view of prodigals, who never address the fair but as the mercenary lure attracts—a scheme to try and reward your passion, which hath shewn itself proof against the times' infection.

SIR CALLAGHAN: Faith, then, it was no bad piece of generalship in you. But now she has surrendered herself prisoner of war, I think I have a right to lay her under contribution—for your kisses are lawful plunder, and mine by the laws of love. (*Kisses her*)

CHARLOTTE: O, Sir Callaghan, you take away my breath.

SIR CALLAGHAN: O you are a clever little creature. Upon my honour, her breath is as sweet as the sound of a trumpet.

GROOM: Why, the knowing ones are all taken in here—double distanced; zounds! she has run a crimp[1] upon us.

MORDECAI: She has jilted us confoundedly.

SIR ARCHY: By the cross of Saint Andrew I'll be revenged; for I ken a lad of an honourable faimily, that understands the auncient classics[2] in aw their perfection: he is writing a comedy, and he shall inseenuate baith their characters intill it.

---

[1] Deceit.

[2] Scottish claims to learning were often ridiculed. Cf. *TSS* pp. 235–7.

MORDECAI: And I will write a satire upon her, in which she shall have an intrigue with a life guard man, and an opera singer.

GROOM: I can't write; but I tell you what I'll do—I'll poison her parrot, and cut off her squirrel's tail, damn me.

SIR CALLAGHAN: Hark'ee, gentlemen, I hope you will ax my lave for all this—if you touch a hair of the parrot's head, or a hair of anything that belongs to this lady; or, if you write any of your nonsensical comedies, or lampoons, I shall be after making bold to make a few remarks on your bodies—hah! I have an excellent pen by my side, that is a very good critic, and that can write a very legible hand upon impertinent authors.

SIR ARCHY: Hut awa, hut awa, Sir Callaghan, donna talk in that idle minner, sir—oor swords are as sharp and as responsible as the swords of other men. But this is nai time for sic mitters; ye hai got the lady, and we hai got the wullows. I am sorry for the little Girgishite here, because he has bespoke his nuptial chariot, and aw his leeveries—and, upon honour, I am sorry for my vary guid freend the squeere; the lady's fortune would hai been vary convenient till him, for, I fancy, he is fetlock deep in the turf—and, upon honour, I am sorry for the lady, for she has missed being matched intill the hoose of Macsarcasm, which is the greatest loss of aw.

SIR CALLAGHAN: The whole business is something like the catastrophe of a stage play; where knaves and fools are disappointed, and honest men rewarded. (*Exeunt omnes*)

FINIS

The True-born Irishman

or

THE IRISH FINE LADY

A COMEDY

In Two Acts

Theatrical Note

The True-Born Irishman was a great success when first performed in Dublin, and Macklin often revived it, both in the capital and the major country towns. It is not known which version was used when Andrew Cherry played the lead at Bath in 1801: more likely the printed one.

In 1910, the play was produced by the Theatre of Ireland Company in Dublin. Joseph Holloway noted that 'it proved vastly entertaining and surprisingly up to date in most of the opinions expressed by Murrough O'Dogherty ... many of the home-thrusts put into O'Dogherty's mouth met with instant applause and seemed quite topical of the moment'. 'Jack Point' said, in the *Saturday Herald*: 'It brings us in touch with a period when the Irish capital was in very truth a capital, and when, in matters theatrical and otherwise, Dublin was not content with being a feeble imitation of London ... *The True-born Irishman* ... deserves to live ... as an acting play which is highly amusing, and which conveys a useful lesson'.

The True-born Irishman

DUBLIN		COVENT GARDEN
14 May 1761		28 November 1767

Dramatis Personae

	DUBLIN	COVENT GARDEN
Murrogh O'Dogherty	Mr. Macklin	Mr. Macklin
Count Mushroom	Mr. Woodward?	Mr. Woodward
Counsellor Hamilton		Mr. Dyer
Major Gamble		Mr. Morris
Pat Fitzmungrel	Mr. Messink	Mr. Dunstall
James		
John		
William		

(Three Newsmen: only in the London production as *The Irish Fine Lady*)

Mrs. Diggerty	Mrs. Dancer	Miss Macklin
Lady Kinnegad		Mrs. Green
Lady Bab Frightful		Mrs. Evans
Mrs. Gazette		Miss Helm
Mrs. Jolly		Mrs. White
Katty Farrel		Mrs. Pitt

Time: from Noon to Evening.

Scene: Dublin, a Room in Mr. O'Dogherty's House.

The True-born Irishman

ACT I

Enter o'DOGHERTY[1] *and* SERVANT

o'DOGHERTY: Who's there?

SERVANT: Sir.

o'DOGHERTY: Is John come in yet?

SERVANT: No, sir.

o'DOGHERTY: Be sure send him to me as soon as he comes in. (*Exit* SERVANT)

Enter JOHN

JOHN: I am here, sir.

o'DOGHERTY: Well, John, how is my brother after his journey?

JOHN: The counsellor gives his compliments to you, sir, and thanks you for your enquiry: he is very well, and will wait on you as soon as he is dressed.

o'DOGHERTY: Mighty well—what is that you have in your hand, John?

JOHN: It is nothing for you, sir—it is a card for my mistress, from Madam Mulroony;[2] her man gave it me as I came in.

o'DOGHERTY: Pray, let me see it—'Mrs. Mulroony makes her compliments to Mrs. Murrogh O'Dogherty, and likewise to Mr. Murrogh O'Dogherty, and hopes to have the favour of their company on Sunday the 17th instant, to play at cards, sup, and spend the evening, with Lady Kinnegad,[3] Mrs. Cardmark, Miss Brag, Mr. Mushroom, Cornet Basilisk, Sir Anthony All-night, Major Gamble, and a very jolly party.'—Here, John, take it to your mistress—I have nothing to say to it. (*Exit* JOHN) Well done,

---

[1] The family of Ó Dochartaigh were lords of the Inishowen peninsula from the fourteenth century, under whom the MacLochláinns held their land.

[2] The Ó Maolruinaidhs belong originally to Fermanagh.

[3] A village in Westmeath.

Mrs. Mulroony—faith, and it well becomes your father's daughter, and your husband's wife, to play at cards upon a Sunday. She is another of the fine ladies of this country, who, like my wife, is sending her soul to the devil, and her husband to a gaol as fast as she can. The booby has scarce a thousand pounds a year in the world, yet he spends above two thousand in equipage, taste, high life, and jolly parties—besides what his fool of a wife loses to that female sharper, my Lady Kinnegad, and her jolly party; which, if I may judge by my own wife, is at least a good two thousand more; so that by the rule of subtraction, take four thousand pounds a year out of one, and in a very little time nothing will remain but a gaol, or an escape in the packet on Connought Monday.[1]

Enter WILLIAM *shewing in* COUNSELLOR HAMILTON[2]

WILLIAM: Counsellor Hamilton. (*Exit* WILLIAM)

O'DOGHERTY: Counsellor, you are welcome to Dublin.

COUNSELLOR: Brother, I am extremely glad to see you.

O'DOGHERTY: By my faith, and so am I you. Odzooks give us a kiss, man: I give you my honour I am as glad to see you in Dublin at this juncture, as I should to see a hundred head of fat bullocks upon my own land, all ready for Ballinasloe[3] fair.

COUNSELLOR: Sir, your humble servant. That is a great compliment from you, brother, I know.

O'DOGHERTY: It is a very true one I assure you.

COUNSELLOR: Well, I see by the newspapers that my sister is returned from her coronation[4] frolic, and in health I suppose, or you would have wrote me word had it been otherwise.

O'DOGHERTY: Yes, yes, she is in health indeed, and returned with a vengeance.

COUNSELLOR: Pray what is the matter?

O'DOGHERTY: Ogho! enough is the matter, the devil an inhabitant in Swift's Hospital for Lunatics,[5] is in a worse pickle than she is.

[1] i.e. Sunday, reputedly devoted to unsabbatical dissipation in Connacht.

[2] The Hamiltons are of Scottish descent, from James I's plantation of Ulster: there were Hamiltons on both sides at the Battle of the Boyne. Counsellor, i.e. barrister.

[3] On the Galway-Roscommon border, noted for the great annual cattle fair on the first Tuesday in October. The MS. substitutes Cork.

[4] She had been to see the coronation of George III, 22 September 1761.

[5] St. Patrick's Hospital, in Bow Lane, founded with Swift's legacy in 1757—'He gave the little wealth he had To found a house for fools and mad'.

COUNSELLOR: You surprise me!—in what respect, pray?

O'DOGHERTY: Why, with a distemper that she has brought over with her from England, which will, in a little time, I am afraid, infect the whole nation.

COUNSELLOR: Pray, what may that be?

O'DOGHERTY: Sir, it is called the Irish Fine Lady's delirium, or the London vertigo;[1] if you were to hear her when the fit is upon her —O, she is as mad—the devil a thing in this poor country but what gives her the spleen and the vapours—then such a phrenzy of admiration for every thing in England—and, among the rest of her madness, she has brought over a new language with her.

COUNSELLOR: What do you mean by a new language?

O'DOGHERTY: Why a new kind of a London English, that's no more like our Irish English, than a coxcomb's fine gilded chariot like a Glassmanogue noddy[2]—why, what name do you think she went by when she was in England?

COUNSELLOR: Why, what name dare she go by but Dogherty?

O'DOGHERTY: Dogherty!—ogho—upon my honour she startles when she hears the name of Dogherty, and blushes, and is much ashamed as if a man had spoke bawdy to her—no, no, my dear, she is no longer the plain, modest, good-natured, domestic, obedient Irish Mrs. O'Dogherty, but the travelled, rampant, high-lifed, prancing English Mrs. Diggerty.

COUNSELLOR: Ha, ha, ha! Mrs. Diggerty! ridiculous!

O'DOGHERTY: Ay, ridiculous indeed! to change her name—was there ever such impertinence? But do you know, brother, among the rest of your sister's whims and madnesses, that she is turned a great politician too concerning my name.

---

[1] This was not new. In W. Philips's *St. Stephen's Green* (1700: though set in Dublin, it has very little local colour) a character recently returned from London says: 'I have brought over new fashions, new tunes, and new plays'; and in C. Shadwell's *Hasty Marriage* (1717: also set in Dublin) a young Irishwoman is gently mocked for admiring things English and being contemptuous of her own country.

[2] Illustrated and described by Constantia Maxwell, *Dublin under the Georges* (1946), pp. 255, 267–8: 'a low single two-wheeled horse chaise, capable of holding two persons, drawn by one horse, with a seat for the driver on the shafts'—a rattling and rickety conveyance; cf. also *Hibernia Curiosa* (1769). The MS. substitutes a donkey-drawn cart for sand. Glasmanóg is the Irish name of the street north of the Liffey called Constitution Hill. At this time the name referred to the area between the present (disused) Broadstone station and the North Circular Road, west of the Royal Canal.

COUNSELLOR: Ha, ha, ha! a politician!—Why how in the name of wonder and common sense can politics and the name of Dogherty be connected?

O'DOGHERTY: O it's a wonder indeed!—but strange as it is, they are connected—but very ridiculously as you may imagine.

COUNSELLOR: But, prithee, by what means?

O'DOGHERTY: Why, you must know, we are to have an election shortly for the county that I live in, which young Lord Turnabout wants to carry for one of his own gang; and as the election in a great measure depends upon my interest, the young fox, knowing the conceit and vanity of my wife, has taken her by her favourite foible, and tickled it up, by telling her that if I direct my interest properly, it would not be difficult to procure me a title. Now, sir, this piece of flattery has stirred up such a rage of quality and title in her giddy head, that I cannot rest night or day for her importunity—in short, she would have me desert my friends, and sell myself, my honour, and my country, as several others have done before me, merely for a title, only that she may take place of a parcel of foolish idle women, and sink the ancient name of Dogherty in the upstart title of Lady Thingum, my Lady Fiddle Faddle, or some such ridiculous nonsense.

COUNSELLOR: But, sir, pray pause a little upon this business—my sister's vanity, I grant you, may be ridiculous—but though you despise titles and ostentation, yet, as your interest can certainly make the member, were I in your circumstances, I would have a voice in the senate of my country—go into parliament for the county yourself.

O'DOGHERTY: Ogh, I have been among them already, and I know them all very well. What signifies my sitting among hundreds of people with my single opinion all alone. When I was there before I was stigmatised as a singular blockhead, an impracticable fellow, only because I would not consent to sit like an image, and when the master of the puppets pulled the string of my jaw on one side, to say aye, and on t'other side, to say no, and to leap over a stick backwards and forwards, just as the faction of party and jobbers, and leaders, and political adventurers directed—ah, brother, brother, I have done with them all—O, I have done with them all.

COUNSELLOR: What, and after all your expence of opposing government right or wrong, and supporting your patriots, will you give them all up?

O'DOGHERTY: Indeed I will—I was patriot mad I own, like a great many other fools in this distracted country—sir, I was so mad that I hated the very name of a courtier as much as an illiterate lay-swaddling[1] methodist does that of a regular clergyman. But I am cured of that folly; for now I find that a courtier is just as honest a man as a patriot—my dear, they are both made of the same stuff; ah, I have at last found out what sort of an animal a patriot is.

COUNSELLOR: Aye!—and pray, brother, what sort of an animal is he?

O'DOGHERTY: Why, he is a sort of political weathercock, that is blown about by every wind of society, which the foolish people are always looking up at, and staring, and distracting themselves with the integrity of its vicissitudes—to-day it is blown by the rough, rattling tempest of party; next day by the trade-wind of sly, subtle, veering faction; then by the headlong hurricane of the people's hot foggy breath; huzza boys, down with the courtier, up with the patriot, till at last the smooth, soft, gentle warm breeze of interest blows upon it, and from that moment it rusts to a point, and never stirs after—so there is your puff patriot for you—ogh, to the devil I pitch them all.

COUNSELLOR: Ha, ha, ha! I am glad to find, brother, that you are come to that way of thinking at last, and I wish you had had the same notions years ago; it would have saved you many thousands.

O'DOGHERTY: Indeed, and that it would—however, experience is an excellent tutor, and as you are a young man, and just coming into the world, mine may be of some service to you; take this judgment from me then, and remember that an honest quiet country gentleman who out of policy and humanity establishes manufactories, or that contrives employment for the idle and the industrious, or that makes but a blade of corn grow where there was none before, is of more use to this poor country than all the courtiers, and patriots, and politicians, and prodigals that are unhanged—so there let us leave them, and return to my wife's business.[2]

---

[1] Swaddler, the Irish nickname for a Methodist preacher. The MS. substitutes terms more familiar in England.

[2] This and the immediately previous speeches seem to express Macklin's own views. During the eighteenth century, the measures ruining Irish trade for England's benefit, and the preferment of

COUNSELLOR: With all my heart, I long to have a particular account of her conduct.

O'DOGHERTY: O, brother, I have many grievances to tell you of, but I have one that is more whimsical than all the rest.

COUNSELLOR: Pray, what is it?

O'DOGHERTY: Why you must know, brother, I am going to be a cuckold as fast as I can.

COUNSELLOR: Ha, ha, ha! that's a comical grievance indeed.

O'DOGHERTY: O stay till you hear the story, and I'll engage you will say it is as comical a cuckoldom as ever was contrived.

COUNSELLOR: I am glad to find, sir, it is of so facetious a nature—pray let me hear this business.

O'DOGHERTY: Sit down, then, brother, for I have got a little touch of my gout, let us sit down for a moment, and I will let you into the whole affair.

COUNSELLOR: Pray do, sir, for you have really raised my curiosity. (*Sits*)

O'DOGHERTY: You must know, brother, there is an English coxcomb in this town just arrived among us, who thinks every woman that sees him is in love with him, and this spark, like another Paris of Troy, has taken it into his head to make a Helen of my wife, and a poor cuckoldy Menelaus of me.

COUNSELLOR: Ha, ha, ha! Pray who is this spark?

O'DOGHERTY: Why, the name of this cuckold-maker is Mushroom, but from his conceit and impertinence, the women and jokers of this town have dignified him with the title of Count Mushroom.   Sir, he is the son of a pawn-broker in London, who having a mind to make a gentleman of his son, sent him to the university of Oxford; where, by mixing in the follies and vices of irregular youth, he got into a most sanguine friendship with young Lord Oldcastle, who you know has a large estate in this country, and of whose

---

Englishmen, were supported in the Irish Parliament (in which no Catholic could sit) by the Court party, made up of Englishmen and their Irish jackals, which held the strings of corruption and so was normally sure of its majority.   Some members, however, caring about Irish prosperity, constituted the Patriotic party and strove steadfastly against such evils: they had the powerful outside support of Swift's pen.   But not all the patriots were honest: some were only concerned to make nuisances of themselves in order to be bought off with places, pensions, or titles.   The dislike and distrust of politics and politicians which Macklin often voiced is evident here.   To have been an M.P., and to evade the penal restrictions upon Catholic land-holders, a forbear, or O'Dogherty himself, must have turned Protestant.

ancestors mine have held long and profitable leases,[1] which are now near expiring—in short, sir, this same count Mushroom and my lord became the Pylades and Orestes of the age, and so very fond was my lord of him, that out of sheer friendship to the count, he got his sister with child.

COUNSELLOR: Ha, ha, ha! that was friendly indeed.

O'DOGHERTY: O yes, it was what you may call modern friendship, taste, and *bon ton*; and my lord being a man of gratitude, in return made him agent in this country, and sent him over to settle his affairs here. And the count and I being in treaty to renew these leases with my lord, and we not being able to agree upon the terms, the coxcomb sends my wife a warm billedoux, in which he very gallantly tells her that she shall decide the difference between us, and settle the leases at her own price, only upon the trifling condition that he may be permitted now and again to be the occasional lord of her ladyship's matrimonial manor.

COUNSELLOR: Impudent rascal! And, pray, what says my sister to all this?

O'DOGHERTY: Why, she does not know a word of the matter.

COUNSELLOR: No! pray how came you to be acquainted with his letter then, and his designs upon my sister?

O'DOGHERTY: Why there is the joke: it was by the help of Katty Farrel, my wife's woman, by whose assistance I carry on a correspondence with the fellow in my wife's name, unknown to her; and by that means I shall not only detect and expose the fellow, but get an excellent bargain of the leases, which are to be signed this very day.

COUNSELLOR: But, sir, I hope you won't accept of leases upon those terms.

O'DOGHERTY: O, I have no time to moralise with you on that point, but depend upon it I will convince you before I sleep of the propriety of my taking the leases:[2] Lord, what signifies it; it is only a good bargain got from a foolish lord by the ingenuity of a knavish agent, which is what happens every day in this country, and in every country indeed.

---

[1] The position of such middlemen between absentee landlord and peasant was often abused, but by some held conscientiously and beneficently.

[2] Hamilton, as befits a lawyer and an Ulster Scots-Irishman, is a bit of a precisian; but O'Dogherty is going to score off a scoundrel and an English absentee in possession of Irish land.

Enter JOHN

JOHN: Sir, Mr. Mushroom and Mr. Sharp the attorney are below.

O'DOGHERTY: O, they are come about the leases.   I will wait on them, John.   (*Exit* JOHN)   Now, brother, you shall see one of the pertest and most conceited impudent coxcombs that has ever yet been imported into this land, or that disgraced humanity.

MUSHROOM: (*Without*)   My compliments, Mrs. Katty, to your lady, I will be with her in the twinkling of a star, or in less time than a single glance of her own immortal beauty can pass to the centre of an amorous heart.

O'DOGHERTY: Orra[1] now did you ever hear such cursed nonsense.

Enter MUSHROOM

MUSHROOM: My dear Diggerty, I kiss your hands.   I am come on purpose—I beg ten thousand pardons—I understood you were alone —you are busy I presume.

O'DOGHERTY: Indeed, count, we are not.   This gentleman is a relation —my wife's brother—Counsellor Hamilton, whom you have so often heard me talk of, and with whom I desire you will be acquainted.

MUSHROOM: Sir, I feel a superlative happiness in being known to you, I have long expected and long wished for it with a lover's appetite; therefore, without waiting for the dull advocation of experience, or the pedantic forms of ceremony, I beg you will honour me with a niche in your esteem, and register me in the select catalogue of your most constant and most ardent friends and admirers.

COUNSELLOR: O dear sir, you are superabundantly obliging—this is such a favour—

MUSHROOM: No, no, no—none, none—give me your hand, Hamilton, you are my friend Diggerty's friend, and that's enough—I'll serve you—say no more—I'll serve you—rely upon me—I live in this town quite *en famille*—I go about every where, am of no party but those of love, pleasure and gallantry—the women like me and commend me at cards, tea, scandal and dancing—the men, at wit, hazard, jolly parties, a late hour and a bottle—I love ease, hate ceremony, and am at home wherever I go—that's my system,

---

[1] The frequent Irish interjection, *ara,* difficult to translate, expressing mild expostulation.

Hamilton—ha, is not that taste, life, philosophy, and *summum
bonum*—ha, my dear, at home wherever I go, an't I, Diggerty?

O'DOGHERTY: O, indeed, to give you your due, count, you are never
bashful in any place.

MUSHROOM: Never, never, my dear.

O'DOGHERTY: No, faith, nor none of your family, I believe.

MUSHROOM: Ha, ha, ha! never, never, my dear Diggerty—bashfulness
is a mark of ignorance, an uncourtly, vulgar disease—what we
men of the world are never infected with—but, my dear Diggerty,
I am come on purpose to settle with you; my attorney with the
leases is below, for I know that my lord would be loth to lose you
as a tenant, and as I am convinced it would be for his interest you
should have the lands, why we will even sign and seal at once
upon your own terms—for really I think tenants in Ireland want
encouragement—they are racked too high—they are indeed—it is
a shame they should be racked so high.

O'DOGHERTY: Faith, count, there's many a true word spoke in jest.

MUSHROOM: Upon my honour I am serious—you want encouragement
in trade too.

O'DOGHERTY: But do you really think so?

MUSHROOM: I do upon my honour, and I will speak to some people of
consequence about it on the other side, as soon as I return.

O'DOGHERTY: Orra but will you?

MUSHROOM: I will upon my honour.

O'DOGHERTY: O aye, you politicians promise us the devil and all while
you are among us, but the moment you get o't'other side, you
have devilish bad memories.

COUNSELLOR: You seem to like Ireland, sir.

MUSHROOM: O immensely, sir—it is a damned fine country, sir—and
excellent claret[1]—excellent claret upon my honour! 'tis true, indeed, it is not such claret as we drink in London—however, upon
the whole, it's a pretty, neat, light, soft, silky, palatable wine, and
I like it mightily—but your fish in this here country is horrid.
There you want taste, Hamilton—that there is an article of the
sçavoir vivre, in which you are totally ignorant—quite barbarous—

---

[1] In the eighteenth century claret was the main drink of the Irish upper classes, and they prided
themselves on its quality.

COUNSELLOR: Aye! in what respect, sir?

MUSHROOM: Oh, my dear Hamilton, how can you ask such a question—you, you, now—who have been in London!—why, you eat all your fish here too noo—

COUNSELLOR: Too noo?

MUSHROOM: Yes, all too noo—why you eat it the very day—nay, sometimes the very hour it comes out of the water—now that there is a total want of taste—quite barbarous.

O'DOGHERTY: O yes, brother, we eat all our fish in this here country too noo—too noo a great deal. Now, I fancy, count, we should keep our fish before we dress it, as you keep your venison, till it has got the hot gout.

MUSHROOM: Ha, ha, ha!—the hot gout—ha, ha, ha! Oh, I shall expire —my dear Diggerty, I honour your hot gout—but your French is a little *en Irlandois*—*en Provence*—*haut goût* is the word.

O'DOGHERTY: Yes, yes—I understand you—Fogo.[1]

MUSHROOM: Ha, ha, ha!—Hamilton, you are a little odd in this here country in some points—your friend there—is—you understand me—however, upon the whole, take you altogether, you are a damn'ed honest, tory rory, rantum scantum, dancing, singing, laughing, boozing, jolly, friendly, fighting, hospitable people, and I like you mightily.

OMNES: Ha, ha, ha!

COUNSELLOR: Upon my word, sir, the people of Ireland are much obliged to you for your helter skelter, rantum scantum portrait of them.

O'DOGHERTY: Indeed and that we are; and so you like us mightily.

MUSHROOM: I do upon honour, and I believe I shall marry one of your women here, grow domestic, and settle among you.

O'DOGHERTY: Orra but will you do us that honour?

MUSHROOM: I really intend it.

O'DOGHERTY: Faith then you will be a great honour to us, and you will find a great many relations here, count; for we have a large crop of the Mushrooms in this here country.

MUSHROOM: O sir, I don't doubt it, for we are a numerous family both in England and Ireland—but I beg pardon, my dear Diggerty, I

---

[1] So in print and MS. An obvious mistake for 'hogo', a 17th century anglicization of *haut goût* —a high or putrescent flavour, taint, or stench.

must rob you of my company for a moment to pay my devoirs to your lady; I know she is impatient to see me upon a particular affair—I will return upon the wings of diligence, then sign, squeeze wax, and dedicate to wit, mirth, and convivial jollity—Hamilton, yours, yours—my dear Diggerty, give me thy hand—from this moment set me down as thy unalterable friend—for I intend to be well with thy wife this very evening. (*Aside and exit*)

o'DOGHERTY: Sure there never was so conceited and so impudent a coxcomb as this puppy.

Enter KATTY FARREL

o'DOGHERTY: O, here is Katty Farrel. So, Katty, do you see who's here, child?—your friend the counsellor.[1]

KATTY: Sir, your humble servant, I am glad to see you look so well. I hope all your good family are in health.

COUNSELLOR: All very well, I thank you, Mrs. Katty.

o'DOGHERTY: Well, well, now your ceremonies are over, let us to business—is your fine mistress dressed yet?

KATTY: Yes, sir—but she has had a sad misfortune.

o'DOGHERTY: What is that, Katty?

KATTY: The money, sir, that you gave her to pay the mercer's bill, from Covent Garden, that was sent after her, she lost last night to my Lady Kinnegad, and some more of them, at brag[2]—but do not take any notice that I have told you of it, for she intends to borrow as much from Mr. Mushroom for a day or two as will pay the bill.

COUNSELLOR: Why, the woman has lost all sense of shame. (*Aside*)

o'DOGHERTY: Katty, that must not be. She must not do so mean a thing upon any account, as to borrow money of Mushroom. I will let you have the money to pay the bill, and do you say you borrowed it of your brother, or some friend or other, for her.

KATTY: I will, sir. (*Exit.* MRS. DIGGERTY, MUSHROOM, etc. *laugh very loud without*)

o'DOGHERTY: So, the toilet council is broke up at last—here she comes, as fantastically fine as a fine lady in a play. Ogho, what a head[3] she has.

Enter MRS. DIGGERTY *and* MUSHROOM

MRS. DIGGERTY: Brother, I am veestly glad to see you.

---

[1] The kind of servant-employer relationship implied here is characteristically Irish.
[2] A card game, in its essentials identical with poker.
[3] Extravagantly dressed hair.

COUNSELLOR: Welcome from England, sister.

MRS. DIGGERTY: I am imminsely obligated to you, brother.

COUNSELLOR: I hope it answered your expectation, sister.

MRS. DIGGERTY: Transcendently.

COUNSELLOR: I am glad it pleased you.

MRS. DIGGERTY: Ravishingly.

COUNSELLOR: Indeed!

MRS. DIGGERTY: Beyond all degrees of compirison.

O'DOGHERTY: O yes—beyond all degrees of compirison.

MRS. DIGGERTY: Veest! imminse! extatic!   I never knew life before—every thing there is high, tip top, the grand monde, the bun tun—and quite teesty.

O'DOGHERTY: O yes, every thing there is quite teesty, brother.

MRS. DIGGERTY: Well, count, do you know that you pleased me veestly last night; I never saw you in such high humour—brother, I believe you do not know Mr. Mushroom, an English gentleman; pray let me have the honour of introducing him to you.

COUNSELLOR: I have had that honour already, sister.

MUSHROOM: Yes, madam, Hamilton and I are old acquaintance.

O'DOGHERTY: O yes, they are old acquaintance, they have known each other above these two minutes.

COUNSELLOR: Pray how do you like London, sister?

MRS. DIGGERTY: O, the place of the world, brother.

COUNSELLOR: Then Dublin I suppose—

MRS. DIGGERTY: O, dear brother, don't neem them together.

O'DOGHERTY: O no, you must not neem them together.

MRS. DIGGERTY: Upon my honour, Dublin, after seeing London, looks like Irishtown or Ring's-end:[1] O, every thing I set my eyes on here gives me the *ennui*, and the *countre cure*.

O'DOGHERTY: O yes, every thing here gives her the contre cœur; that is a disease she has brought over with her from London that we know nothing of here.

MRS. DIGGERTY: The streets are so narrow, the houses so dirty, and the people so ridiculous! then the women, count! ha, ha, ha!—I can't

[1] At the time villages where the south bank of the Liffey reaches Dublin Bay. In the later eighteenth century the Pigeonhouse breakwater at Ringsend was the usual landing-place for passengers to Dublin, who noted the insalubrious squalor, and compared the villages to Wapping and Rotherhithe (which the MS. substitutes): cf. Maxwell, *op. cit.*, pp. 98, 243, 253, 255.

help laughing when I think of them. Well, I am convinced that the women of this here country who have never travelled, have nothing of that—a—a—non chalance, and that jenny-see-quee that we have in London.

o'dogherty: O no, brother! the women have nothing of that jenny-see-quee, that she has brought over with her from London.

mrs. diggerty: But, Mushroom—I don't know if what I am going to tell you be conceit or real; but, upon my honour, when I first came from England—you must know, brother, I came over in the picket.

o'dogherty: O yes, brother, she came over in the picket.

mrs. diggerty: Yes, sir, I came over in the picket, and we had a great orage—I don't believe, Mr. Diggerty, you know what an orage is.

o'dogherty: Indeed you may take your oath I don't, my dear.

mrs. diggerty: That is, sir, becase you have not been in foreign parts —then I will tell you what an orage is—sir, an orage is a storum.[1]

o'dogherty: Madam, I thank you for your intelligence—indeed you are very learned and very obliging.

mrs. diggerty: And so, as I was saying, count, we had a great storum, and the picket—I shall never forget it—the picket landed us about twenty miles from Dublin—and so, do you know, I say, Mushroom, that I fancied, being just come from England, that the very dogs here when they barked, had the brogue, ha, ha, ha!

omnes: Ha, ha, ha!

mushroom: Why then, by all that's gothic, madam, I have thought so a thousand times.

mrs. diggerty: You have!

mushroom: I have, upon honour.

mrs. diggerty: Have you ever observed it, brother? Mr. Diggerty, what do you think? Hav'n't the dogs of this here country the brogue?

o'dogherty: Indeed and that they have, my dear, and the cows too, and the sheep, and the bullocks, and that is as strong as ever your own mother had it, who was an O'Gallagher.[2]

---

[1] Though the indications are not elaborate nor always exact, Mrs. Diggerty is clearly shown over-correcting in her attempt to cultivate an English accent, e.g. 'picket', but at times falling back into her native pronunciation, e.g. 'storum'.

[2] The father of Mrs. Diggerty and the Counsellor had married into the old Irish family of Ó Gallchobair, descended from a seventh-century king of Ireland, and like the Ó Dochartaighs and MacLochláinns, associated with Donegal.

MRS. DIGGERTY: Oh!

O'DOGHERTY: Not two of whose ancestors could ever speak three words of English to be understood.

MRS. DIGGERTY: You are a strange rude man, Mr. Diggerty, to tell me of my mother's family—you know I always despised my mother's family—I hate the very name of Gallagher, and all the old Irish whatever.

COUNSELLOR: The present company excepted, sister—your husband, you know—

MRS. DIGGERTY: O, I never think of him.

COUNSELLOR: Ha, that's polite indeed.

O'DOGHERTY: O no, she never thinks of me.

COUNSELLOR: Well, but sister, you have given us no account of the coronation,[1] no doubt you were there.

MRS. DIGGERTY: There! O moundew!—what a quistion! Why I was in every part of it—ax Mushroom else.

MUSHROOM: Every where, every where—she was every where, and with every body.

O'DOGHERTY: Well, well—then I suppose it was very fine; but after all, now, was it as fine as our riding the fringes[2] here, or the lord lieutenant going to the parliament house?

MRS. DIGGERTY: He, he, he! O shocking! don't neem them together—now that is so Irish—but, brother, what would have afforded you the highest entertainment, was the city feast. O that there was imminse.

O'DOGHERTY: O yes, that there was imminse, brother, and much finer than this here.

COUNSELLOR: Then you were at the city feast too, sister?

MRS. DIGGERTY: O dear yes! the court never stirred without me.

O'DOGHERTY: No, indeed, the court never stirred without her.

MRS. DIGGERTY: And the lord mayor made a point of having me there: so I went with her grace, a friend of mine, and a peerty of the court, as one of the household—but the minute I went in every

[1] In the MS., Mrs. Diggerty expatiates at some length upon the coronation.
[2] Every three years, on 1 August, the Lord Mayor rode the franchises, called 'fringes' in Dublin; i.e., he went in procession with the City Guilds round the boundaries of his jurisdiction. The procession was elaborate and ostentatious, and its fame as a spectacle was widespread. Cf. Maxwell, *op. cit.*, pp. 228–9, and O'Keeffe, *op. cit.*, I, pp. 38–44.

eye was upon me: Lord, it was veestly pleasant to see how the she grocers, the she mercers, the she dyers, the she hosiers, and the she taylors did stare at me—I was very brilliant that's certain— rather more so than I was at the wedding.

O'DOGHERTY: O indeed I don't doubt but you were a sight.

MRS. DIGGERTY: O pray, Mr. Diggerty, be quiet, and don't interrupt me—Well, but, brother, as I was saying, it was imminsely entertaining to hear the awkward city creatures whisper and give their vardee upon me, in their city manner. Lord, is this the handsome Irishwoman?—the famous Irish toast?—the celebrated Mrs. Diggerty—ha!—I don't think she is so handsome, says one—hum!—well enough, says another, only I don't like her nose—pray, doesn't she squint?—says a third—O yes, she certainly squints, says a fourth—and she is a little crooked—but she is genteel—O yes, yes, the city creatures all allowed I was genteel.

O'DOGHERTY: O yes, yes, to be sure they all allowed she was genteel.

MRS. DIGGERTY: But, brother—O Lud! I had like to have forgot—do you know that the count is one of the prettiest poets in England, aye, or in Ireland either?

MUSHROOM: O heavens! madam!

MRS. DIGGERTY: He is, by my honour.

COUNSELLOR: I do not doubt the gentleman's talents in the least, sister.

MUSHROOM: Sir, you are very polite, the lady is pleased to rally, that's all, for my muse is but a smatterer—a slattern—a mere slip-shod lady.

MRS. DIGGERTY: Do not mind him, brother, what I say is true. He is a mighty pretty poet, and to convince you that he is, I will shew you some verses that he indited upon me, as I was dancing at court—(*Pulls them out*)—Here they are, brother. Count, will you be so obliging as to read them to my brother?

MUSHROOM: Madam, as the sublime bard politely sings, the nod of beauty sways both gods and men, and I obey. Gentlemen, the title will at once let you into the whole of what you are to expect in this little production. 'An extempore on the famous Mrs. Diggerty's dancing at court'—Now attend—

> When beauteous Diggerty leads up the dance
> In fair Britannia's court,
> Then ev'ry heart is in a prance,
> And longs for Cupid's sport.

> Beaux ogle, and pant and gaze,
> Belles envy and sneer, yet praise,
> As Venus herself were there;
> And prudes agree, it must be she,
> It must be she—or Diggerty,
> It must be she—or Diggerty,
> Or Diggerty, the fair.

(Bows very low to MRS. DIGGERTY)

That's all, gentlemen, that's all—only a *jeu d'esprit*, as I told you; a slight effort of a muse, bound in the silken chains of beauty and delight. (*He bows, she curtseys*)

COUNSELLOR: Conceited coxcomb! (*Aside*)

MUSHROOM: And now, madam, I have a favour to beg of you.

MRS. DIGGERTY: O command it—what is it?

MUSHROOM: Why, madam, as the celebrated Doctor Thomas Augustine Arne[1] has honoured this hasty offspring with an alliance of his harmonious muse, and as your ladyship has frequently heretofore enlivened it with your vocal glee, shall we beg that you will once more animate these verbal images with a touch of your Promethean pipe.

MRS. DIGGERTY: O dear, count, you are veestly panegyrical.

COUNSELLOR: Aye, aye, come, sister, as you have the tune oblige us with it.

MRS. DIGGERTY: I will try, brother, what I can do—but, by my honour, I have a great big cold—hem—hem!—

MUSHROOM: The worse your voice, madam, the more your taste will shine.

MRS. DIGGERTY: Nay, count, voice or no voice, I will make an effort—Sol-la-mi-fa-sol, &c.—Upon my honour I have no more voice than a kitling.

SONG

(*During the song* MUSHROOM *beats time conceitedly, but so as not to interrupt her, or interfere with her acting it*)

MUSHROOM: Bravo! bravissimo! carissimo! novelissimo! transcendissimo! and every superlativissimo in the sublime region of excellentissimo!

---

[1] 1710–78: a leading English composer and musician, closely involved with the theatre. Presumably it was his son who was present when Macklin killed Hallam. Cf. p. 10 above.

O'DOGHERTY: Come, count, now if you please we will go down, and sign the leases, and dispatch the attornies.

MUSHROOM: With all my heart.   (*Exit* O'DOGHERTY)

MRS. DIGGERTY: You dine here, count.

MUSHROOM: Do I breathe! do I exist!   I will but just step down, sign the leaves, and return on the wings of inclination—*ma chère belle sans adieu.*   (*Exit*)

MRS. DIGGERTY: *Au revoir*—well, he is a most humourous creature, and mighty witty: don't you think so, brother?

COUNSELLOR: Very witty, indeed, and I suppose understands a lady's toilet—

MRS. DIGGERTY: The best of any man in the world, the most handy creature about a woman—and such teest—but, brother, you must sup with us to-night—I have a few friends—a private peerty this evening: Lady Kinnegad, Lady Pam, old Lady Bab Frightful, Mrs. Gazette, Mr. Mushroom, Pat Fitzmungrel, Major Gamble, Mrs. Cardmark, and half a score more—quite a private peerty— you must be with us, brother—we are to have a little gambling and dancing, and are to be mighty jolly—I shall expect you— yours, yours—I must go finish my toilet.   (*Exit*)

COUNSELLOR: What a strange turn this woman's mind has taken—she is far gone I see, and must be pinched to the quick—and shall this very night.   (*Exit*)

END OF THE FIRST ACT

ACT II

Enter O'DOGHERTY *and* MRS. DIGGERTY

O'DOGHERTY: Well, but, my dear, why will you be in such a passion? Why will you not hearken to reason?

MRS. DIGGERTY: Mr. Diggerty, I will hear no reason; there can be no reason against what I say—you are the strangest man—not be a lord—sir, I insist upon it—there's a necessity for a peerage.

O'DOGHERTY: Oh! then only shew me the necessity, and all my objections will vanish.

MRS. DIGGERTY: Why, sir, I am affronted for want of a title: a parcel of upstarts, with their crownets upon their coaches, their chairs, their spoons, their handkerchiefs—nay, on the very knockers of their doors—creatures that were below me but t'other day, are now truly my superiors, and have the precedency, and are set above me at table.

O'DOGHERTY: Set above you at table?

MRS. DIGGERTY: Yes, sir, set above me at table wherever I go.

O'DOGHERTY: Upon my honour then that's a great shame. Well, well, my dear—come, come, my dear, don't be in such a fluster.

MRS. DIGGERTY: Fluster! why sir, I tell you I am ready to expire whenever I go into the great world.

O'DOGHERTY: At what, my dear?

MRS. DIGGERTY: At what—Egh! how can you ax such an ignorant quistion? Can there be anything more provoking to a woman of my teest and spirit, than to hear the titles of a parcel of upstart ugly creatures bawled in one's ears upon every occasion—my Lady Kinnegad's coach there—my Lady Kilgobbin's chair there—My Lady Castleknock's servants there—my Lady Tanderagee's[1] chariot there. And after all these titles only consider how my vile neem sounds. (*Cries*) Mrs. Diggerty's servants there—Mrs. Diggerty's chair there—Mrs. Diggerty's coach there—it is so mean and beggarly I cannot bear it—the very thought of it makes

[1] Kilgobbin, a village ten miles south of Dublin: Castleknock, a village seven miles to the west; Tanderagee, a town in east Armagh.

Mr M--k--n Orator.

CARICATURE OF MACKLIN, ORATOR

(*By courtesy of the British Museum*)

me ready to burst my stays and almost throws me into my hysterics. (*Throws herself into a couch*)

O'DOGHERTY: Nay, my dear, don't be working yourself up to your fits, your hysterics, and your tantrums now.

MRS. DIGGERTY: My life is miserable. (*Rises*) You cross me in every thing, you are always finding fault with my routs, and my drums, and my fancy ball—t'other night you would not make up a dress for it, nor appear at it—O fie, fie, fie—but you are true Irish to the very bone of you.

O'DOGHERTY: Indeed I am, and to the marrow within the bone too; and what is more, I hope I shall never be otherwise.

MRS. DIGGERTY: Ridiculous weakness! Pray, sir, do you not think the English love their country as well as the Irish do theirs?

O'DOGHERTY: O indeed I believe they do, and a great deal better; though we have a great many among us that call themselves patriots and champions, who, at the same time, would not care if poor old Ireland was squeezed as you squeeze an orange—providded they had but their share of the juice.[1]

MRS. DIGGERTY: Pooh, pooh! nobody minds what you say—you are always abusing every body in power—well, sir, you see the English are improving in teest every day, and have their burlettas and their operas, their Cornelys, their Almacks, their macaronies—[2]

O'DOGHERTY: O my dear, I tell you again and again, that the English can never be precedent to us. They, by their genius and constitution, must always run mad about something or other, either about burlettas, pantomimes, a man in a bottle, a Cock-lane ghost,[3] or something of equal importance. But, my dear, they

---

[1] This speech is altered and expanded in the MS.; presumably the irony might have been missed in London. The English love their country better because they have more of such 'patriots and champions'.

[2] Burlettas, musical farces; Mrs. Cornelys, from 1763 onwards, organised subscription entertainments at Carlisle House in Soho Square; Almack's, the famous Assembly Rooms in King Street, St. James's; a group of young exquisites about 1760 brought foreign tastes back from the Continent— the name probably derives from the Macaroni Club, so called to stress the members' preference for foreign cooking.

[3] In 1749 an advertisement appeared announcing that on 16 January a man would enter a wine-bottle on the Haymarket stage, and the theatre was wrecked in the riot which followed his non-appearance—it was rumoured that the hoax was planned by Lord Montagu, who had laid a bet that people were credulous enough to swallow it; in 1762 a man called Parsons got his daughter to impersonate a ghost—the Cock Lane ghost was the subject of a serious investigation in which Dr. Johnson took part; cf. Boswell, *Life of Johnson* (ed. G. B. Hill, 1887), I, pp. 406–8. The MS. adds other instances of popular English credulity.

can afford to run mad after such nonsense; why, they owe more money than we are worth; stay till we are as rich as they are, and then we may be allowed to run mad after absurdities as well as they.

MRS. DIGGERTY: Mighty well, sir, mighty well!   O, mighty well.

O'DOGHERTY: Heyday, what's the matter now?

MRS. DIGGERTY: But I see your design—you have a mind to break my heart—(*Sobs and cries*) yes, you argue and contradict me for no other end—you do every thing to fret and vex me.

O'DOGHERTY: Pray explain, my dear—what is it you mean?

MRS. DIGGERTY: Why, sir, ever since I returned to this odious country I have been requesting and begging, and praying, that you would send to London only for the set of long-tailed horses, that I told you I admired so—but no, I cannot prevail, though you know my Lady Kilgobbin, my Lady Balruddery,[1] my Lady Castleknock, and, in short, every lady of figure all run upon long tails—nobody but doctors, apothecaries, lawyers, cits, and country squires drive with short tails now—for my part, you know I detest a short tail.

O'DOGHERTY: Well, my dear, I have sent for your brother to town, on purpose to settle all these points between us, and if he thinks it proper that you should have long tails, you may have them as long as my Lady Kilgobbin's, my Lady Balruddery's tails, or any tails in the universe; and as to the title, if it can be had, why we will submit that to him likewise.

MRS. DIGGERTY: I know it can be had—and so let me have no more trouble about it, for a title I will have—I must be a lady as well as other people—I can't bear being a plain Mrs. Diggerty any longer —(*Cries*)

O'DOGHERTY: Well, well, my dear, we will try what we can do—you must be a lady! yes, yes, you shall be a lady; but by the blood of the O'Dogherty's, it shall be a broken-backed lady.   A hump shall be your patent, my dear.   (*Aside and Exit*)

MRS. DIGGERTY: An obstinate man! not accept of a title—in short, there's no living without it.   Who's there?

Enter JOHN

JOHN: Madam.

MRS. DIGGERTY: Nobody come yet?

[1] i.e. Balrothery, a village twenty miles north of Dublin.

JOHN: No. madam.

MRS. DIGGERTY: What's o'clock?

JOHN: A quarter past seven, madam.

MRS. DIGGERTY: Are the candles lit, and the cards ready?

JOHN: They have been ready this half hour, madam.

MRS. DIGGERTY: Shew the company into this room.

JOHN: Yes, madam. (*Exit. A loud knocking, three servants without*)

WILLIAM: Lady Kinnegad.

JAMES: Lady Kinnegad.

JOHN: Lady Kinnegad.

Enter JOHN, *shewing in* LADY KINNEGAD

JOHN: Lady Kinnegad, madam. (*Exit*)

LADY KINNEGAD: My dear Diggy—what, all alone—nobody come?

MRS. DIGGERTY: Not a mortal, I have been fretting this hour at being alone, and had nothing to divert me but a quarrel with my husband.

LADY KINNEGAD: The old fogrum![1] what, he won't open his purse strings, I suppose—but you should make him, for he is as rich as a Jew.

MRS. DIGGERTY: Aye, but he is as close-fisted as an old judge—Lord, he has no notion of anything in life, but reading musty books, draining bogs, planting trees, establishing manufactories, setting the common people to work, and saving money.

LADY KINNEGAD: Ha, ha, ha! the monster! (*A loud knocking*)

WILLIAM: Major Gamble.

JAMES: Major Gamble.

JOHN: Major Gamble.

Enter JOHN *and* MAJOR GAMBLE

JOHN: Major Gamble, madam. (*Exit*)

MRS. DIGGERTY: Major, how is your gout to-day?

MAJOR GAMBLE: I don't know how the devil it is, not I—hobbling up your stairs has made me sweat—Lady Kinnegad, I kiss your hands; I ask your pardon, but I must sit down—I cannot stand— I got cold last night, and I feel it to-day—what, is there nobody come yet but us?—nothing going forward (*A loud knocking*)

WILLIAM: Lady Bab Frightful.

JAMES: Lady Bab Frightful.

---

[1] An antiquated or old-fashioned person.

JOHN: Lady Bab Frightful.

LADY KINNEGAD: Here she comes, as Mushroom says, nature's contradiction—youth and age, frost and fire, winter and summer, an old body and a young mind.

Enter JOHN *and* LADY BAB FRIGHTFUL

JOHN: Lady Bab Frightful, madam.   (*Exit*)

MRS. DIGGERTY: My dear Lady Bab!

LADY BAB: My dear Diggy—Lady Kinnegad, I kiss your hands—O, major—why, you had like to have ruined us all last night—the bank was just broke—well, I am a perfect rake—I think I was one of the last this morning.   I danced till five.

LADY KINNEGAD: As the old saying is, Lady Bab, you can never do it younger—live while we live, that's the rule of happiness, you have good spirits, a good jointure, and nobody to controul you—you amiable creature.

LADY BAB: Yes, I thank my stars, I never want spirits.   Tol, lol, lol (*Sings*)—I could dance till morning.   (*A loud knocking*)

WILLIAM: Mrs. Jolly.

JAMES: Mrs. Jolly.

JOHN: Mrs. Jolly.

Enter JOHN *and* MRS. JOLLY

JOHN: Mrs. Jolly, madam.   (*Gives a card to* MRS. DIGGERTY, *and exit*)

MRS. JOLLY: So, good folks.

MRS. DIGGERTY: Madam, your most obedient.

MRS. JOLLY: What, all idle!—no loo[1]—no brag—no hazard[2]—nor no dancing begun yet, and Lady Bab here—but where's Mushroom? —I've such a story for him.   Where's the count, Diggerty?

Enter JOHN *with a note and exit*

MRS. DIGGERTY: O he will be here, never fear, madam—O, this is a card from Gazette—(*Reads*) 'Dear Dig, I cannot be with you at seven; but before you have played two hands, expect me—three short visits at the Green, one in Merrion-street, two in the Mall, two in Britain-street, three words at the Castle with his Excellency,[3] and then I am yours for the night, and whilst I am———Gazette.'

---

[1] A round card game, in which the losers of tricks pay into a pool which is taken by the winner.

[2] Dicing.

[3] From St. Stephen's Green, via Merrion Street, the Mall (now O'Connell Street) and Britain Street (now Parnell Street), to Dublin Castle would have been a journey of some two Irish, or two-and-a-half English miles.

LADY KINNEGAD: Well said, Gazette!—she will spread more scandal in these short visits than truth can remove in a twelvemonth. (*A loud knocking*)

WILLIAM: Mr. Fitzmungrel.

JAMES: Mr. Fitzmungrel.

JOHN: Mr. Fitzmungrel.

LADY KINNEGAD: O, here's Fitzmungrel! drunk, I suppose, according to custom.

LADY BAB: And brutal, according to nature; yes, yes, he's drunk, I see. I will be gone, for I know he will be rude.

LADY KINNEGAD: No, no, stay—let us all share in his abuse, pray.

Enter JOHN

JOHN: Mr. Fitzmungrel, madam. (*Exit*)

Enter FITZMUNGREL, *drunk and singing*

FITZMUNGREL: My dear Mrs. O'Dogherty—but I know you do not love to be called O'Dogherty, and therefore I will call you by your English name. Mrs. Diggerty—my dear Diggerty, I have not been in bed since I saw you.

MRS. DIGGERTY: Why, where have you been, Fitz?

FITZMUNGREL: At the Curragh, my dear, with Pat Wildfire, Sir Anthony All-Night, Sir Toby Ruin, Dick Bashaw, and half a score more, and a fine chase we had—haux, haux, my honies—over, over, haux—but I was resolved to be with you, my little Diggerty, because I promised, so I smoked it away to town—drove myself in my own phaeton, and was over-turned just as I came to dirty Dublin.

MRS. DIGGERTY: Why you are all dirty!

FITZMUNGREL: Yes, I had a fine set down in the dirtiest spot of the whole road.

MRS. DIGGERTY: I hope you are not hurt.

FITZMUNGREL: Not I, my dear—haux, haux, whoop—no, no, my dear Diggerty, I am like a cat, I always light upon my legs—haux, haux, whoop—ha, my dear angelic cousin, Lady Bab Frightful—by heavens, you are a beautiful creature and look like the picture of good luck—well, shall we have another bank to-night?—here, take this note into your bank. (*Gives a note*) I will go take a nap in the next room in my old chair, and when you have made it five hundred, wake me, my little Babby—do you hear?

LADY BAB: I will, I will—that's a good man, go, and take a nap.

FITZMUNGREL: My dear cousin, thou'rt the beauty of our family.

LADY BAB: Well, well—go sleep—go sleep.

FITZMUNGREL: The beauty of our family, Bab—another Venus, as handsome as Medusa—and you are besides a good-natured, old, young, middle-aged, giggling girl of threescore—so I'll go take my nap—haux, haux, tally ho—whoop!   (*Exit*)

MRS. DIGGERTY: He is horrid drunk.

LADY KINNEGAD: And what is worse, he is a greater brute sober than drunk.   (*A loud knocking*)

WILLIAM: Mrs. Gazette.

JAMES: Mrs. Gazette.

JOHN: Mrs. Gazette.

LADY KINNEGAD: Here she comes, that knows every body's business but her own, ha, ha, ha!

MAJOR GAMBLE: I will swear she is in as many houses every day as Faulkner's Journal.[1]

Enter JOHN *and* MRS. GAZETTE

JOHN: Mrs. Gazette, madam.   (*Exit*)

MRS. GAZETTE: My dear Diggerty, you got my billet—I came to you as soon as possible—but where's Mushroom? I do not see him.

MRS. DIGGERTY: He will be here, madam.

MRS. GAZETTE: My dear Jolly, why you look in high bloom to-night —Major, how's your gout?—Lady Kinnegad, your most devoted —O, but Diggerty, I have a piece of news—they say your husband's to have a peerage.

OMNES: Ha, ha, ha!

MRS. DIGGERTY: It is very true, madam, very true—we are to be entitled.

MRS. GAZETTE: Why not? I am sure there are those that have not half your fortune, who have got peerages.   And pray, my dear, what is your title to be?—you must consult me upon it.

MRS. DIGGERTY: Why, I have thought of several, but know not which to pitch upon—I am distracted about it, I have thought of nothing else this week—I wish you would all advise me—it must be something new, elegant, and uncommon—and teesty—yes, I must have it teesty—see, here is the list of titles—if you will all step into the

[1] The leading Dublin newspaper of the day.

drawing-room, we will determine upon one, and then sit down to
our peerties—come, *allons, sans cérémonie*—I'll shew you the way
—come, major— (*Exeunt all but the Major*)

MAJOR GAMBLE: Aye, aye, pack along—I'll hobble after you—get the
hazard ready—but I must sit by the fire, I am cursed lame—
'sblood, I have trod upon some damned shell or pebble—O damn
it—curse the shell—but Lady Bab's bank will be worth touching.
(*Exit*)

Enter O'DOGHERTY *and* KATTY FARREL

O'DOGHERTY: They are all gone to their nightly devotions—well, and
what did she say when you gave her the money?

KATTY: O sir, she was overjoyed, and so thankful—but she will lose it
all again to that Lady Kinnegad.

O'DOGHERTY: Not to-night, Katty; her brother was in the room before
them to prevent her playing; he is resolved to settle all affairs with
her this very night. But what makes this Mushroom stay so long?
Sure he will come.

KATTY: O never fear, sir—you never saw a man so eager, and so full of
expectation.

O'DOGHERTY: And so you have really dressed him up in your lady's
clothes?

KATTY: I have, sir, indeed—and he is ten times fonder of himself—if
possible—as a woman, I think, than he was as a man.

O'DOGHERTY: Ogh, I will engage I will cure him of his passion for
himself, and for all Irish women, as long as he lives.

KATTY: Here comes my mistress, and her brother with her, sir.

O'DOGHERTY: Come, come, quick; let us get out of their way, for he is
resolved to startle the lady, and waken her, if possible. Let us
leave them to themselves, for I reckon they will have a sharp
brush. (*Exeunt*)

Enter MRS. DIGGERTY *and* HAMILTON

COUNSELLOR: Madam, madam, you shall hear me.

MRS. DIGGERTY: Was there ever so rude, so abrupt a behaviour, to
force me from my company thus?

COUNSELLOR: 'Tis what your insolent disease demands; the suddenness
and abruptness of the shock is the chief ingredient in the remedy
that must cure you.

MRS. DIGGERTY: What do you mean, sir?

COUNSELLOR: I will tell you, madam—you are not ignorant that your husband took you without a fortune; that he generously gave the little our father left you to your younger sister, with the benevolent addition of two thousand pounds—you know, too, that by marriage articles, upon a separation or your husband's death, you are entitled only to a hundred pounds a year; which cautious pittance his prudence wisely insisted on, as a necessary check upon the conduct of giddy, female youth, and thoughtless vanity, when matched with the tempered age of sobriety and discretion—now, madam, I am commissioned to inform you, that the doors are open, and that the stipulated sum will be punctually paid you, as your vicious appetite shall demand; for know, that neither your husband's love, my affection, nor a residence in this house can be enjoyed by you another hour, but on the hard condition of a thorough reformation.

MRS. DIGGERTY: Sir!

COUNSELLOR: Madam, it is true; for if female vanity will be mad, husbands must be peremptory.

MRS. DIGGERTY: Pray, sir, do not speak so loud.

COUNSELLOR: Why not?

MRS. DIGGERTY: The company will hear you.

COUNSELLOR: I know it—and I intend that they shall.

MRS. DIGGERTY: Oh, oh, oh! I shall be ashamed for ever—pray do not speak so loud—bless me, brother, you startle me—what is it you mean?

COUNSELLOR: Will you hear what I have to say? Will you attend to the dictates of a brother's love, with modest patience, and virtuous candour?

MRS. DIGGERTY: I will.

COUNSELLOR: Sit down—know then, in your husband's judgment, the sums you have squandered, and those you have been cheated of by your female friends, is your least offence—it is your pride, your midnight revels, insolence of taste, rage of precedency, that grieve him; for they have made you the ridicule of every flirt and coxcomb, and the scorn and pity of every sober person that knows your folly; this reflects disgrace upon your friends, contempt upon the spirit and credit of your husband, and has furnished whispering suspicion with stories and implications, which have secretly fixed an infectious stain upon your chastity.   (*Both rise*)

MRS. DIGGERTY: My chastity!   I defy the world!

COUNSELLOR: Aye, madam, you may defy it; but she who does, will find the world too hard a match for her.

MRS. DIGGERTY: I care not what slander says—I will rely upon my innocence.

COUNSELLOR: But I will not, madam, nor shall you—it is not sufficient for my sister, or your husband's wife, or female reputation, to rely on innocence alone—women must not only be innocent, they must appear so too.

MRS. DIGGERTY: Brother, I don't know what you mean by all this.   I beg you will explain.

COUNSELLOR: I will—know then, this coxcomb Mushroom—

MRS. DIGGERTY: Mushroom!

COUNSELLOR: Mushroom—as a man of wit and spirit—thought himself obliged to take some hints your levity had given him.

MRS. DIGGERTY: I give him hints—brother, you wrong me.

COUNSELLOR: Pray hear me—this spark, I say, like a true man of intrigue, not only returns your hints with a letter of gallantry, but bribes your own woman to deliver it.

MRS. DIGGERTY: My woman!

COUNSELLOR: The same.

MRS. DIGGERTY: I am ignorant of all this, and will turn her out of the house this instant.

COUNSELLOR: Softly! hear the whole! the maid, instead of carrying the letter to you, delivers that, and many others, to her master, who, in your name, hand, stile, and sentiment, has answered them all, and carried on an amorous correspondence with the gentleman, even up to an assignation; and, now, at this very instant, the spark is preparing for the happy interview, and has made the town the confidants of his good fortune.

MRS. DIGGERTY: O heavens!

COUNSELLOR: Now judge what your husband, brother, and your friends must feel, and what the world must think of her, whose conduct could entitle a coxcomb to such liberties.

MRS. DIGGERTY: Brother, I shall make no defence—the story shocks me! and though I know my own intentions, yet what people may say—but, be assured, I shall be more prudent for the future—perhaps I have been to blame—pray advise me—only say what I shall do to be revenged upon the fellow for his impudence, and what will convince my husband, you, and all the world of my innocence, and I will do it. I protest you have given such a motion to my heart, and such a trouble and a trembling, as it never felt before.

COUNSELLOR: It is a virtuous motion—encourage it—for the anxiety and tears of repentance, though the rarest, are the brightest ornaments a modern fine lady can be decked in.

KATTY *and* O'DOGHERTY *without*

O'DOGHERTY: I shall be in here with the counsellor, Katty, and the moment he comes, bring me word.

KATTY: I shall, sir.

COUNSELLOR: Here your husband comes.

MRS. DIGGERTY: I am ashamed to see him.

Enter O'DOGHERTY

O'DOGHERTY: Well, brother, have you spoke to her?

COUNSELLOR: There she is, sir—and as she should be—bathed in the tears of humility and repentance.

O'DOGHERTY: Ogh, I am sorry to see this indeed—I am afraid you have gone too far. If I had been by, I assure you, brother, you should not have made her cry—Yerrow,[1] Nancy, child, turn about, and don't be crying there.

MRS. DIGGERTY: Sir, I am ashamed to see your face—my errors I acknowledge—and for the future—

O'DOGHERTY: Pooh, pooh—I will have no submissions nor acknowledgements; if you have settled every thing with your brother, that is sufficient.

MRS. DIGGERTY: I hope he is satisfied—and it shall be the business of my life—

O'DOGHERTY: Pooh, pooh! say no more I tell you, but come, give me a kiss, and let us be friends at once—there—so, in that kiss now, let all tears and uneasiness subside with you, as all fears and resentment shall die with me.

COUNSELLOR: Come, sister, give me your hand, for I must have my kiss

---

[1] The Irish interjection *dhera*, not easily translatable, implying mild disagreement.

of peace too. I own I have been a little severe with you, but your disease required sharp medicines.

o'dogherty: Now we are friends, Nancy, I have a favour or two to beg of you.

mrs. diggerty: Pray, command them.

o'dogherty: Why, then, the first thing that I ask is, that you will send away that French rascal the cook, with his compots and combobs, his alamodes and aladobes, his crapandoes and frigandoes, and a thousand outlandish kickshaws, that I'm sure were never designed for Christian food; and let the good rough rumps of beef, the jolly surloins, the geese and turkies, cram fowls, bacon and greens; and the pies, puddings and pasties, that used to be perfectly shoving one another off the table, so that there was not room for the people's plates; with a fine large cod too, as big as a young alderman—I say, let all those French kickshaws be banished from my table, and these good old Irish dishes be put in their places; and then the poor every day will have something to eat.

mrs. diggerty: They shall, sir.

o'dogherty: And as to yourself, my dear Nancy, I hope I shall never have any more of your London English; none of your this here's, your that there's, your winegars, your weals, your vindors, your toastesses, and your stone postesses;[1] but let me have our own good, plain, old Irish English, which I insist is better than all the English English that ever coquets and coxcombs brought into the land.

mrs. diggerty: I will get rid of these as fast as possible.

o'dogherty: And pray, above all things, never call me Mr. Diggerty—my name is Murrogh O'Dogherty, and I am not ashamed of it; but that damned name Diggerty always vexes me whenever I hear it.

mrs. diggerty: Then, upon my honour, Mr. O'Dogherty, it shall never vix you again.

o'dogherty: Ogh, that's right, Nancy—O'Dogherty for ever— O'Dogherty!—there's a sound for you—why they have not such a name in all England as O'Dogherty—nor as any of our fine

---

[1] Vulgar pronunciations: cf. Thomas Sheridan, *The Brave Irishman* (1787) I, 'I saw him go into the blue postices;' also Marryat, *Peter Simple* (1834), Chap. III, where the coachman says that the best inn is 'the Blue Postesses, where the midshipmen leaves their chestesses, call for tea and toastesses, and forget to pay for their breakfastesses'. Today we would spell 'postses'.

sounding Milesian[1] names—what are your Jones and your Stones, your Rice and your Price, your Heads and your Foots, and Hands, and your Wills, and Hills and Mills, and Sands, and a parcel of little pimping names that a man would not pick out of the street, compared to the O'Donovans, O'Callaghans, O'Sullivans, O'Brallaghans, O'Shaghnesses, O'Flahertys, O'Gallaghers, and O'Dogherty's[2]—Ogh, they have courage in the very sound of them, for they come out of the mouth like a storm; and are as old and as stout as the oak at the bottom of the bog of Allen, which was there before the flood—and though they have been dispossessed by upstarts and foreigners, buddoughs and sassanoughs,[3] yet I hope they will flourish in the Island of Saints, while grass grows or water runs.

Enter KATTY

KATTY: Mr. Mushroom is come, sir.

O'DOGHERTY: What, in his woman's clothes?

KATTY: Yes, sir.

O'DOGHERTY: Impudent rascal! and where have you put him, Katty?

KATTY: In the back parlour, sir.

O'DOGHERTY: Odzooks! Katty, go down, and shew him up here—this is the largest room to exercise the gentleman in—begone, quick, and leave all the rest to me.

KATTY: I am gone, sir. (*Exit*)

O'DOGHERTY: My dear, you must act a part in this farce, the better to bring the rascal into ridicule.

MRS. DIGGERTY: Any thing to be revenged of him for his ill opinion of me.

O'DOGHERTY: Step into your own room, then, and I will come and instruct you how to behave. (*Exit* MRS. DIGGERTY) And, brother, do you go and open the affair to the company, and bring them here to listen to the count's gallantry, and to be witnesses of his making me a cuckold.

COUNSELLOR: I warrant you I will prepare them for the scene. But, brother, be sure you make the gentleman smart. (*Exit*)

---

[1] Cf. p. 59, n. 1, above.

[2] The choice of names has interest. All belong to the old Irish aristocracy. The Ó Donnabháins have been in south-west Cork since the Anglo-Norman invasion. The Ó Suileabháins have been prominent in Irish history since then, and belong to Cork and Kerry. For the other names, cf. p. 47, n. 1; p. 59, n, 2; p. 83, n. 1; p. 95, n. 2.

[3] Irish *bodach*, oaf, lout; *sasanach*, Englishman.

o'DOGHERTY: Ogh, leave him to me—by the honour of the whole Irish nation I will make him remember the name of Diggerty, as sensibly as his school-master ever did *hic, haec, hoc, genitivo hujus*—an impudent rascal! make a cuckold of an Irishman—what, take our own trade[1] out of our hands—and a branch of business we value ourselves so much upon too—why, sure that and the linen manufacture[2] are the only free trade we have—O, here the company come.

Enter all the company

LADY KINNEGAD: Well, where is this count, this hero of intrigue?

o'DOGHERTY: Below stairs.

LADY BAB: And in woman's clothes, Mr. Dogherty?

o'DOGHERTY: And in woman's clothes, Lady Bab, come to make a cuckold of me; and if you will all hide yourselves in the next room, you may see how the operation proceeds—hush—here he comes—get in, get in—and do not stir—here he is—begone.

(*They all retire—exit* o'DOGHERTY)

Enter KATTY, *and* MUSHROOM *in woman's clothes*

KATTY: Step into this room for a moment, sir, and I will let my mistress know you are here—I protest I should not have known you.

MUSHROOM: Should not you? Ha, ha, ha! Why I think I do make a handsome woman, Mrs. Katty.

KATTY: Handsome! why you are a perfect beauty! you are the very picture of a Connaught lady, that visits my mistress—well, I will go and see if the coast is clear, and let her know you are come.

MUSHROOM: Do, dear Mrs. Katty, and tell her my soul is all rapture, extacy, and transport, and rides upon the wings of love.

KATTY: I will, I will, sir. (*Exit*)

MUSHROOM: A man must speak nonsense to these creatures, or they will not believe he loves them. I shall have more intrigues in this country than I shall know what to do with; for I find the women all like me. As to Lady Kinnegad I see she is determined to have me.

LADY KINNEGAD: Indeed! Conceited puppy!

---

[1] Irishmen were regarded in England as notorious rakes: cf. *TSS*, pp. 113, 119–20, 127, 190–1, 198.

[2] The Irish linen trade, which did not compete with English manufactures, was exempt from the restrictions imposed on Irish trade in general.

MUSHROOM: But she is gross, coarse, and stinks of sweets[1] intolerably.

LADY KINNEGAD: Rascal!

MUSHROOM: Gazette is well enough; I am sure I can have her. Yes, she's a blood, but she won't do above once and away.

MRS. GAZETTE: Saucy fellow!—but once indeed—I assure you!

MUSHROOM: Jolly has some thoughts of me too, I see—but she's an idiot, a fool—damned silly.

MRS. JOLLY: Mighty well, sir—very well—

MUSHROOM: But of all the spectacles that ever attempted to awaken gallantry, sure Nature never formed such another antidote as poor Lady Bab.

LADY BAB: Oh! the villain!—an antidote—an antidote—

MUSHROOM: She always puts me in mind of an old house newly painted and white-washed.

LADY BAB: I will go tear his eyes out.

MUSHROOM: Then she is continually feeding that nose of hers, and smells stronger of rappee than Lady Kinnegad does of the Spice Islands.

LADY KINNEGAD: Oh! the rascal!

MUSHROOM: That Kinnegad is a damned tartar; she and Mrs. Card-mark have fleeced poor Diggerty horridly—when I get Diggerty to England, I will introduce her to my lord; for by that time I shall be tired of her. O, here the party comes.

Enter MRS. DIGGERTY *and* KATTY

My angel! my goddess!

MRS. DIGGERTY: O dear Mr. Mushroom, how could you venture so? I am ready to die with apprehension, lest my husband should discover you.

MUSHROOM: Never fear, my charmer; love despises all dangers, when such beauty as yours is the prize.

MRS. DIGGERTY: But I hope, Mr. Mushroom, your passion is sincere?

MUSHROOM: Madam, the winged architect of the Cyprian goddess has fabricated a pathetic structure in this breast, which the iron teeth of Time can never destroy.

MRS. DIGGERTY: O dear Mr. Mushroom, you are veestly kind.

KATTY: Come, come, madam, do you lose no time, retire to your chamber, there you will be safe, here you may be interrupted.

[1] Perfumes, not sweetmeats.

MRS. DIGGERTY: Do you step and send the servants out of the way.

MUSHROOM: Do, do, dear Mrs. Katty.

KATTY: I will, I will.   (*Exit*)

MUSHROOM: Dear creature, do but lay your hand upon my heart, and feel what an alarm of love and gratitude it beats.

KATTY and O'DOGHERTY without

O'DOGHERTY: Well, but, Katty, if she is so very ill, that is the very reason why I must see her.

MUSHROOM: Zounds! your husband's voice!

MRS. DIGGERTY: O heavens!

Enter KATTY

KATTY: My master, my master!

MRS. DIGGERTY: What will become of me?

KATTY: Run you down the back stairs, madam, and leave him to me.

MRS. DIGGERTY: Dear sir, farewell; for heaven's sake, don't discover yourself.

MUSHROOM: No, no, madam, never fear me, not for the world.

MRS. DIGGERTY: Adieu.   (*Exit*)

MUSHROOM: What the devil shall I do, Mrs. Katty?

KATTY: Sit you still, sir, at all events—I will put out the candles. (*Puts them out*)   He will take you for my mistress; pretend to be very ill; leave the rest to me.   Sure you can mimic a fine lady that has the vapours or the cholic.

MUSHROOM: O nobody better!—nobody better—

Enter O'DOGHERTY with a pistol

O'DOGHERTY: Heyday! what, in the dark, my dear?

KATTY: Yes, sir, my mistress is very ill, and cannot bear the light.

O'DOGHERTY: What is her complaint?

KATTY: The cholic, sir.

O'DOGHERTY: The cholic, sir! and what good can darkness do the cholic sir—get candles.

MUSHROOM: Oh, oh!—no candles—no lights, pray, my dear, no lights.

KATTY: No, no lights—my lady has the head-ache, as well as the cholic, and the lights make her much worse; therefore, pray let her sit in the dark, she will soon be well—are you any better, madam?

MUSHROOM: A great deal, but no lights, pray—oh, oh!—no lights! **no** lights!

115

O'DOGHERTY: Well, my dear, you shall have no lights, you shall have no lights—leave us, Katty—I have some business with your mistress. (*Exit* KATTY) How are you, my dear? are you any better?

MUSHROOM: O, a great deal, my dear.

O'DOGHERTY: I am mighty glad of it, my soul. But now, my dear, I have long wanted to have a little serious conversation with you upon a business that has given me the utmost uneasiness, nay indeed the utmost torture of mind; so without farther ceremony, and in one word, to come to the point—I am jealous, my dear.

MUSHROOM: How! jealous!

O'DOGHERTY: Indeed I am, as are half the husbands of this town, and all occasioned by one man, which is that coxcomb, count Mushroom.

MUSHROOM: He is a very great coxcomb, I own, my dear.

O'DOGHERTY: You may say that with a safe conscience—and a great jackanapes he is too into the bargain; though, I must own, the fellow has something genteel in him notwithstanding.

MUSHROOM: O yes, my dear, he is a very pretty fellow—that all the world allows.

O'DOGHERTY: It is very true, but his prettiness will be his ruin; for as he makes it his business and his glory to win the affections of women, wherever he goes, and as he has made conquests of several married women in this town, there are half a dozen husbands of us that have agreed to poison him.

MUSHROOM: How! poison him! O horrid! why that will be murder, my dear.

O'DOGHERTY: O, that is none of our business—let him look to that—we must leave that to the law—the fellow is always following you to the play-house, balls, and routs, and is constantly smiling at you, and ogling, and sighing—but if ever I catch him at those tricks again, as sure as his name is Mushroom, I will put the lining of this little pistol into the very middle of his scull.

MUSHROOM: Oh, oh, oh!

O'DOGHERTY: He told me this morning that he had a new intrigue upon his hands this afternoon—I wish I knew where it was; by all that's honourable, I would help the husband to put eight or ten inches of cold iron into the rascal's bowels.

MUSHROOM: Oh, oh, oh!

O'DOGHERTY: What is the matter, my dear? what makes you start and cry out so? Give me your hand—why you are all in a tremor! Ogho, why you have got the shaking ague.

MUSHROOM: I am mighty ill—mighty ill—

O'DOGHERTY: Why you are all in a cold sweat—you had best go up stairs and lie down.

MUSHROOM: No, no, no!—oh, no!—

O'DOGHERTY: Why you shall have some immediate help—here, Katty—John—William—who's there?

Enter WILLIAM

WILLIAM: Did your honour call, sir?

O'DOGHERTY: Fly this minute to the next street to Mr. Carnage the surgeon, and bid him hasten hither to bleed my wife; then run as fast as you can to Doctor Fillgrave, and tell him my wife is very ill, and must be blistered directly. Begone—fly—

WILLIAM: I will, sir. (*Exit*)

MUSHROOM: Soh! what the devil shall I do now. I shall certainly be discovered. (*Aside*)

O'DOGHERTY: How are you now, my dear?

MUSHROOM: O better, better, a great deal.

O'DOGHERTY: O, but for fear of the worst, I will have you bled plentifully, my dear, and half a score good rousing blisters laid on by way of prevention; for it is a very sickly time, my life.

MUSHROOM: Aye, so it is, my soul. But, my dear, I begin to be a little better; pray send the maid hither.

O'DOGHERTY: What do you want with the maid, my angel?

MUSHROOM: I want her upon a particular occasion, my love—oh, oh, oh!

O'DOGHERTY: Very well, my dear, I'll send her to you. I think we have the count of the three blue balls in a fine pickle; but I have not done with him yet. I have laid a ridiculous snare for him, if he will but fall into it, that will not only expose him to the world, but cure him for ever, I think, of trespassing upon matrimonial premises. (*Aside and exit*)

MUSHROOM: Was ever poor devil so sweated! I wish I were out of the kingdom! I shall certainly be poisoned among them! they are a damned barbarous people. I have often heard of the wild Irish,[1] but never believed there were such till now. Poison a man, only for having an intrigue with a friend's wife. Zounds, we never mind such things in England; but they are unpolished beings here.

Enter KATTY, *with two candles*

MUSHROOM: Oh! Mrs. Katty, get me out of the house, or I am a dead man—he suspects I have a design upon his wife, and carries a loaded pistol to shoot me.

KATTY: O heavens, sir—I don't know what to do with you—here comes my poor mistress, frightened out of her wits too.

Enter MRS. DIGGERTY

MUSHROOM: O, madam! if you don't contrive to convey me out of the house some way or other, I shall be detected, poisoned, shot, or run through the vitals.

MRS. DIGGERTY: I am so distracted. I cannot think—you must even discover yourself to him, and say you came hither in that disguise out of a frolic.

MUSHROOM: Zounds, a frolic! Madam, he is as jealous as a Spanish miser, or an Italian doctor; he has a pistol in his pocket loaded with a brace of balls[2]—he would shoot me, run me through the body, or poison me directly, should he discover me—have you no closet, or cup-board? Dear Mrs. Katty, cannot you contrive to get me out of the house in some shape or other?

KATTY: Why yes, sir, I have a contrivance that I think might save you.

MUSHROOM: What is it? what is it? quick, quick, for heaven's sake; for he certainly has a pistol in his pocket—he shewed it to me.

KATTY: Why, sir, I have a large portmanteau trunk, by the help of which, I think, you might be safely conveyed out of the house, if you would but submit to be shut up in it.

MUSHROOM: Submit! zounds! any thing, any thing, dear Mrs. Katty, to save my own life and a lady's honour. Why, child, it is an excellent contrivance, and, in my condition, perhaps the only one that could relieve me. For heaven's sake, let me see it—where is it?

KATTY: It stands just without the door here in the passage. (*Brings it in*) Here it is, sir, if it is but big enough—that's all the danger.

[1] A very old cliché.
[2] i.e. double-barrelled, not double-loaded.

118

MUSHROOM: Zounds! let me try it—let me try it—quick—quick—put in my clothes[1]—there—cram me in—buckle me up—stay, stay—leave this end a little open for air, or I shall be stifled—very well—excellent well—Mrs. Katty—there—cram me in—it will do—snug—snug—damned snug—

MRS. DIGGERTY: Now call the men to carry it up to your room.

KATTY: Here, John, William.

SERVANTS: (*Without*) Madam.

KATTY: Come here quickly.

Enter JOHN *and* WILLIAM

KATTY: Here, take this portmanteau on your shoulders, and carry it up to my room—make haste. (*The servants turn it up endways, with* MUSHROOM'S *head to the ground, then raise it on their shoulders*)

Enter O'DOGHERTY

O'DOGHERTY: Where are you going with that portmanteau?

JOHN: Up to Mrs. Katty's room.

O'DOGHERTY: Set it down here[2]—what have you got in this portmantle, Katty?

KATTY: It is, sir—it is—

O'DOGHERTY: What, what is it?

KATTY: Why it is—it is—

O'DOGHERTY: Speak this minute, or I will put my sword up to the hilts in it.

MUSHROOM: Ah! hold, hold—my dear Diggerty, hold—'tis I—'tis I—

O'DOGHERTY: I—who the devil is I?

MUSHROOM: Mushroom—your friend Mushroom.

O'DOGHERTY: What!   Count Mushroom![3]

MUSHROOM: The same—the very same—

O'DOGHERTY: Hold the candle—aye, it is my friend the count indeed.

MUSHROOM: Zounds, my dear Diggerty—you have dropped the hot wax on my face—do pray let me out.

O'DOGHERTY: And so this was the new intrigue you told me of this afternoon.

MUSHROOM: Ah, my dear Diggerty, I was but in jest, upon my honour.

---

[1] i.e.—tuck my petticoats into the portmanteau with me.   Comic business is called for.

[2] They set the portmanteau down on end with Mushroom still inverted.

[3] About this point the portmanteau is opened to disclose Mushroom upside down.

O'DOGHERTY: Aye, now you are right, count—the intrigue was but in jest on my wife's side, indeed—here, ladies, come hither, and see this hero of intrigue and taste that they all admire so much.

MUSHROOM: Ah, dear Diggerty, don't expose me.

Enter the company

OMNES: Ha, ha, ha!

O'DOGHERTY: Here, John—set him upon his legs on the ground[1]—so—there—Lady Kinnegad, pray let me introduce you to the knight of the leathern portmantle.

LADY KINNEGAD: Count, your most obedient—I would salute you, but I am coarse and stink of sweets.

MUSHROOM: Ah, my dear lady, that was only the wanton vanity of a coxcomb upon the verge of paradise as he thought.

MRS. JOLLY: Your humble servant, count—I would strive to extricate you, but, as you know, I am an idiot, a fool—ha, ha, ha!

MUSHROOM: O dear Mrs. Jolly—

LADY BAB: Yes, and I am like an old house newly painted and white-washed, and I stink of rappee.   I think a little rappee would not be amiss to clear your eyes, and refresh your spirits, and there is some for you.   (*Throws snuff in his face*)

MUSHROOM: O dear Lady Bab, this is (*Sneezes*) cruel—(*Sneezes*) indeli-cate—(*Sneezes*) and intolerable—(*Sneezes*) but I beg you will let me out of this confinement.

O'DOGHERTY: Indeed I will not, for I intend that other people shall enjoy your situation as well as I—this is Lady High-Life's night —all the world is there—so here, John, take this portmantle on your shoulders to Lady High-Life's, with my compliments, and never stop till you take it upstairs to the ball-room, and there set it down—they will be extremely glad to see their old friend, the count of the three blue balls.

MUSHROOM: Mr. Diggerty—madam—ladies—

OMNES: Away with him—away with him.   Ha, ha, ha!   (*He is carried off*)

O'DOGHERTY: Now, gentlemen and ladies, you may go plunder one another at cards and dice as fast as you can—and, like the count,

[1] They turn the portmanteau, with Mushroom in it, the other way up.

make yourselves objects for a farce—if every fine lady and cox-comb in this town were turned into a farce, faith we should be the merriest people in all Europe—but ours is over for to-night, and pretty well upon the whole.

> *Indeed, I think 'tis very fairly ended:*
> *The coxcomb's punished;*
> *The fine Irish lady's mended.*

FINIS

The School for Husbands

or

THE MARRIED LIBERTINE

A COMEDY

In Five Acts

Theatrical Note

The School for Husbands, in spite of Scottish and other opposition, but supported by the Irish in the audience, just managed to last for nine nights, so that the author was able to enjoy his three benefits. Although it is not so weak a play as one might therefore suppose, this is the whole of its theatrical history.

The School for Husbands

COVENT GARDEN   28 JANUARY, 1761

Dramatis Personae

Lord Belville	Mr. Macklin
Townly	Mr. Davies
Captain Manwaring	
Serjeant Bates	Mr. Buck
Reynolds	
Corporal	
Four Recruits	
Two Servants	
Lady Belville	Mrs. Ward
Harriet	Mrs. Abegg
Angelica	Miss Macklin
Lucy	Mrs. Green
Pert	Mrs. Pitt

Time: from 7 in the evening until 10.

Scene: Act I, a Room in Lord Belville's House.
Acts II to V, Harriet's Dressing Room.

Prologue

When the chaste Muse, to mend a vicious age
Polished her mirror, and adorned her stage,
Poetic Justice taught the moral Bard,
That Virtue only could deserve reward;
Satire's keen edge that Folly ought to fear,
And Vice deep branded, wear a lasting scar.
But soon, corrupted by unjust applause,
Succeeding Poets quite reversed her laws;
Vice they tricked out with ornaments of Art,
And poured the enchanting poison on the heart;
Then guilty Passion Gallantry became,
And faithless vows were polished into Fame.
Deluded maid with Love-o'er-flowing eyes
Gave to each dear, false Dorimant the prize;
Nay, wrongs to wedlock had imputed merit,
Husbands but sinned from taste, and wives from spirit.
Thus meanly witty, and with talents dull,
They made a brothel what was Virtue's school.
Far from such flowery paths to-night we tread,
And pick our way where thorny duties lead;
An injured wife's licentious husband draw,
Vice hang in effigy that 'scapes the Law;
Favoured by Fortune, honoured by his birth,
In parts abounding, wanting but in worth,
A slave to Passion, Ridicule shall shew
With Folly's cap disgracing Wisdom's brow.
How just the draught, the colouring how true,
With all its failings we submit to you:
Indulge a zeal that something would supply
In this vacation of true Comedy;
Nor scorn the well-meant effort of a heart
That labours from affection to the art;

And to requite you—may true Genius fire
Some chosen masters to assume the lyre!
Where Johnson's[1] Art may Shakespeare's Nature meet,
Steele's moral page light up with Congreve's wit;
That varying tints united may produce
Life's finished picture for a nation's use.
Then virtuous Bards shall wholesome truths dispense,
Teach by example—and assist their Prince
(Whose life to Morals with more force can draw
Than all the galling fetters of the Law):
Nor let the Stage be unimproved alone,
While Crowds are learning Virtue from the Throne.

[1] i.e. Ben Jonson.

The School for Husbands

ACT I

Enter LADY BELVILLE *and* PERT

LADY BELVILLE: Most abandoned man! can no ties bind him? no obligations, however, sacred, restrain him?

PERT: 'Tis a terrible story indeed, madam.

LADY BELVILLE: Dishonoured, ruined Julia! my heart bleeds for her poor distracted mother. Pert—

PERT: Madam.

LADY BELVILLE: Order the chair this instant.

PERT: 'Tis ready, madam; your ladyship ordered it before.

LADY BELVILLE: I will go directly to Harriet and Angelica, and join in any contrivance, any revenge.

PERT: Aye, do, madam—behave with spirit, as Lady Belville should do; expose him to the world. It is a shame he should use your ladyship so—running after every thing that has but a pettycoat on—and, begging your ladyship's pardon, you are wrong to bear it so patiently.

LADY BELVILLE: I have borne it till it has almost broken my heart; but I will let him see I know his odious practices.

PERT: Aye, do, my lady: do not die under his ill usage, as his first lady did; but tell him he is only an old—why he is old enough to be your father—nay, your grandfather for aught I know—and yet to have such tricks.

LADY BELVILLE: Did not the footman say Mr. Townly was here?

PERT: Yes, madam; he is waiting to speak with your ladyship.

LADY BELVILLE: Desire him to walk in.

PERT: Aye, that is right; consult him, my lady—for though he is my lord's nephew, he is a modest gentleman, and will advise you properly.

LADY BELVILLE: Well, well—prithee do not be so talkative, but send him in.

PERT: Yes, yes, I shall send him in to be sure, madam—Ah! bless me from such husbands! (*Exit*)

LADY BELVILLE: Degenerate man! to prostitute his dignity and character thus—debase his blood, and mix with every creature wretchedness or vice prepares for him! but I am at length determined he shall see himself in all his infamy.

Enter TOWNLY

LADY BELVILLE: Mr. Townly, your servant.

TOWNLY: Your ladyship's most obedient—you seem disordered.

LADY BELVILLE: No wonder, sir—'tis impossible to be otherwise, while your uncle behaves in the manner he does.

TOWNLY: Has any thing particular happened, madam?

LADY BELVILLE: Nothing particular, sir, for baseness is his practice; but something new has happened in his abandoned pleasures—O, Mr Townly, the wickedness of it!

TOWNLY: Bless me, madam! what can be the cause of this emotion? I protest I am almost afraid to enquire into particulars—but if they may be mentioned—

LADY BELVILLE: Sir, I have no secrets but my lord's, and those, in justice to my own character, the world must know—you recollect a visit we made last summer in the country to the clergyman of our parish?

TOWNLY: Perfectly, madam.

LADY BELVILLE: Charmed with the modest mien and manners of their eldest girl, my god-daughter, and willing to ease the industrious parents of part of their burthen, I brought Julia to town, and placed her with my own milliner—her innocence all her inheritance, and her sole future dependence my protection.

TOWNLY: I know the girl, have often seen her here. His vicious gallantry has not wronged her, I hope.

LADY BELVILLE: O, the libertine—Reynolds, the prime agent of his vices, and he have seduced and secreted her: not half an hour since her mistress was here, and informed me of the whole transaction.

TOWNLY: I am amazed at his indiscretion: it will ruin his interest in the county—the election is just coming on too.

LADY BELVILLE: His interest—his interest, Mr. Townly—is that the only consideration? where is his honour—where is mine?—I, who was a kind of guardian to the girl—where is his morality, his duty to society and his Maker?

TOWNLY: Nay, madam, I am not his advocate.

LADY BELVILLE: But I will confront him, charge him with his crimes—pluck off the specious mask, expose him to the world.

TOWNLY: Dear madam, think a moment. This is the language of passion; for heaven's sake reflect.

LADY BELVILLE: What can I do? it is impossible I should longer conceal my wrongs.

TOWNLY: I earnestly intreat, madam, you will submit your resentment and conduct but for this night to my direction. I am come from Harriet and Angelica, in consequence of a letter you received from them yesterday.

LADY BELVILLE: Pray, what do they intend?

TOWNLY: Particulars they have not yet let me into. My lord in his rambles has light on Miss Harriet, and is most deeply smitten with her—quite a sighing swain.

LADY BELVILLE: That I know by her letter.

TOWNLY: And she and my tyrant Angelica have contrived some trick to be revenged on him, which they beg to consult your ladyship upon—and they have pressed me into their service.

LADY BELVILLE: And do you think, Mr. Townly, it will be prudent in you to be concerned in such a scheme? I think you had better not be seen in it—as to me, I care not what I do to expose him.

TOWNLY: There, madam, I am against you—I would not expose him; but if by a private shame we can make a friend reflect, and see a folly that injures his fame and fortune, I think it is the greatest service we can do him. However, I am so far of your ladyship's judgment, that I am resolved to keep behind the curtain till I see how their scheme operates—not that his knowing that I was privy to his disgrace would give me the least concern, for though I am his nephew, I am not his dependant; and upon my honour I think it my duty to come into any means, even the most harsh, that may check this shameful vice of his.

LADY BELVILLE: Shameful indeed!

TOWNLY: Pray be advised: try this experiment to-night. It is now past seven; at eight he is to be with Harriet.

LADY BELVILLE: How can that be? the House will not be up then: they are expected to sit late, and I know he intends to speak—which he never does till towards the close of a debate.

TOWNLY: Depend upon it, madam, he will contrive to keep his appointment with a new mistress though the nation were undone by it—especially one of Miss Harriet's youth and beauty.

Enter PERT

PERT: My lord is come from the House, madam.

LADY BELVILLE: Where is he?

PERT: Writing in the library, madam. He is in a mighty fuss because Reynolds is out of the way. Some body rings—I suppose it is Reynolds; I will go down and observe them. (*Exit*)

TOWNLY: He is now going to Harriet's—you had better get there before him—let me prevail—come, madam, resolve. The fear of being publicly exposed, though it should not reclaim, may at least lay him under a prudent restraint for the future.

LADY BELVILLE: It is easier to acquire a hundred virtues, Mr. Townly, than to part with one vice that is become a predominant pleasure—but, however, I will go and join in any scheme that will make him see his odious character.

TOWNLY: That is well resolved, madam—then you had better go directly.

LADY BELVILLE: I must see him first.

TOWNLY: When you have had your interview with him, we shall expect you.

LADY BELVILLE: You may.

TOWNLY: Your ladyship's most obedient. (*Exit*)

LADY BELVILLE: Your servant, sir. Poor Julia! Oh! the profligate! but I deserve it all: in his first marriage I knew him well—but friends would flatter, and vanity would believe, in spite of sharp presentiments to the contrary, that my youth and beauty would reclaim him—well, that is past—incorrigible man! how shall I resolve? bear his usage longer I cannot—and to join with these girls in exposing him seems imprudent, nay dangerous; and yet some expedient is necessary. I will see him first—he is here—how punctual in his vice.

Enter LORD BELVILLE *and* SERVANT

LORD BELVILLE: Where can Reynolds be? send the chair men to look for him—he must be found. And d'ye hear, William, in the meantime do you lay out my plain brown clothes, my tie periwig, and the surtout I wore when I was ill—and get a hackney coach.

SERVANT: I shall, my lord.   (*Exit*)

LORD BELVILLE: My dear, your servant.   (*She turns short upon him with a look of indignation*)   Why that angry aspect? madam, you seem out of humour.

LADY BELVILLE: You know I have reason to be so.

LORD BELVILLE: Not I, upon my honour.

LADY BELVILLE: You do.

LORD BELVILLE: Ha, ha, ha! nay, if your ladyship is determined to be out of humour, I am passive—you know I never dispute your pleasure, my dear.

LADY BELVILLE: Ha, ha, ha! you are mighty facetious this evening, my lord.   (*Laughing with him sneeringly*)

LORD BELVILLE: I confess, I should be always glad to laugh my friends out of their follies—I think mirth is a much better remedy, than anger or musty morals.

LADY BELVILLE: Ha, ha, ha! very true, my lord—and I wish the experiments were tried upon a near friend of mine.

LORD BELVILLE: Ha, ha, ha! whenever your ladyship pleases—I am ready—for—ha, ha, ha! I know I am the friend: I have some foibles, I own.

LADY BELVILLE: Foibles, foibles! you have, ha?   Oh!—is the House up?

LORD BELVILLE: N-no, my dear.   I believe they will sit late, but—a—it was hot—crowded—I found myself not very well, so—

LADY BELVILLE: Did you speak, my lord?

LORD BELVILLE: O yes; yes, yes—I spoke a good while—your friend Lord Hillington spoke to-day for the first time, my dear—made a very good figure—very well indeed, very decent upon honour —so I left them to themselves.

LADY BELVILLE: What, you have an engagement, I suppose—ha, ha! some new beauty?

LORD BELVILLE: Well, why—ha, ha, ha! I am glad to see you can laugh, and resume your good humour.   No, my dear, I have no engagement or attachment to any beauty but yours—there my love and heart are both devoted.

LADY BELVILLE: Ha, ha, ha!   O, you civil, sincere creature.

LORD BELVILLE: Why, I am sincere now, notwithstanding your severe look, and ironical smile. My life, I am going to Arthur's[1]—I promised to spend the evening there with some of those military blades that are returned from the expedition:[2] you know one loves to hear the particular observations of different people upon so particular an affair, my dear—and so—but I hope we shall not make a late sitting of it, though.

LADY BELVILLE: Ha, ha, ha! very true, my lord—so you are going to Arthur's? (*Very gravely*)

LORD BELVILLE: Yes.

LADY BELVILLE: Pray look me full in the face, my lord.

LORD BELVILLE: With all my heart, my dear, for it is a very handsome one.

LADY BELVILLE: Upon your honour, you are to spend this evening at Arthur's—upon your honour?

LORD BELVILLE: Ha, ha, ha! well, I vow you have a most excellent talent for humour, when you have a mind to exert it; but you are so exact at times—do you think, my dear, I would tell a falsehood?

LADY BELVILLE: (*Echoing him in manner very reproachfully*) O, not for the world—ha, ha, ha! but—a—I would not have you take such pains at times to let me know where you are a-going—because it only betrays you into a circumstance that least becomes a gentleman.

LORD BELVILLE: Upon my honour I am going to Arthur's.

LADY BELVILLE: He, he, he! I beg pardon; I thought you had been upon the wing to visit your late conquest. (*Sneeringly*)

LORD BELVILLE: Madam!

LADY BELVILLE: To celebrate your triumph over humanity and every social tie, in the person of that unfortunate victim to your vice—the poor ruined Julia.

LORD BELVILLE: Julia!

LADY BELVILLE: Or perhaps, my lord, you are going to see your new born son at Chelsea.

LORD BELVILLE: My dear, you want discretion; your peevishness begins to be a little troublesome—I cannot answer all these idle suggestions. (*Angrily*)

[1] A well-known club-house in St. James's Street.
The conquest of the French settlements in Canada in 1760.

LADY BELVILLE: You cannot, indeed, my lord—for daring as your vice is, and practised as you are in female ruin, this cruelty upon Julia, and treacherous outrage upon my hospitality, you cannot answer to your own humanity or the world's censure.

LORD BELVILLE: Well, well; I will not throw away my reason upon you now; but I will speak to you when you are calm, and convince you of your error in this affair; for at present you see with jealous eyes—and as to the world, my dear, you are wrong there too—it is not so severe upon my foibles as your ladyship fancies.

LADY BELVILLE: Mistaken man—I know your flatterers make you think your vices are hidden from the world's eye, but you are deceived. They are the subjects of every tongue, the poisoned weapons with which your enemies secretly stab your fame.　My heart has often felt the shamefullest, sharpest proofs of their odious notoriety—as you sit in public, if you but address a woman, I hear the tongue of censure whisper your designs against her honour, and aggravate your character with all the circumstances of ridicule and infamy.　I hear myself, my children pitied—and O, shame—I see the hand of scorn pointing at their noble father as an abandoned detested libertine.

LORD BELVILLE: Madam, your warmth rises a little too high; it grows licentious, beyond the bounds of decency or toleration—be advised, restrain it—you had better.

LADY BELVILLE: No, my lord; duty and affection—however it may offend—compel me to hold a mirror to your vices.

LORD BELVILLE: What do you mean, madam?

LADY BELVILLE: Have you not now—now, my lord—now, this instant —deserted your country and your friends?

LORD BELVILLE: How? wherein?

LADY BELVILLE: The importance of this day's question in Parliament, you declared to me but this very morning, to be most interesting both to yourself and your friends—yet have you not basely neglected it?　Nay, is not every interest, public and private, sacrificed to levity and wanton pleasures?

LORD BELVILLE: Your accusation is malicious—I have discharged my duty.

LADY BELVILLE: You have not.

LORD BELVILLE: That, madam, is not a wife's province to determine—my character, and conduct, are my own concern.

LADY BELVILLE: And mine, my lord—I have an interest, an equal interest, in your fame, your honour, and your fortune; and cannot see them perish, and mine with them, without feeling and resentment.

LORD BELVILLE: Madam, I know not what you mean, or who has advised you to this sudden, this extraordinary behaviour. If you persist, there is but one measure—you shall have a proper appointment[1] whenever you please.

LADY BELVILLE: How, my lord!

LORD BELVILLE: I am determined.

LADY BELVILLE: I understand you: ungrateful man, is this your humanity; this your return for my patience and affected blindness to a vice that has undone your fame, wasted your fortune, and destroyed my peace? But you shall never have an opportunity again to menace me with a separation.

LORD BELVILLE: That, madam, is entirely in your own option.

LADY BELVILLE: 'Tis well, my lord—remember you drive me to extremities. I have long borne your shameful courses, but be assured my patience ends here—if it be in my power to expose, or to revenge your ill usage, expect the worst that can be contrived by an injured wife's resentment. (*Exit*)

LORD BELVILLE: This is astonishing—I cannot account for this extreme warmth; sure there must be more in it than I immediately comprehend. It is impossible this affair of Julia could at once stir up all this spirit; it has stung her, I see; and the doctrine of divorce too has touched the quick of her ladyship's pride, and startled her a little—aye, but that will have a good consequence; it will cool her resentment, and make her return to her usual patience and discretion—ha, ha, ha! she will weep for a day or two in private, dine and sup in her dressing room, complain to her female friend, her lap-dog, and looking glass; be invisible to the world, out of humour with her maid; pout, look foolish, beg pardon, and so come to herself—but after all, has she not some little cause of complaint? Why, I am afraid were I to submit that question to be tried by my conscience I should have a verdict against me: but

[1] A suitable allowance for her maintenance, on separation.

let pleasure try the cause—which is nature's supreme judge—and I am sure I shall be acquitted. I married her for love, and she is still young, agreeable—nay faith, to do the woman justice, handsome—and perhaps were she the property of another I suppose I should not care what expence or trouble it cost me to come at her. But possession—possession is a lazy dull circumstance: it tires nature, makes her careless and sleepy; she loves new objects. Well; wives and moralists may preach up what they will, but variety is nature's prime bliss: every man that can should enjoy it —and all would if they durst.

Enter REYNOLDS

LORD BELVILLE: Reynolds, where have you been? did you not know I have an engagement this evening?

REYNOLDS: I did, my lord, but there was a necessity for my going out.

LORD BELVILLE: What have you there?

REYNOLDS: Your lordship's clothes, surtout, and tie periwig. Have you seen my lady?

LORD BELVILLE: Yes.

REYNOLDS: Has she said anything particular?

LORD BELVILLE: She has been in a violent passion, and mentioned something about Julia and Chelsea.

REYNOLDS: O, she knows every thing about Miss Julia.

LORD BELVILLE: So I understand—but how could that happen?

REYNOLDS: My lord, I will tell you the whole affair: I am but just come from Miss Julia.

LORD BELVILLE: What carried you thither?

REYNOLDS: Why, while your lordship was at the House, about an hour ago, Miss Julia's mistress came here. Joe luckily shewed her into the stucco room, where my lady came to her—upon which I whipped into the next room, and overheard every word they said.

LORD BELVILLE: Oho! now the mystery is cleared—I wondered how she got her intelligence.

REYNOLDS: But the worst is, her mistress has found out where Julia lodges.

LORD BELVILLE: No!—

REYNOLDS: She has indeed, my lord; that was the reason why I went out: for, as she told my lady she had not been at the lodging yet— oho! then, thinks I, your going there now shall be to very little

purpose—so I ran away to Miss, and in a violent hurry told her
you had ordered her to take another lodging directly; made her
pack her things into a hackney coach, and hurried away as fast as
we could drive.

LORD BELVILLE: And where have you taken a lodging?

REYNOLDS: That we might not be dogged, I made the coach drive into
the city to Blackfriars, whence we took water, landed at Cuper's
Gardens,[1] and from thence walked up towards the bridge, to the
lodgings your honour had for the little mantua maker, when she
lay in—and there I left her frighted out of her wits.

LORD BELVILLE: You have managed cleverly, Reynolds—well, I must
begone, (*Looking at his watch*) it is three quarters after seven, and
eight is the hour appointed. Come, take off this heavy finery,
and give me my sober, modest Staffordshire garb.

REYNOLDS: Will your honour please to put them on here?

LORD BELVILLE: Where is my wife?

REYNOLDS: Just gone out in a hackney chair.

LORD BELVILLE: O, then I will dress me here.

REYNOLDS: Stay, stay, my lord—the sleeve is wrong there. Does your
honour think you shall succeed with this lady; at last, my lord?

LORD BELVILLE: We have no impediments but conscience and fears,
Reynolds—for being bred up in the country, under an old parson
her uncle, and a religious aunt, she has no idea of love without
matrimony.

REYNOLDS: Your lordship will soon cure her of that folly.

LORD BELVILLE: This night, I hope.

REYNOLDS: You say she never was in London before, my lord.

LORD BELVILLE: Never.

REYNOLDS: And is she so very handsome, my lord?

LORD BELVILLE: O, an angel—her cheek, Reynolds, is like the blushing
rose: she has not only beauty, but virtue in her mien and aspect;
she looks like the child of innocence and love—her very awkwardness; nay, her ignorance, and even her provincial dialect—for she

[1] Cuper's Bridge (a jetty or landing-stage) was on the South Bank of the Thames, nearly opposite
Somerset House. Cuper's Gardens was an open area behind it. In the *Survey of London and
Westminster* (1733) 'Cupid's Stairs' appears where 'Cuper's Bridge' is marked in John Rocque's map
of London (1746). It was noted for fireworks, was a resort 'for the profligate of both sexes', and
was suppressed as a place of public entertainment in 1753. Cf. Wheatley, *London Past and Present*
(1891), I, p. 483. Dodsley (*London and its Environs*, 1761, II, p. 209) calls it 'a seat of luxury and
dissipation'. Cf. also Boswell, *ed. cit.* V, p. 295.

has a most barbarous West Country accent—add grace and novelty to her charms.

REYNOLDS: How lucky it is, my lord, that she falls into such good hands.

LORD BELVILLE: Why, her charms will not be thrown away, Reynolds—my wig—so—I think I make a very grave sober figure.

REYNOLDS: Your honour always looks in that dress, like an honest justice of the quorum.

LORD BELVILLE: Ha, ha, ha! yes, I think I am a little in that style, Reynolds; that is what I pass for with this girl—here, take this sword; my Staffordshire gravity will look more sober and profound without it.

REYNOLDS: Your lordship will have no occasion for that weapon, I believe, to-night—ha, ha, ha!

LORD BELVILLE: Ha, ha, ha! no, Reynolds, I do not think I shall. If I am not at home before twelve, let Sampson be with his chair at three o'clock near the back door, and wait till I come.

REYNOLDS: He shall, my lord—but stop one moment, pray, my lord There is something forgot that you will want, should you chance to stay all night.

LORD BELVILLE: What is that, Reynolds?

REYNOLDS: Your lordship's night cap.

LORD BELVILLE: That is well remembered—very well remembered indeed, Reynolds.

REYNOLDS: I will put it into this pocket of the surtout. You know, my lord, you are always apt to catch cold on these occasions, for the caps you meet with are never so warm as your lordship's.

LORD BELVILLE: True, true, Reynolds—I got a devilish cold the other night, for want of it. Is there a hackney coach?

REYNOLDS: 'Tis ready, my lord.

LORD BELVILLE: Very well. Do you step over to Julia: let her know I shall see her to-morrow at twelve, and bid her keep up her spirits. (*Going*)

REYNOLDS: I shall, my lord—but what shall we do with that little girl near the King's Road, that we brought to town with us? She does nothing but cry from morning to night—she says your lordship promised her a fine house, and a chariot, and that she should see the King, the play, and the opera every night.

LORD BELVILLE: Ha, ha, ha! O, the idiot! Do you pay off the lodging, Reynolds: take a place for her in the Cirencester stage coach; give her five guineas, and send her down to her friends again—they will be glad to receive her.

REYNOLDS: I'll take care, my lord. She shall be packed off with the first coach—but, my lord—I beg your lordship's pardon—one word, if your lordship pleases—your honour was so good as to say, your honour would speak about my brother; and I hear the commissions are all to be filled up to-morrow.

LORD BELVILLE: Why, it is done: I spoke yesterday—he has an ensigncy[1] in an old regiment—and as to the place in the excise for your friend, I have not yet seen any of the Commissioners;[2] but you may depend upon it, it shall be done.

REYNOLDS: Your honour is very good. I will come with the chair myself, and wait till your honour comes.

LORD BELVILLE: Yes, yes, Reynolds—I have taken care of your brother; and the General assured me, he should have a company[3] as soon as possible, in a very little time.

REYNOLDS: Your honour is always very good. You look mighty grave and sober in that dress—I dare swear you will succeed. William, get the coach ready below. (*Lights* LORD BELVILLE *out*)

END OF THE FIRST ACT

[1] The lowest commissioned rank in the infantry, now 2nd lieutenant.
[2] The Commissioners of Excise, controlling the tax administration, were the appointing body.
[3] i.e. be promoted to captain.

ACT II

Enter LUCY *and* TOWNLY

LUCY: John, get candles, quick.   Please to walk in here, sir.

TOWNLY: Heyday, Mrs. Lucy—I hope you are not going to lead me into your lady's bed chamber.

LUCY: No, sir—only into her dressing room: her bed chamber is reserved for somebody else to-night.

TOWNLY: Pray, where is Angelica, Mrs. Lucy?

LUCY: Ha, ha, ha!   O sir, you cannot see her at present; you will by and by, I warrant you—he, he, he! she is upon some extraordinary business that will surprise you—take my word for it—he, he, he! so whimsical—you will die with laughing.

TOWNLY: Then, pray, Mrs. Lucy, let my merry death come from you —what is this mighty secret that she is about?

LUCY: O, no sir: I cannot tell it you—but here comes Miss Harriet; she I suppose will let you into the whole affair.

Enter HARRIET

HARRIET: Well, Mr. Townly, have you seen the lady?

TOWNLY: Yes, madam.

HARRIET: And what success? have you prevailed? will she come?

TOWNLY: Madam, she is as ripe for your purpose as a wife's vengeance can make her.

HARRIET: That is charming.

TOWNLY: Brim full of resentment.

HARRIET: Delightful.

TOWNLY: There has been such a breach between my lord, and her, this evening.

HARRIET: Better and better; that is just what we wanted.

TOWNLY: I expect her every moment.

HARRIET: Lucy, go you down, and when Lady Belville comes shew her up into this room.

LUCY: Yes, madam.   (*Exit*)

HARRIET: Are you not surprised, Mr. Townly, at being led into a lady's dressing room at this time of night?

141

TOWNLY: Why, it has an air of adventure, I must acknowledge, madam —a fertile imagination might draw warm conclusions from it.

HARRIET: Well, sir, this dressing room is to be the scene of your uncle's gallantry—we have laid such a plot against him; but for these two days have deferred executing it, in hopes Angelica's brother would have been in town to assist us: we expect him every hour. Well, Mr. Townly, I could not have conceived, had I not experienced it, that any man could be such a dupe to women, as I find he is—we have drawn such promises of expence from him— ha, ha, ha! I believe Lucy has got a hundred pounds out of him already.

TOWNLY: I know him, madam; his expence in women is immoderate: if he likes the object, any sum may be drawn from him. In short, he is a perfect Don Quixote in these affairs—continually seeking adventures—quite infatuated with the itch of intrigue. It is a kind of madness in him—ha, ha, ha! one part of his character is, that most of his idle evenings are spent in walking about in a mean shabby dress, and peeping into milliners' shops, habit warehouses, and lace chambers, in quest of new faces—ha, ha, ha!

HARRIET: Ha, ha, ha! ridiculous! at his age too—why, he must be near sixty, Mr. Townly.

TOWNLY: Madam, this distemper increases with his years—he grows worse and worse every hour. Why, he went after a Dulcinea of the scullery as a footman, t'other day, and was locked into a coal vault till three in the morning—where he caught a cold that had liked to have killed him.

HARRIET: Ha, ha, ha! poor gentleman.

TOWNLY: Madam, he is at all: nothing escapes him—this girl that makes such a noise about town—though he could ill afford it, what do you imagine his lordship squandered away upon her, for one evening's *tête-à-tête*?

HARRIET: Really, sir, I am no judge of these matters.

TOWNLY: Only the trifling sum of two thousand.

HARRIET: Incredible!

TOWNLY: It is so—but it is a fact. No French financier in time of public distress is more extravagant or whimsical in his gallantries to the ladies. O, madam, he has lavished most profusely upon two or three of distinguished rank in this town; even to the dis-

142

tressing of his affairs—the famous toilette[1] that is so admired for its elegance and splendour was of his lordship's furnishing, and the bouquet and necklace of his presenting.

HARRIET: Yes, yes, that lady is notorious: she makes no secret of her receiving presents: I know from where she had her fine set of Dresden[2] too—but her quality sets her above the scandal of prostitution.

Enter LUCY

LUCY: Lady Belville is come, madam.

HARRIET: Did I not bid you shew her up?

LUCY: She is here, madam.   (*Exit*)

Enter LADY BELVILLE

HARRIET: I am extremely glad to see your ladyship.

LADY BELVILLE: Dear Miss Harriet, I am under the utmost confusion for the trouble that you, and your cousin Angelica have had upon my account—and shall ever acknowledge the tender concern you have both shewn upon this occasion.

HARRIET: Pray, madam, no apology—both my cousin and I have a singular pleasure in serving your ladyship.

LADY BELVILLE: I believe it, my dear.   Mr. Townly, your servant.

TOWNLY: I am glad to see your ladyship here.

LADY BELVILLE: But pray, my dear, how long has my lord been this violent lover of yours?

HARRIET: About ten days, madam.   The adventure began thus—the day after we came to town, my sister Sally, another young lady, and I—towards the dusk of the evening—were walking in the Green Park; where my lord in a grave, shabby undress, for some time hovered about us.   We were in a laughing giddy humour, and knowing his character for amorous adventures, and being convinced that he had no knowledge of us, we flirted, tittered, ran, coquetted, and used every pretty little female trick we could think of, to encourage our knight errant's pursuit.   At length, seeing us destitute of a squire, he with great modesty made up to us, and offered his service to see us home.   I, to disguise myself and heighten the joke, instantly talked a broad West Country dialect, and put on all the awkward bashfulness and rustic simplicity I

---

[1] Equipment for the toilet table, not dress.
[2] Expensive and much esteemed porcelain.

could assume; for I was the charming nymph that had pierced his heart, and moved his eloquence—in short, we were idle enough to let him wait on us home; and ever since he has pestered us with visits, letters, proposals, and gallantries of every kind—and my mad cousin Angelica being in the secret, she would not let me rest till I came into a plot of hers against his lordship; which is to be put into execution this very evening.

TOWNLY: Does my lord know, madam, that you have any knowledge of Lady Belville?

HARRIET: That is impossible, I believe: for neither my cousin nor I had the honour of her ladyship's acquaintance before last autumn at Bath; and as we have not visited since we have been in town, 'tis probable he knows nothing of it—unless her ladyship has mentioned the acquaintance.

LADY BELVILLE: Never—I am but just come to town myself. But pray, my dear, does my lord know whom he is addressing?

HARRIET: Ha, ha, ha! no, no madam, we are both cheats, rank impostors—and in our reciprocal frauds, a great part of our mirth consists.

LADY BELVILLE: I do not understand you, my dear.

HARRIET: Why, madam, he does not appear here as Lord Belville— but as one Mr. Jackson, a grave, sober, country gentleman of Staffordshire, who is come to town upon law business.

TOWNLY: Ha, ha, ha! quite the man of intrigue.

LADY BELVILLE: Shameful!

HARRIET: And I, to be even with him, am not Harriet Wingfield, but one Miss Margery Packington—a raw, ignorant, unexperienced, country thing, bred up in the old fashioned ridiculous whims of religion, morality, and good works; and am just come up to London town for the first time, to see the Court, and the lions, Saint Paul's and the world; and to learn fashions and manners, and genteel behaviours—ha, ha, ha! (*Assuming her West Country accent*)

TOWNLY: Ha, ha, ha! excellent—why, you are a good comedian, Miss Harriet.

HARRIET: This, sir, is a fair contention between male and female art— he intends to ruin me, and I, with this lady's permission, intend most maliciously to laugh at him.

LADY BELVILLE: My dear, laughing will be but a poor consolation to my heart.

HARRIET: Madam, with your assistance we may proceed a step or two further—ha, ha, ha! But there is some part of his conduct in this affair, that I believe is ten times more ridiculous than anything you ever heard of him.

TOWNLY: Pray, what may that be, madam?

HARRIET: Why, sir, the best joke is that in the midst of his passion for me, while he is vowing, flattering, swearing, and convincing me of his love, and honourable intentions, he is underhand making the warmest advances to my woman—ha, ha, ha! and yesterday made her a formal proposal.

TOWNLY: Ha, ha, ha! admirable—madam, that is the man; his very characteristic—voracious—never satisfied.

LADY BELVILLE: My dear Harriet, there is nothing new in this to me; it is a meanness I have often experienced even under my own roof.

TOWNLY: But come, Miss Harriet, I think the sooner you make us acquainted with your plan of operation, the better. What is your scheme? what do you intend to do with this gallant?

HARRIET: Sir, for the particulars you must consult your madcap mistress Angelica; she is our commander in chief: all I can tell you at present is, that—ha, ha, ha! she has got into a new suit of her brother's regimentals, that were left here when he went abroad——and his old servant, Bates, whom he has made his serjeant, and left behind to recruit, is to assist in our plot against my lord.

TOWNLY: Ha, ha, ha! ridiculous—ha, ha, ha! the mad creature—why she has wonderful spirits, is a good mimic; and I fancy will make a very smart cavalier—and where is the wild creature now?

HARRIET: Within, sir, with Lucy and the maids—equipping for action.

Enter LUCY

LUCY: Well, madam, we are dressed—we are all dressed—I have just sent the serjeant in to settle her sword—such a little captain—so stout, so brisk, and so lively—O, you would die with laughing to see her—Odzooks, she is ready to jump out of her breeches with courage.

OMNES: Ha, ha, ha!

TOWNLY: Aye, aye—I will warrant the madcap has spirits enow.

LUCY: Spirits! why, she cocks her hat, folds her arms; and stares, and struts, and swears, and swaggers, and talks nonsense—ha, ha, ha! just like a real captain.

OMNES: Ha, ha, ha!

LUCY: See, see—here she comes, and her serjeant with her.

Enter ANGELICA *and* SERJEANT: *as she enters she sings a few bars of 'Happy, happy pair'; and as she sings addresses the ladies alternately in affected military airs—and during her singing the maid in admiration mimics her in dumb shew: and at the end of the singing they all cry out, 'Bravo, Bravo'.*

OMNES: Bravo! Bravo!

LUCY: Aye, madam: bravissimo!

ANGELICA: Madam, I am your ladyship's most devoted and most affectionate slave, in all times, places, occasions, and conditions—by night or by day; sleeping or waking; by land or by sea; in peace or in war—I beg, madam, you will command the heart and sword of a man, who lives only for the fair sex—but particularly the divine Lady Belville; who is the theme of my muse, the idol of my heart, and will ever be the toast of my soul—while there is claret, burgundy, or champaigne in the universe, dem me!

OMNES: Ha, ha, ha!

LADY BELVILLE: O, dear captain, you overwhelm me—why, you are the very spirit and quintessence of wit, and military gallantry.

ANGELICA: Your ladyship's politeness is unanswerable, and obliging above the superlative; or may a French bullet terminate the existence of your eternal admirer—Townly, how dost thou do, my boy? give me thy hand. Well—and how—ha? how do you like us, my dear, ha?—do our regimentals look spruce, smart, and *dégagée*? and our sword hang upon the *qui vive*, ha? ready for action? is our *chapeau bien troussé*? have we a *fierté* in it?—that is, does it look impudent, and swear in a fellow's face? Dem me, my dear, turn out, I am your man—follow me, that's all. (*Noses*[1] TOWNLY *like a bully*)

OMNES: Ha, ha, ha!

TOWNLY: Upon my honour, madam—

ANGELICA: How sir? Madam?

[1] Pushing her face insolently right up to Townly's.

146

TOWNLY: I beg pardon: captain, I mean—I never saw a more compleat son of Mars; in dress, figure, spirit, and martial deportment.

ANGELICA: Aye, but have I the true, alert, impudent forwardness of a military stripling; that wants to establish a character by shewing his courage, when there is no occasion for it?

LUCY: Well, I vow, madam, you are mighty comical, and do act it so cleverly.

ANGELICA: Hark'ee, Townly, do you think now, my dear, that you and I could make a riot at Vauxhall—ha, ha! break a lamp, or a waiter's head; and by the help of half a dozen friends bully a pert attorney's clerk, or a swag bellied rosy drunken citizen—that had no sword—make love to their women, and carry it off with a 'Dem me, do you prate—kick the rascal—break his head, run him through—talk to gentlemen and men of honour—a parcel of scoundrels, poltroons, bourgoises—dem me, bourgoises, rascally bourgoises'?

OMNES: Ha, ha, ha!

TOWNLY: Admirable! pray, let me observe you—sure you are the very coxcomb that really made the riot last summer at Vauxhall.

ANGELICA: Ha, ha, ha! then you think that I shall pass—and that I am tolerably pert.

TOWNLY: As pert as a city apprentice that had just put on regimentals; and was resolved to rise into note, by being troublesome to every man, and impertinent to every woman.

ANGELICA: My dear Townly, thou art an obliging fellow, or may victory forsake me—ha, ha, ha! but I am afraid you flatter me.

TOWNLY: What do you think, serjeant? Does she not look quite militair? Might she not pass upon the parade at the head of a company for a compleat modern hero?

SERJEANT: Aye, that she would, your honour, better than half the military green horns that are idling and swaggering about this town.

LUCY: Hark, a coach stops—he is come; that is his sober two knocks— tap, tap. (*Knocks without*)

HARRIET: Lucy, run you down: bring him up here; and when you have acted your scene, then let me try how I can act mine.

LUCY: I shall, madam. (*Exit*)

ANGELICA: Quick, quick, Harriet: get ready; you will not be dressed time enough; off with your hoop, and on with your fine, awkward, tawdry sack;[1] your rusticity and West Country accent, in an instant—and let me see that you shed the tears of credulous innocence, with all the art of a true town syren.

HARRIET: Never fear my hypocrisy—I warrant I play my part: adieu. (*Exit*)

ANGELICA: And now, madam, answer me sincerely—can your jealousy stand the fire of your husband's gallantry while, like another serpent, he displays himself in all the tricks and arts of seduction against the youth and beauty of that provoking Eve that just left us?

LADY BELVILLE: With the most intrepid indignation.

ANGELICA: I am afraid of you—but, however, I will try you: if you will march this way, then, I will escort you where you may reconnoitre every thing that passes in the enemy's camp

LADY BELVILLE: With all my heart.

ANGELICA: This way; follow me then.   (*Exeunt*)

SERJEANT: She is a merry one; but she was always a good humoured girl.   Her brother will be here by and by; ha, ha, ha! how he will stare to see her got into his breeches—but here the party comes; I believe we shall sweat his lordship a little before we have done with him.   (*Exit*)

Enter LUCY *and* LORD BELVILLE

LUCY: Please to walk in here, sir.

LORD BELVILLE: Well, how do you do, Mrs. Lucy?

LUCY: At your service sir.

LORD BELVILLE: I hope I am not past my time.

LUCY: Not at all, sir.

LORD BELVILLE: Well, Mrs. Lucy—and how—hah! why, you look as handsome as ar angel this evening.

LUCY: Do I, sir?

LORD BELVILLE: You know you do, hussy.

LUCY: Sir, you are pleased to say so, but I am afraid you flatter me.

LORD BELVILLE: No, no, I never flatter: well, where is your lady—is she at home, Lucy?

LUCY: At home—to be sure, sir.   Did not you appoint being here this evening; and do you think she would be abroad—no, no, no, poor

[1] A loose gown: a rustic girl would not have worn the fashionable hoop to extend her skirts.

lady, not for the world—she is a little busy writing letters to send into the country—but I will let her know that you are here.

LORD BELVILLE: No, no; stay, Mrs. Lucy—you shall not disturb her—besides, I want to have a little private conversation with you, Mrs. Lucy.

LUCY: If you please, sir.

LORD BELVILLE: Well, what do you think, Mrs. Lucy, of what I proposed to you yesterday?

LUCY: Lord, sir; how should I know what to think of it? I suppose you were but in joke.

LORD BELVILLE: I tell you, I am serious. You and I must be friends—we must, we must—here, Lucy, here is a bit of paper; I promised you something if I succeeded—take it, you fool—and now give me a kiss as a proof that we are friends. Nay, nay; you shall kiss me, hussy—and heartily, too, for now I look upon you as my own.

LUCY: He, he! he, he! there is no refusing you any thing—um—um—Lord, Mr. Jackson, you are enough to—(*Leering at him after she has broken from him*) —n—nagh, how can you be so wicked?

LORD BELVILLE: Come, come—now we are friends, and that we have but one interest, tell me honestly how affairs stand with your mistress—she gave me a blushing, bashful, silent kind of promise at parting yesterday, that this night should crown my happiness. What do you think of it, Lucy—are there any hopes?

LUCY: Why, I do not know, sir. She is so distracted, between love, sin, fear, and religion, that I do not know what to think of it—one moment she consents—the next she is frighted out of her wits, and would not do such a thing for the world, without marriage. Now, I was thinking of a little innocent joke, that I know would quiet her scruples at once.

LORD BELVILLE: What is that, Lucy?

LUCY: Why, sir, it is only a blind, for as she is a poor, ignorant, country soul, you know we may persuade her it is real.

LORD BELVILLE: But what is it, Lucy?

LUCY: Why it is, sir—I don't know the name of it, but it is a writing men give to women sometimes beforehand.

LORD BELVILLE: A contract?

LUCY: Aye, aye, a contract—that is the name of it.

LORD BELVILLE: Pooh, pooh! that will take up time. I was going to propose that myself—but that is too tedious; I want things to be concluded this very night.

LUCY: Why, so they may, sir. Cannot you get the contract prepared directly, and only invent some excuse or other, why you defer the marriage for a few months, and leave the rest to me—I will engage it will do.

LORD BELVILLE: Dear Lucy—if you can compleat it to-night—

LUCY: We can do nothing without the contract, sir.

LORD BELVILLE: I will go to my lawyer, and return with one in half an hour, but had we not best feel her pulse beforehand—propose it to her slily at a distance to see how she relishes it?

LUCY: Yes, I think that step will be very proper, first. I will go let her know you are here: poor soul, how she will tremble with love and fear when I tell her you are come; for she loves you to distraction —perfectly doats on you. But I will let her know you are come. (*Exit*)

LORD BELVILLE: Aye, do, do. There was no succeeding without the assistance of this baggage; now I think it may be done—and this very night. Ha, ha, ha! old Ovid's judgment I find is still infallible; secure the maid, the mistress soon will follow. Ha, ha, ha! what a flattering salvo[1] is a contract to a female mind, that is struggling between religious fears, and amorous desires—I will give her twenty, if that will bring her to my arms. However, I must take care it does not rise in judgment against me—let me see —it will be given in the name of Jackson. I have secured the maid: aye, but the sure stroke will be the old one; take it along with me in the morning—that makes it a compleat vision, and leaves her in a true female fool's paradise.

Enter HARRIET *and* LUCY.

LUCY: Nay, nay—come, madam; hold up your head, and look at him. Do not tremble and blush so. Lord, what are you afraid of—he will not eat you.

HARRIET: Naw; dawn't ye naw, dear Lucy; dawn't ye ask me to do zuch a graceless thing—dear naw, dawn't.

LUCY: Nay, but you promised him last night.

---

[1] From Latin *salvo*, I save: an expedient for saving a person's reputation, or soothing offended pride or conscience.

HARRIET: Naw—why dost talk zo, Lucy? why, he does knaw himzelf it to be a zin; and that I has scruples upon my mind.

LUCY: Then fairly tell him your scruples at once; he will satisfy them every one.

HARRIET: Naw, dawn't ye naw—dawn't ye draaw me to my ruin, Lucy: I thought zure ye were my friend.

LORD BELVILLE: What is the matter? I hope you are not afraid of me.

LUCY: Yes, she is, sir. She loves you so, she says, that she is afraid to trust herself with you.

LORD BELVILLE: I am sorry for that—whom should you trust yourself with, my angel, but with him who doats on you, who lives but for your sake; and whose life should be sacrificed to give you a moment's pleasure?

LUCY: Look you there—now, madam, did I not tell you so?

HARRIET: I pray ye, Mr. Jackson, forbear: ye have made me miserable enough already, by draawing my love upon ye; dawn't ye quite ruin me.

LORD BELVILLE: Do not talk of ruin, my life—don't: why, I mean to love, to live, to die with you. I do, by heaven!

HARRIET: Nay: pray, zir, dawn't ye zwear, dawn't ye zwear; for they do zay there be lords and great folks in this town, that will zwear and promise anything to a woman beforehand—if zo be that ye be one of those, zir, I does beg that ye will ztop—for I has an aunt and uncle in the country, that would break their hearts zhould I be naughty. (*Cries*)

LORD BELVILLE: Do not cry, my life: you shall not be naughty—you shan't, my soul; why, I love you virtuously—by your own heavenly face, and those two living stars, I do.

HARRIET: Aye, aye, zo ye do zay, Mr. Jackson—zo ye do zay; but if ye loved me with all your heart and soul, as I does ye, ye'd marry me.

LORD BELVILLE: Marry you, my dear—nay, dry up your tears—I would marry you with all my soul: but there are reasons, when you hear them, that you yourself would think me mad, if I married—are there not, Lucy?

LUCY: Yes, yes, there are reasons doubtless; and very strong ones—tell her what they are, sir—you had as good as tell them at once.

LORD BELVILLE: My dear, I did not care to make you acquainted with them, because I thought that they would grieve you—but you must know, I have a grandfather of immense age, who cannot possibly live three months, and were I to marry during his life, he would disinherit me of a vast estate.

LUCY: Is not that a very good reason, now? can you have a better? Come, madam, resolve—he will marry you the instant his grandfather dies. Won't you, sir?

LORD BELVILLE: Upon my honour—by truth, by your angelic self, I will.

LUCY: And in the mean time he will give you a bond, a marriage contract—or if you insist upon it, he will take his book oath to marry you. Won't you, Mr. Jackson?

LORD BELVILLE: Anything, anything, my angel; I will sign or swear anything to quiet your fears.

HARRIET: Aye, but will that contract keep it from being a zin, Lucy? Will it be as good as a marriage?

LUCY: Just the same, madam.

LORD BELVILLE: Why, it will be a marriage in conscience, my dear.

HARRIET: Will it? O, if it will be a marriage in conscience—

LORD BELVILLE: It will indeed: and when one is married in conscience, you know, my dear, one is married in heaven; and when one is married in heaven—why then, one has nothing to do but to go to bed. Ha, Mrs. Lucy?

LUCY: Very true, sir, very true.

LORD BELVILLE: Why, it is not the priest that makes the marriage, my dear.

HARRIET: No?

LORD BELVILLE: No, my angel.

HARRIET: O, lack! pray, who then?

LORD BELVILLE: Why, the intention, the love, and the integrity of the parties.

HARRIET: O dear me! they always told me, it was the parson and the ring.

LORD BELVILLE: Not in the least, my life—nothing but love, and sleeping together.

HARRIET: Oho! is that all? that can zoon be done, then.

LUCY: Well, well, sir; we are satisfied. Go; bring the contract, and then you may talk to the purpose.

LORD BELVILLE: Shall I, my love?

HARRIET: In truth I be afraid, Mr. Jackson.

LUCY: Psha! Go, bring the contract I tell you, and leave her to me.

LORD BELVILLE: Well, let her promise that she will only just let me see her bed chamber, to-night, when I come back—only see it.

LUCY: Come, promise him, madam.

HARRIET: Well! Heigh ho! if it be no zin.

LORD BELVILLE: None, none; my love, give me a kiss to seal the promise. (*Kisses her*)

HARRIET: O fye! how can you do zo?

LORD BELVILLE: Now another; as earnest of what I am to expect at my return. (*Kisses her again*)

HARRIET: Nay—pray ye, Mr. Jackson.

LORD BELVILLE: Raptures—and paradise!

LUCY: Well, well; begone, sir; the sooner you go, the sooner you will come back—let her alone, now—do not say a word more. I tell you it will do—it will do.

LORD BELVILLE: I have done—I have done.

LUCY: When you return, ring at the back door, that the servants may not see you. I will let you in—and send your chair away; be sure.

LORD BELVILLE: Dear Lucy—

LUCY: Hush—not a word, but fly.

LORD BELVILLE: Mum—I am gone; we have her; we have her, Lucy.

LUCY: Yes, yes; she is safe—begone, begone.

LORD BELVILLE: You are an excellent girl: we have her; we have her. (*Exit*)

HARRIET: See him into his coach, Lucy, for fear he should return and surprise us.

LUCY: I will, madam. (*Exit*)

HARRIET: You may appear; he is gone.

Enter LADY BELVILLE *and* TOWNLY

HARRIET: Where is Angelica?

TOWNLY: She saw enough of the party, she said, and is gone down with the serjeant to the recruits to instruct them in the parts they are to act against his lordship.

HARRIET: Well, madam, how do you like our comedy? Are not we a couple of finished impostors? and is not my gallant a proper object for laughter and satire?

LADY BELVILLE: His character is almost too licentious for the stage—so monstrous the innocent would not believe it natural. Was there ever any thing so wicked, so perfidious as the contract? Pray, my dear, what use do you intend to make of it against him?

HARRIET: That we must consult our general upon. If you please, madam, we will step to Angelica, and hold a council of matrimonial and female revenge, of which your ladyship shall be president.

LADY BELVILLE: With all my heart.

HARRIET: Come, sir; will your honour assist? As you are going to enter into the hostile state of matrimony, being of our council may inform you how dangerous it is to provoke our sex too far—and teach you to behave with decency to a wife, though you cannot with affection.

TOWNLY: I shall be proud to know my duty, madam, from so learned a board. (*Exeunt*)

END OF THE SECOND ACT

ACT III

Enter ANGELICA *and* TOWNLY

ANGELICA: Nay, prithee, dear love-sick gentle swain, be not so impor-
tunate; time your addresses better—am I in a condition now to
hear soft nonsense? Ha, ha, ha! upon my honour you are a bad
judge of a female mind. Never throw away your assiduities and
fine speeches, Mr. Townly, upon your mistress, when her spirits
are in a hurry, and her vanity in pursuit of another object—which
you know is my case at present. Why, I can no more think of
love, while my spirits are in this uproar—I vow I could as soon
think of turning nun.

TOWNLY: Madam, you have a brilliant wit, I allow, and a most resistless
eloquence. I admire them both as much as you can do—yet I
could wish they would condescend to lend a little attention one
moment.

ANGELICA: Sir, in the name of my wit and eloquence, I thank your
admiration; but it is impossible to grant your request, for the
witty, and the eloquent, sir, never love to hear any body but
themselves.

Enter LADY BELVILLE *and* HARRIET

ANGELICA: Oh! you are come most timely to my relief—what do you
think, ladies, the gentleman's private business was?

LADY BELVILLE: Some new distress, perhaps against my lord?

ANGELICA: No, madam, that would have been sensible and seasonable:
it was only to declare the impatience of his passion.

TOWNLY: And do you blame me for my impatience?

ANGELICA: Yes, I do, sir: a general might as well think of his amours
in the hour of action, as we talk of our affairs in the present
conjuncture—but to business.

HARRIET: Why indeed, Mr. Townly, your passion is a little out of time.

ANGELICA: Sir, you were called into our cabinet to assist us in punishing
my lord, and in redressing this lady for the general weal—and like
a selfish minister you would neglect the business of the nation to
gratify your own private passion.

155

TOWNLY: I plead guilty, madam.

ANGELICA: Behave with more patriotism, or we shall dismiss you from our councils—but to business. Well, ladies, is the contract finished according to the alterations?

HARRIET: Yes, my dear; Lucy is copying it fair.

LADY BELVILLE: But pray, Miss Harriet, if I understand you right, you intend the contract to be in your own hand writing, and drawn up by yourself.

HARRIET: True, madam.

LADY BELVILLE: Then, if it be in Lucy's hand, will not my lord distingnish if from yours?

HARRIET: No, madam; he has never seen my hand, for all letters and cards from me, were written by Lucy—no, no, I was determined my gallant should never have anything under my hand: therefore as I borrowed a false name, I made use of a false hand.

Enter LUCY

LUCY: I have done it, madam; here it is.

HARRIET: Very well; give it me.

TOWNLY: Pray, madam, what paper's that?

ANGELICA: An instrument of business, sir—the Magna Charta of our sex against the falsehood and tyranny of yours. You see we have not been idle, sir; public business has been going on, notwithstanding your love and dalliance. Where's the serjeant, Lucy?

LUCY: Below, with his recruits, madam—shall I call him up?

ANGELICA: By all means: my lord will soon be here.

LUCY: Who is below there? John?

JOHN: (*Without*) Madam.

LUCY: Send Bates up.

JOHN: (*Without*) Yes, madam.

HARRIET: I long till we come to the contract.

LADY BELVILLE: It must be a most ridiculous scene. I cannot conceive what will be the event of it—or how he will behave under the detection of his infamy.

ANGELICA: Suspend your curiosity, madam: we shall shew him in proper colours, never fear. Whatever virtues or vices he has in him, I will engage we produce them. O, there is nothing shews the heart and latent spirit of these boasted lords of creation, so well as woman—you see, madam, they have all been fools and bubbles,[1] from Marc Anthony down to his lordship, when once they come into our hands—ah! if we could but keep from deceiving ourselves, we might do what we pleased with them.

Enter SERJEANT

ANGELICA: Serjeant, we must prepare for our ambuscade: you remember your orders?

SERJEANT: Very well, noble captain: and I will answer with my life, I execute them to please you—I'll warrant I'll bully him.   (*A bell rings*)

LUCY: Hark!   (*Bell rings again*)   —the back door bell—'tis he.

ANGELICA: To your arms, ladies: to your arms—quick, fly—the enemy is in our camp—away—away to your respective posts.

LUCY: Aye, aye—begone all: I'll go down and let him in.   (*Exit*)

ANGELICA: Come, my fair lady of the enchanted castle—ha, ha! the giant is come to devour you—but I, your trusty and right hardy knight, will lay him weltring in his purple gore, or grace his triumphs with my headless trunk.   Harriet, you to your frights and your fears: and prepare your bed chamber; and leave the door to the back stairs unlocked: be sure.

HARRIET: (*Going*)   I shall.

ANGELICA: Have you the contract?

HARRIET: Yes, yes.   (*Exit*)

ANGELICA: Begone, then.   Mr. Townly, you will give that lady safe convoy into that chamber again, whence you may overhear the parley.

TOWNLY: Victory attend you!   Come, madam, this way if you please.

LADY BELVILLE: Adieu, noble captain!   Success, and no quarter.

ANGELICA: None—none, madam.   Virtue never does give any to vice.   (*Exeunt* TOWNLY *and* LADY BELVILLE *at the folding doors*)[2]   Serjeant, you know when to make your attack?

SERJEANT: I warrant your honour.

ANGELICA: As soon as Lucy leaves him, that is your signal to enter; and be sure to bluster and swagger: we are in no danger, Bates, from his courage, for Lucy says he has no sword on.

---

[1] Cf. p. 75, n. 1, above.

[2] This can only mean that the sliding flats or shutters open and the exit is through them.   Cf. Introduction, p. 9 above.

SERJEANT: If he had, madam, I would engage to bully him—I know how to deal with such chaps.

ANGELICA: To your post then.

SERJEANT: I am gone, your honour. (*Exit*)

ANGELICA: I hear them advance: I must go, and prepare my mine—if it be sprung properly, I think we shall blow his lordship up. (*Exit*)

Enter LUCY *leading* LORD BELVILLE

LORD BELVILLE: It is a long dark way, Lucy, from the back door to your lady's bed chamber.

LUCY: The shortest way always seems long to a lover, sir.

LORD BELVILLE: Very true, Mrs. Lucy, very true—ha, ha, ha! well, Lucy, here is the contract ready signed: see, here is my name at the bottom, in large letters—Anthony Jackson.

LUCY: Ha, ha, ha! you need not have given yourself that trouble.

LORD BELVILLE: Why, what is the matter? she has not changed her mind, I hope.

LUCY: No, no, sir; far from that—quite the reverse. Would you believe it, sir! I have worked her up to such a pitch of credulity and impatience, that by the help of a brother of mine who is a lawyer, she has drawn up a contract in her own hand.

LORD BELVILLE: Ha, ha, ha! O, charming! just as we could wish it. Upon my honour though, you frightened me, Lucy—I was afraid she had repented, and that her matrimonial qualm had come over her again.

LUCY: No, no, sir; no danger: we have her as safe as love and credulity can make her, so you have nothing to do but to sign her foolish paper—and go to bed, sir.

LORD BELVILLE: Admirable: give me your hand, Lucy. Kiss me, hussy —(*Kisses her*) you jade, you have managed it to my wish.

LUCY: Yes, sir: I believe you will find I have managed it to some purpose; but you must sign the contract.

LORD BELVILLE: Pooh! ha, ha, ha! fifty of them—ha, ha, ha! Come, come, I am impatient till I sign it.   Let us go in to her. (*Going*)

LUCY: Hold! are you mad, sir.

LORD BELVILLE: Why?

LUCY: Hush!

LORD BELVILLE: What is the matter?

LUCY: Softly, I say.

LORD BELVILLE: Why, what?

LUCY: Be quiet—not a word.

LORD BELVILLE: Ha!

LUCY: He is going, I believe.

LORD BELVILLE: Going? Who?

LUCY: I thought I heard him move.

LORD BELVILLE: Who?

LUCY: Hush! softly! her brother.

LORD BELVILLE: Brother!

LUCY: No—he is not stirring.

LORD BELVILLE: What brother?

LUCY: Speak softly, I say—a brother of hers, an officer that is with her, sir—a young desperate rakehell, who is just come from America, and is going there again to-night, or to-morrow morning. I am sure we shall be glad when he's gone.

LORD BELVILLE: Why so, Lucy?

LUCY: O sir, he is the most quarrelsome, riotous, fighting—he does not care what mischief he does—continually in scrapes and round-houses[1]—he almost killed a watchman the other night in Covent Garden—is fighting duels every week, and has killed a man or two already.

LORD BELVILLE: Why do not they hang the rascal? Such fellows are a pest to society—they study nothing but fencing and how to get into quarrels in order to shew their skill. Had you not best step and see what he is about, Lucy?

LUCY: I will, sir.

LORD BELVILLE: But don't stay.

LUCY: No, no, sir. He feels our captain; we shall startle him before we have done with him. (*Aside and exit*)

LORD BELVILLE: A plague on these wrongheaded puppies: these officers always come across me either as rivals, or relations—I hate to have any thing to do where they are concerned. I should not like to be drawn into an affair upon this occasion, and with a madman too—Zounds! I have left my sword behind me: what the devil shall I do?—'twas foolish! if he should find me here I do not know what might be the consequences.

---

[1] Lock-ups, places of temporary detention.

Enter SERJEANT

SERJEANT: We are all ready, your honour.

LORD BELVILLE: What fellow is this? his serjeant, I suppose. I will retire a little. (*Going*)

SERJEANT: Here, you sir—where is the captain? You sir—damn you, why do you not answer?

LORD BELVILLE: What do you mean, rascal? do you know whom you strike?

SERJEANT: Know whom I strike? yes, very well—I strike a unmannerly fellow, that would not give a gentleman an answer: and therefore thought proper to teach him the discipline of ill manners.

LORD BELVILLE: You are an impudent rascal. How dare you lift your hand against any man?

SERJEANT: And who are you that asks such impertinent questions?

LORD BELVILLE: Sirrah, I am a gentleman.

SERJEANT: And, sirrah, so am I a gentleman—one who wears the King's cloth: and if you are affronted, why I am ready to exchange a brace of bullets with you, run you through the body, or give you any other gentleman-like satisfaction you please.

LORD BELVILLE: Give me satisfaction, you impudent fellow!

SERJEANT: You—aye, or any man, sir. Zounds!

LORD BELVILLE: What do you speak so loud for, you rascal?

SERJEANT: Loud! Damme, who am I afraid of? I'll be as loud as a cannon if I please, or——

LORD BELVILLE: Softly, I say.

SERJEANT: Zounds! Do not tell me of softly!

LORD BELVILLE: You are the impudentest fellow! do you know where you are, or whom you speak to, fellow?

SERJEANT: Fallow! fallow, sir! damme, sir, not your fallow!

LORD BELVILLE: I tell you not to speak so loud. What do you want, sir? what do you want?

SERJEANT: What is that to ye, what I want? damn ye, I want my captain—Fallow! for three pinches of snuff I would cram your fallow down your throat with my sword, and would teach ye how to behave yourself another time to a gentleman that has the honour of wearing the King's military marks of his favours and distinctions. (*Exit*)

LORD BELVILLE: The fellow is mad! a gentleman—ha, ha, ha! impudent

160

rascal—but that I am not in a position to have an interview with his captain, I would have the scoundrel punished severely. I fancy he is decamping; I hear somebody going down stairs: yes, he's going, that's lucky—he might have interrupted us—O, here she comes herself.

Enter HARRIET *and* LUCY

LUCY: Come, come madam: he is gone; cheer up—all's safe; give me the contract. Here, sir, is the bond; and pen and ink.

HARRIET: Indeed, zir, I most zincerely does beg your worship's pardon, for making ye tarry zo long, but in truth zir, it was not out of ill manners, therefore I hopes ye will not think it of me.

LORD BELVILLE: I do not, my charmer.

HARRIET: Ye must know the true reason was, I had a brother with me, a mad, giddy brained spark, who horrified me out of my wits—because as how ye must knaw he is a captain, zir—and would kill me about his honour, if he thought I zhould dare to let any gentleman zpeak to me without his particular licence had for that very occasion: zo I ztayed till he was gone lest he zhould fight with ye and be for killing me—for he is a perfect reprobate at quarrelling, and cares not whom he murders.

LORD BELVILLE: You did very prudently, my dear: and is he gone?

HARRIET: O yes; yes, he is gone; I zaw him out of the house, and yet I trembles at the thought of him. He is going this very night to fight the Cherokees and the wild men in America.

LUCY: Come, come sir: here is the contract that the lady has drawn up herself—sign it, and make her happy; I will read it to you.

LORD BELVILLE: No, no; there is no occasion for reading it—whatever her virtuous heart has thought proper to dictate to this fair hand, I shall sign implicitly.[1] (*Kisses her hand*)

LUCY: Here, sir: come to the table then; and sign it at once.

LORD BELVILLE: With all my soul—I would sign with my heart's blood. (*Signs it*) Here, my angel, take this pledge of truth and everlasting love. (*Gives it to her*)

LUCY: Nay, madam, do not hang down your head and blush, but look up: turn to him, and meet his honest passion with joy—for now it is an honest passion.

HARRIET: Heigh ho! is it, Mr. Jackson?

[1] Without a doubt or enquiry.

LORD BELVILLE: It is, my life—honest and virtuous as law and love can make it.

HARRIET: I dawn't knaw what to zay, zir; my heart moves as it would jump to my mouth. I be zcared out of my wits, lest what I be doing zhould be a zin—and lest ye zhould be false hearted—but I will rely on your goodness and your honour.

LORD BELVILLE: You may, my life. Justice shall invent new words and punishments for my name and person, if I deceive you.

LUCY: Come, come, sir; go and undress, and my lady will come to you.

LORD BELVILLE: Will you, my life?

HARRIET: Yes— (*Sighs and looks at him*) my angel.

LORD BELVILLE: Oh! that kind look—that yes has shot through my heart—I shall die with—

LUCY: Well, well, sir—do not die here: nay, nay, no soft looks and sighs here—begone, sir—go, go, sir—take her while she is in the humour.

LORD BELVILLE: I will, I will: do not let her stay—you are an excellent girl—

LUCY: Go, sir.

LORD BELVILLE: And have managed it nicely. (*Exit into the bed chamber*)

LUCY: Yes, I have managed it nicely, if you knew all—ha, ha, ha! he is in the trap.

HARRIET: Ha, ha, ha! shut the door.

LUCY: It is.

HARRIET: Fasten it.

LUCY: Yes—there.

HARRIET: You may come forth. (*Knocking at the folding doors*)
   Enter TOWNLY *and* LADY BELVILLE, *first peeping out*

HARRIET: We have him: he is undressing; going to bed.

TOWNLY: Why, Miss Harriet, you are an incomparable actress.

LUCY: Speak softly, sir.

HARRIET: He cannot hear us.

TOWNLY: I never saw a character better personated.

LADY BELVILLE: Very artful indeed—you have outdone him in his own hypocrisy.

LUCY: You must not stay too long, madam; Mrs. Angelica will begin the sport without you—to your post, quick—go in, madam, there. (*Exit* HARRIET) I will shut you together, (*Shuts the door*) and now the captain may begin as soon as he pleases—come, madam, let us begone.

TOWNLY: I would give twenty guineas, I could be a spectator of the scene.

LADY BELVILLE: We shall hear it all.

LUCY: Away, away, away. (*Exeunt*)

ANGELICA: (*Within*) Here, this way, serjeant; break open the door.

SERJEANT: (*Within*) I will have it open in a crack—hah; hah; hah —it's done. (*Noise of bursting the door*)

ANGELICA: (*Within*) Where is the villain? Shoot him. Fire. (*A pistol goes off*)

LORD BELVILLE: (*Within*) What do you mean, sir? are you going to murder me?

ANGELICA: (*Within*) Shoot the rascal.

HARRIET: (*Within*) No! Pray, dear brother, do not kill him.

ANGELICA: Fire! again I say, why do not you fire, you rascal, when I command you? (*Another pistol goes off*)

Enter LORD BELVILLE *half undressed*, ANGELICA *and* SERJEANT *with drawn swords, and* HARRIET *holding* ANGELICA

LORD BELVILLE: Help! Murder! Murder! Lights! Lights!

ANGELICA: Let me come at the villain.

LORD BELVILLE: What, do you mean to murder me?

ANGELICA: Guard the door, serjeant—let not man, woman or child stir out.

SERJEANT: They shall go through me if they do. (*Exit*)

ANGELICA: Let me go, vile woman. Hold off your hands.

HARRIET: Ye zhall not get from me, brother; nay, why will you ztrive zo? I does beg ye will not murder him.

LORD BELVILLE: No sir, do not murder me.

HARRIET: His intentions be honourable.

LORD BELVILLE: Yes, sir, my intentions are honourable.

ANGELICA: Honourable villain! did I not detect you in her bed chamber? are you not undressed? was she not with you? Let me go—by the honour of a soldier, he shall have as many holes through his body as there are stars in the firmament.

HARRIET: O dear! O dear! good now, brother—why, zure ye be mad. Do but hear him first, and kill him afterwards.

ANGELICA: Well, speak, sir; what have you to say?

LORD BELVILLE: Why, sir, upon the honour and veracity of a gentleman—

ANGELICA: Zounds, sir! no flourishing about honour and veracity with me, but speak to the point.

LORD BELVILLE: Sir, you are so very hot: madam, will you speak to your brother—you know my intentions were honourable.

HARRIET: Nay, good brother, be not so rash, but hear me.

ANGELICA: Well; what have you to say—for your seducer, and for your own wickedness?

HARRIET: Brother, ye does wrong me—I be not wicked, nor is he a villain, but an honest and zober gentleman, of Ztaffordshire.

ANGELICA: Of Staffordshire?

LORD BELVILLE: Yes, sir, of Staffordshire.

ANGELICA: Silence, sir: go on, madam—of Staffordshire—well, what then?

HARRIET: What then? why then, he is an honest gentleman, and loves me in an honourable way.

ANGELICA: What is his name?

HARRIET: Why, brother, that is what I was going to tell ye; but ye were in zuch a passion, ye zcare one out of one's wits—his name is Jackson.

ANGELICA: Jackson! is your name Jackson, sir?

LORD BELVILLE: Yes, sir.

ANGELICA: Of Staffordshire? this is all invention; I know every family in Staffordshire—there is no such name there.

LORD BELVILLE: You are right, sir: we are but lately settled in that county—originally a Cornish family.

ANGELICA: Damn your family, sir—what is all this to your designs upon my sister?

HARRIET: I tell ye his designs be honourable, brother—were they not, Mr. Jackson? why do ye not zpeak for yourself, and tell the truth?

LORD BELVILLE: Yes, they were honourable; indeed, sir.

ANGELICA: How? which way? prove it—convince me.

HARRIET: Why, brother, we be married. Why do not ye confess the truth, I zay, Mr. Jackson?

LORD BELVILLE: What does she mean? (*Aside*) Yes, sir, we are married.

ANGELICA: Married! Sir, I ask your pardon most sincerely; then I sheath my sword. Why did you not let me know this sooner?

HARRIET: Ye were zo impatient, brother, ye would not hear a body.

ANGELICA: When were you married?

HARRIET: About ten minutes ago.

ANGELICA: So lately! where is the parson?

HARRIET: We had none, brother—ours was a marriage in conscience.

ANGELICA: Conscience! do you mean to impose upon me, sir? explain this moment, sir, or this sword draws.

HARRIET: O, dear! pray, brother, do not kill him—nay, ye may ztruggle, but ye zhall not get away from me.

ANGELICA: Let him explain then.

LORD BELVILLE: Why, sir, the fact is, I have given the lady a contract.

ANGELICA: How?

HARRIET: And that, ye know, brother, is a marriage in conscience—is it not, Mr. Jackson?

LORD BELVILLE: It is, madam.

ANGELICA: A marriage in conscience! a contract! there must be some juggle in this.

HARRIET: No, indeed and indeed, brother, there is no juggle in it; for here be the contract, in plain written hand—if ye do not believe me, look at it yourself.

ANGELICA: Let me see this contract—give it me. (*Reads*) 'Anthony Jackson of the County of Stafford Esquire having made my honourable addresses to Margaret Packington, of the Parish of Saint George in the County of Middlesex, spinster, do by this writing under my hand solemnly promise to perform the same. But as a large fortune is depending on the will and power of the said Anthony Jackson's grandfather, he the said Anthony Jackson doth request that the said Margery Packington will defer the marriage for three months, at the expiration of which time, he doth solemnly promise to wed the said Margery Packington; or whenever she shall demand the performance of this his promise of wedlock, and in the mean time he doth acknowledge her as his lawful wife as far as oaths, honour, this writing, and conscience can bind him—as witness my hand, Anthony Jackson.' O, very well, very well—is this your hand, Mr. Jackson?

LORD BELVILLE: It is, sir.

ANGELICA: Do you acknowledge it?

LORD BELVILLE: I do, sir.

ANGELICA: Very well, sir.

LORD BELVILLE: Sir, I assure you upon my honour, I meant the lady fair—I would not deceive her for the world. I wish I were out of the house. (*Aside*)

ANGELICA: It is mighty well, sir. Sergeant.

Enter SERGEANT

SERJEANT: Here, your honour.

ANGELICA: Is not our chaplain in the house?

SERJEANT: He is, your honour.

ANGELICA: Desire him to come hither directly, to marry a couple.

LORD BELVILLE: Hah!

SERJEANT: He shall be with your honour in the flashing of a cannon. (*Exit*)

ANGELICA: By the honour of my name, and the reputation of a soldier, the deed shall be done before this sword be sheathed.

LORD BELVILLE: This is worse and worse—what the devil shall I do? (*Aside*)

ANGELICA: You seem not to relish my proposal, sir.

LORD BELVILLE: Sir, as you may so easily imagine, there is no honour I should be so proud of, as an alliance with your family—yet could it be deferred for a few days—

ANGELICA: Not a moment—Zounds, sir, this sword—and let me tell you, sir, if your are a gentleman, and a man of honour, you ought not to hesitate a moment.

LORD BELVILLE: I grant it, sir—but consider what a vast fortune we should lose by it. My grandfather, sir—

ANGELICA: Damn your grandfather, sir! and your grandmother! and your whole generation! Am I to suffer ignominy for your avarice? a lady's character, and the honour of a soldier, are of more value than the mines of Mexico and Peru.

LORD BELVILLE: I mean only for a few days.

ANGELICA: Not a moment! my recruits are below waiting for me, and I am to embark with them, for America, within this hour; so that I must see my sister's honour and my own redressed, before I go—nay, this instant—or death—

LORD BELVILLE: Sir, I own I am in your power; I have no weapon, every advantage is against me: but as you are a gentleman, I hope you will not take my life.

ANGELICA: What do you mean, sir?

LORD BELVILLE: If you will give me your honour I shall suffer no insult, I will lay such reasons before you, as will convince you that a marriage is impracticable at present.

ANGELICA: Your life is safe: speak, sir; my honour is passed.

LORD BELVILLE: I shall make no preface or apology, but rely on your word—I am myself greatly to blame, and I sincerely ask yours and the lady's pardon—but—

ANGELICA: Well sir, go on.

LORD BELVILLE: I am—

ANGELICA: What, sir?

LORD BELVILLE: Married already.

ANGELICA: Married!

LORD BELVILLE: Married, sir.

HARRIET: How! and beest thou a married man, Mr. Jackson?

LORD BELVILLE: I ask your pardon, madam, but it is too true.

HARRIET: Alas! alas! what a villain has I zet my heart upon! (*Cries*)

ANGELICA: Retire, idiot; and weep within—what could you expect but deceit? Leave us.

HARRIET: Oh! Mr. Jackson, ye be a knavish man—but thy life shall answer for the injury thou hast done my vartue, if there be poison, or zword, or gunpowder in the univerzal world. Ah! thou art a villain, a deceitful Ztaffordshire villain. (*Exit crying*)

LORD BELVILLE: What a damned affair this is. (*Aside*)

Enter SERJEANT

SERJEANT: An please your honour, the chaplain has no tawcle[1] about him; but he is gone to borrow a prayer book.

ANGELICA: He may spare the trouble: the villain has deceived my sister, and imposed upon me. He has a wife already. The rascal is no gentleman—he must be an impostor—some low fellow: what punishment shall I put him to, suitable to his meanness and villainy?

[1] i.e. tackle, the equipment for the job.

SERJEANT: Why, if he is a cheat and a sharper, your honour, by law you may press him into the Service. Say but the word—and in half an hour we will hoist him on board, and carry him along with us to America to fight the Cherokees.

ANGELICA: An excellent thought, serjeant—I commit him to your custody, and shall expect to see you both on board as soon as possible.

LORD BELVILLE: Have a care what you do, sir: I am a gentleman of rank.

ANGELICA: I will answer your rank, sir. Secure him, serjeant, and on board with him— (*Exit*)

SERJEANT: I warrant your honour—if he gets out of my clutches, Old Nick shall be his helpmate. Come, sir, march.

LORD BELVILLE: At your peril, sir, lay a finger on me.

SERJEANT: Such another word out of your jaws, and the light shall shine through your carcase, as it would through a sieve, or a cullender—you rascal, do you mutiny? disobey command? Who is below there? Send up some of our people—I will make you understand that you are a lawful recruit: and if you deny it, you shall be shot for the first misdemeanour you commit in the Service.

Enter a CORPORAL *and four* RECRUITS

SERJEANT: Corporal, take that fallow—gag and tie him, neck and heels.

LORD BELVILLE: Do not lay hands on me, I charge you—I am a lord.

CORPORAL: O be quiet—be aisy, my dear soul, for if you was the lord leeftenant of Ireland you must go when you are commanded.[1]

LORD BELVILLE: Stand off, you rascals—don't touch me.

RECRUIT: Oh! blood and thunder! hold your tongue, my dear, when you are well used. (*They lay hold on him*)

LORD BELVILLE: You villains, will you murder me?

SERJEANT: Gag him—bind him—a rascal—

RECRUIT: Ocho! come along, my dear. Push him along behind there, and knock him down if he won't be quiet. (*They force him off in great confusion and noise*)

END OF THE THIRD ACT

[1] The Corporal and speaking recruit are Irishmen, great numbers of whom were serving in the British army.

ACT IV

Enter LADY BELVILLE *and* HARRIET

LADY BELVILLE: They make a hideous noise below, Harriet; what is the matter?

HARRIET: Some misunderstanding among the recruits, I suppose.

LADY BELVILLE: I thought I heard my lord's voice.

HARRIET: You might, madam, for he was very loud.

LADY BELVILLE: What was the dispute?

HARRIET: I cannot say exactly—all I heard of it was, that my lord threatened them, and said they should all suffer for what they were doing. But Angelica is gone down to quell the noise.

Enter TOWNLY

HARRIET: Well, Mr. Townly, what is the matter below?

TOWNLY: O, ha, ha, ha! such a scene: but I could not enjoy it all; I did not dare venture farther than the bottom of the back stairs. I beg your ladyship's pardon—but were he your husband, or my uncle, a million times, I could not help laughing—such a ridiculous figure. If ever he intrigues again, I am much mistaken.

HARRIET: Yes, yes, I believe the gentleman will remember this night's adventure, as long as he lives.

LADY BELVILLE: But pray, what was my lord so loud about?

TOWNLY: Here comes my tyrant, who was in the midst of it all; she can inform you minutely.

Enter ANGELICA

ANGELICA: O Harriet, support me! ha, ha, ha! I shall expire.

LADY BELVILLE: What is the matter?

ANGELICA: Oh! ha, ha! madam, you may be satisfied now: for not only your cause, but the cause of every injured wife in Great Britain, is vindicated up to the most wicked revenge, that ridicule can inflict.

HARRIET: Why, what have you done to him?

ANGELICA: The serjeant led him down prisoner among my brother's recruits, who are waiting for him, to be sent on board as soon as he arrives: to those tender swains, the captive lover told a tale of stately woe that made each hearer burst with laughing—ha, ha, ha! he said he was a peer of the realm!—ha, ha! that he would have them all hanged if they did not release him.

HARRIET: Ha, ha, ha! ridiculous—and did they attempt to set him free?

ANGELICA: O, ha, ha, ha! the reverse—the thought of having a lord amongst them for a fellow soldier furnished the savages with such an infinite fund of wit and insolence, that at last he downright mutinied, and would have forced his way out; raved, roared, and struggled like a madman—upon which the serjeant without the least ceremony fairly gagged him, and with shameful cords of perdurable toughness bound our hero.   Ha, ha, ha, ha!

OMNES: Ha, ha, ha, ha!

TOWNLY: Monstrous!

HARRIET: Delightful!

ANGELICA: And he has equipped him with spatterdashes, knapsack, haversack, pouch, cantine,[1] and all military accoutrements befitting a gentleman soldier upon a march.   Ha, ha, ha, ha!

OMNES: Ha, ha, ha, ha!

TOWNLY: Why, he will run distracted.

ANGELICA: And in that dress, with the droll addition of a grenadier's cap upon his tie periwig, is he sitting in one of the niches of the back parlour, surrounded by a parcel of swearing, taunting, drunken, jolly recruits—silent and sulky as a military coward on the eve of a battle, reflecting upon death.

OMNES: Ha, ha, ha, ha!

TOWNLY: Upon my word, madam, you would make an admirable painter—you have sketched as fair a figure for the genius of a Hogarth, as ridicule could wish.   Ha, ha, ha! he will certainly run mad.

LADY BELVILLE: I pity him not: he who could give such a contract deserves every punishment that justice can devise.

ANGELICA: Stay till we have done with him, madam; I have not spit half my malice at him yet: I'll teach him to give contracts, and go a poaching in masquerade after young country game.

---

[1] Spatterdashes, long gaiters: knapsack, a bag or case of canvas or leather carried on the back and containing the soldier's necessities: haversack, a stout canvas bag carried by a shoulder-strap, holding the day's rations: pouch, for ammunition: cantine (canteen), a small metal vessel for liquid carried on the march.

HARRIET: O lud! what would I give to see my contracted spouse in his present pickle.

ANGELICA: Do not be in a hurry, Harriet—in a very few minutes you shall see him in a much more ridiculous pickle, take my word for it; I have such a distress in my head for him.   I am resolved to try his lordship's patience before I am done with him.

TOWNLY: I think you have made his blood circulate pretty briskly already.

ANGELICA: Pooh! a trifle! a trifle to what I intend—I want to touch the noble delicate part of the animal, that is what I want to come at; and with this lady's assistance, to try if there be such a thing as a tender or humane nerve in any part of his composition.

TOWNLY: Well, madam, suppose your tender and humane nerve found out, what then?

ANGELICA: Why then, sir, I would make my lady fret and play upon it till it went off snap—like the string of a fiddle in a concert.

LADY BELVILLE: My dear, he merits the deepest vengeance our malice can contrive, but you can add nothing to his present vexation: I know his pride; he must feel his situation most severely.

ANGELICA: So much the better, madam, so much the better; for take my word for it, nothing but probing to the quick can bring those voluptaries to a sense of duty and social obligations.   I know the gentry: they are a new species of philosophers, that irreligion and luxury have introduced among us.   I had a lover once of their sect—their doctrine is present pleasure at any expence, hang consequences: they care not whom they injure, so they are but gratified.

LADY BELVILLE: That is, indeed, too much my lord's unhappy character.

ANGELICA: Nay, madam, it is the character of them all.   Fortune and pleasure are the deities they sacrifice to; the temple of virtue is quite erased.   Give them but a fine equipage, deep play, and an admired wanton—and a minister of state may convert the honour of every man of them into a vote, that would sell the nation to Prester John and their boasted liberties to the Great Mogul.[1]

Enter SERGEANT

[1] 'a vote . . . Mogul'—these words are repeated in the last speech in Act IV of *The Man of the World*.

ANGELICA: Well, serjeant, how does our recruit like his new profession?

SERJEANT: We have had the devil to do with him; but he is pretty quiet now, madam. Upon condition I would unbind him, he promised upon his honour that he would not resist again; but he is as melancholy as if he were upon an uninhabited island—he will not speak a word now, nor open his jaws.

ANGELICA: We shall soon cure him of his sullenness.

SERJEANT: He begs hard that he may speak a word or two with Mrs. Lucy.

ANGELICA: By all means indulge him in that, serjeant; let him come up into this room, and we will send Lucy to him.

SERJEANT: Madam, he shall come up in a twinkling. (*Exit*)

ANGELICA: Come, madam, let us go and prepare for our scene—*allons*, to the right about, march. (*Exeunt*)

Enter LORD BELVILLE

LORD BELVILLE: Rascals! villains! was there ever such treatment, to dress me up thus? damn their knapsacks, their cantines, and their insolence: they shall not impose them upon me any longer—I will have such vengeance—Zounds! were this farce known I should become the jest of the whole town—rot this captain—was there ever such a wrongheaded scoundrel? to be sure 'twas a little provoking to find me undressed in his sister's bed chamber—and had he not interrupted us, I might have made Miss Margery useful in her generation: but the fellow really seems to have a taint of madness in his resentment—yet sure he cannot be so far gone as seriously to think of transporting me. What shall I do? Resistance I have tried as far as anger unarmed could exert it—and when I offer to cry out, in order to raise the neighbourhood, the rascals gag and bind, and threaten to stab or shoot me. That ruffian the serjeant, too, has almost poisoned me—he has not only made me take listing money in spite of my teeth, but the rascal—out of his abundant loyalty—has forced nauseous liquors down my throat to the King's health, till I am almost ready to expire.

Enter LUCY

LUCY: O sir! O sir, you have ruined me—I am undone—lost my reputation—how could you be so base, so wicked, so inhuman, to tell us you were a single gentleman—when for ought we know you may have a wife in every county in England? Oh, oh, oh! (*Cries*)

LORD BELVILLE: Do not cry, do not cry, dear Mrs. Lucy—I have but one wife, upon honour.

LUCY: But one! How many would you have? one is as bad as ten thousand—O, there is no believing a word you say—such oaths! such vows! O la, O la, O la! mercy on us—what devils men are when they want to get their ends of a poor woman! why, you would swear any thing. (*Cries*)

LORD BELVILLE: Prithee, Lucy, do not cry so, but hear me.

LUCY: Nay, sir: all you can say now will signify nothing, for the captain's determined, and swears by all the gods and furies, in heaven and hell, that you shall go to America as a recruit—and I—the cruel wicked man—he vows that I shall go along with you to fight the blacks—Oh, oh!

LORD BELVILLE: Zounds! was there ever such a madman? we have but one remedy, Lucy.

LUCY: What is that, sir? (*Cries*)

LORD BELVILLE: You must go instantly to a Justice of Peace, and make oath how I am used by this wild man.

LUCY: O, sir! impossible; that is impossible.

LORD BELVILLE: Why so, Lucy?

LUCY: Why, sir, he has placed a parcel of his recruits and soldiers, terrible looking fellows, at the street door, and all over the house, with orders to run any one through the body, or shoot them, that offers to stir out, make a noise, look out of a window, or do any thing that may alarm the neighbours, or bring assistance.

LORD BELVILLE: Why, this is intolerable—such a breach of all laws.

LUCY: O sir, I have not told you half of what has happened, not half our misery—Oh! my poor, poor mistress—

LORD BELVILLE: Ha! what of her, Lucy?

LUCY: Oh! I cannot tell it you for fears—for grief, for anger, for madness—Oh! Oh! my poor lady—Oh! Oh!

LORD BELVILLE: How! mad?

LUCY: Mad as a bedlamite!

LORD BELVILLE: You amaze me! mad! how happened that?

LUCY: O sir, your dear, lovely, enchanting person, and your sweet bewitching tongue, made such an impression upon her heart—and your oaths, vows, perfidy, the fury of her brother, and the loss of the man she doated on—such a riot and distraction in her poor brain, that she is gone quite, stark, staring, raving mad—Oh! Oh!

LORD BELVILLE: Poor creature.

LUCY: O sir, take care of yourself—take care of yourself, let me advise you—I am quite out of breath at the terror of it; but by some means or other she has got a sword, and runs wild about the house —for no person dares face her, raving, and roaring, and searching for you, sir.

LORD BELVILLE: Ha! for me?

LUCY: Vowing to pierce your heart with that sword, as you had hers with Cupid's dart.

LORD BELVILLE: 'Sdeath, Lucy, lock her up—I may be killed by her— where's her brother? his fury and insolence shall no longer impose upon me. Let me see him—he shall know who I am.

LUCY: Pray, sir, have patience—are you mad too? have you a mind to be murdered? to have me murdered? and my poor lady murdered?

LORD BELVILLE: But this treatment is not to be borne—I will die rather than suffer it.

LUCY: Pray, sir, be patient one moment. Had you not better get off quietly and safely, if you can, than to run the risk of murder?

LORD BELVILLE: Certainly.

LUCY: Very well, then. Stay, sir, stay—I have just hit on a thought that I believe will save us—aye, now I think of it, there is a back door that goes out of the laundry into the garden: if I can but open that, I am sure we may both steal out.

LORD BELVILLE: That is a good thought: run and see, dear Lucy, if it can be opened.

SERJEANT: (*Without*) Where are ye, Jackson?

LORD BELVILLE: Here is that rascal.

LUCY: Step behind this screen—quick, sir—and do not stir upon any account until I come to you. I will engage I get you out through the garden. Let me alone with the serjeant—I will manage him.

LORD BELVILLE: Do, do Lucy: I'll not stir. (*Goes behind the screen*)

Enter SERJEANT

SERJEANT: Come, come, Jackson. Mrs. Lucy, your servant—where is Jackson our recruit, I left here?

LUCY: Did you not meet him? He is gone down the back stairs to the rest of the men.

SERJEANT: Is he? O, then it is well enough, if he be gone down to the men.

Enter ANGELICA *with drawn sword*

ANGELICA: Unhappy woman! mad as the winds! I got her sword from her at last: but the villain that has been the cause of her madness shall suffer for it—his life shall be a continued slavery. Go, you impudent treacherous wretch, and help guard my sister: and lay this sword where she cannot come at it. Begone out of my sight, vile creature. (*Exit* LUCY)

ANGELICA: Where is that villain, serjeant?

SERJEANT: He is below with the men, please your honour.

ANGELICA: Let him be bound, and a strong guard set over him; and let not the sailors, nor any person whatever, have any communication with him till you send him aboard.

LORD BELVILLE: Soh!

SERJEANT: I will take particular care he shall not speak to a soul, nor see sun or moon, till he gets to America.

ANGELICA: What answer did the messenger bring from the lady?

SERJEANT: That she would meet you here, in less than half an hour.

ANGELICA: Very well: as soon as you have seen the recruits into the barge, and that villain safe, come to me to the bagnio, for there the lady and I shall be—but where are my pistols? it is proper to have them about me on this occasion.

SERJEANT: Here they be, sir, charged with a brace of bullets each.[2]

ANGELICA: Aye, these will give a proper reception to any one that shall offer to interrupt us. Be you ready; I shall set out from the bagnio for Gravesend[3] about three in the morning, and you must go with me.

SERJEANT: I shall be sure to attend. I will go now, and see them all aboard in an instant. (*Exit*)

ANGELICA: The injury he has done me is beyond reparation, beyond revenge! Poor Margery! thy madness is a happiness—but I will sacrifice to it.

[1] Originally a bath-house: brothel, house of assignation.
[2] Cf. p. 118, n. 2, above.
[3] On the South bank of the Thames, some 30 miles below London: an important part of the port system. The grave of Pocohontas is at Gravesend.

Enter SERJEANT

SERJEANT: Odswauns! sir, we are all betrayed—all ruined!

ANGELICA: What is the matter?

SERJEANT: Jackson, the villain, has bribed the sentinels, and they have let him get out of the house.

ANGELICA: Let him out! I will have them all shot, every man of them—I will kill them myself. Follow me. (*Exit*)

SERJEANT: I will, sir. A sly rascal—if once we lay hold of him again, I'll prevent his escape effectually, for by Jupiter I will hamstring him. (*Exit*)

LORD BELVILLE: What a damned condition am I in now: he certainly intends to send me away. His sister's madness is unlucky—that has irritated him. If Lucy can but get the garden door open—

Enter LUCY

LUCY: O sir, do not stir—they think you are gone off. I have got the garden door open: but you must not stir till the search is a little cool.

LORD BELVILLE: No; no, by no means.

LUCY: O, heavens, sir! they are coming. Lie close—they will never think of searching for you here. I must leave you: do not stir. (*Exit*)

LORD BELVILLE: Stir! no, rot them—what a situation!

Enter ANGELICA *and* SERJEANT

ANGELICA: You heard what the sentinels swear: he must be in the house—go, search it from top to bottom.

SERJEANT: If he be under the roof, I will find him, unless the devil hides him for his own use. (*Exit*)

ANGELICA: Not to have him with me to America would be such a disappointment.

Enter LUCY

LUCY: Sir, there is a lady below in a chair enquires for you.

ANGELICA: Shew her up—stay, how is my sister now?

LUCY: Very bad, sir—we have tied her down in her bed, poor lady, and have sent for a physician.

ANGELICA: Does she speak?

LUCY: She raves; and calls on Mr. Jackson; and begs to see her dear, dear Mr. Jackson.

LORD BELVILLE: Poor creature.

ANGELICA: This you have contributed to, vile wretch.

LUCY: Indeed, sir, I knew no more of his being a married man, than I do of my dying hour.

ANGELICA: Begone, and shew the lady up. (*Exit* LUCY) The villain! why did I not run my sword through his heart at once? my poor sister—but let me drive her from my thoughts. Grief and resentment now must give way to love and rapture.

Enter LADY BELVILLE

ANGELICA: My life, my bliss, my guardian goddess!

LORD BELVILLE: Hah!

ANGELICA: Welcome as victory, love and honour—O let me taste those lips, and give you love's native welcome to my heart.

LORD BELVILLE: How! by heavens, my own wife!

ANGELICA: And will you at last reward my toils, assiduities, and faithful love?

LADY BELVILLE: Yes, I resign—am determined; the cruel usage of my husband has at length driven me to your arms.

LORD BELVILLE: Soh!

ANGELICA: That is but a cold compliment to my love, madam, and my long solicitude.

LADY BELVILLE: In a commerce of this nature, sir, as there can be no virtue in it, one quality it should have—which is mutual sincerity. On my part, I honestly own you are more indebted to my lord's profligate life, and to resentment, than to the natural warmth of my inclinations or my love—for my regard to him, my patience, my sufferings, and every passion of my heart is now turned to hatred and revenge.

LORD BELVILLE: Very well!

ANGELICA: I know his character well, madam, though I am a stranger to his person: the world condemns him as a libertine; and for his treatment of you, all men hate him.

LADY BELVILLE: The world knows but little of him: but they shall be intimate with him in his most secret vices. I have a perfect history of all his haunts and engagements—the wives, sisters, daughters of his dearest friends are the object of his vices: there is not a corner of the town in which he has not some unhappy wretch that he has seduced. This very evening he is upon some new intrigue; and ten to one at this instant is contriving the ruin of some innocent creature, or suffering the ignominy and shame his vice deserves.

LORD BELVILLE: Hum!

ANGELICA: Well, madam, I hope you are at last cured of your love for him.

LADY BELVILLE: Most unalterably: not two hours since he threatened me with divorce—for which if I be not revenged—

ANGELICA: Let my faithful love, madam, be the sweet instrument of your vengeance upon the dull savage, that had not sense to taste your matchless charms.

LADY BELVILLE: Look you, captain, I own your person is not indifferent to me—but before I take so desperate a step, I have two points to settle. The first is concerning your going to America: that I own shocks me; it will be a severe trial upon my heart to lose the man to-morrow to whom I shall resign myself to-night.

LORD BELVILLE: Furies and hell!

ANGELICA: I have no will, madam, but what your charms inspire; you are the ruler of every passion within this breast: but name your pleasure—love, courage, life shall try their last exertion to obey you.

LADY BELVILLE: Then, sir, from this moment I am wholly yours—by this kiss. Let us retire, and I will give you full instructions how you shall revenge me upon the worst of men.

LORD BELVILLE: Here, madam, is your victim.

LADY BELVILLE: Ah! I am betrayed— (*Exit*)

ANGELICA: Slave! advance a step—you rush on death.

LORD BELVILLE: I defy it.

ANGELICA: You see, I am doubly armed—stir not on your life.

LORD BELVILLE: I am in your power, I know: with me use your discretion; but stir not after her, I charge you.

ANGELICA: This insolence shall be punished without mercy.

LORD BELVILLE: I care not.

ANGELICA: Villain, do you forget the wrong you have done my sister? must you interrupt me in my pleasures too?

LORD BELVILLE: In this I must, though death opposed me. I am bewildered, and know not where I am—lost in a labyrinth of shame: each step brings new perplexities and disgrace; but this last is past the bearing even of a coward's patience.

ANGELICA: The man is mad. What do you mean by this fustian? explain.

LORD BELVILLE: Be the consequence what it may, you shall know me, sir—that lady the law hath made mine, and though my heart hath long been truant, it now severely tells me, I love her more than life.

ANGELICA: Let me understand you, sir. Is the lady that was here, your wife?

LORD BELVILLE: She is.

ANGELICA: Justice, I thank thee! by my sister's virgin fame, it gives me joy—I thought her wrongs were past the power of revenge; but now my vengeance shall be satisfied.

LORD BELVILLE: What mean you, sir?

ANGELICA: To revenge a sister's lost chastity, in the pollution of her betrayer's wife—to make his issue spurious, his infamy notorious, his life odious as unblushing vice.

LORD BELVILLE: In such revenge there is a baseness—a cruelty. You, sir, I have not injured—the cradled infant is not purer than your sister's chastity, for me: I charge you then not to sacrifice your own to an incensed wife's, and a husband's honour to an intended wrong.

ANGELICA: Honour! your honour—where, in what does it consist? how dare you prophane the word with your vicious breath? where was that social guardian, when a married libertine with a forged contract robbed a virtuous lady of her fame, and drove her into madness?

LORD BELVILLE: Sir, I knew her not: I knew not you: let that mitigate.

ANGELICA: You knew yourself, sir: you knew your rank: you knew society—the theory of honour too I find you knew, but not the practice.

LORD BELVILLE: I own my crime; will that appease? 'twas base—be you otherwise: do not persist.

ANGELICA: I will: you are full in my power, and struggling will but increase your misery. I know the pangs your heart must feel: but when you think upon the wrongs you have done to me—when you reflect how many comfortless fathers, and distracted mothers, your vice has made, how many forsaken wretches it has thrown upon an unpitying world—conscience will inform your heart there is but justice in your punishment.   That, sir, ought to alleviate your anguish; and to that consolation my equity resigns your dying honour.   (*Exit*)

LORD BELVILLE: Diseases stop his purpose! I will not lose her thus.   In spite of shame or death I must speak to her, or my heart will burst with helpless rage.   (*Exit*)

END OF THE FOURTH ACT

ACT V

Enter LADY BELVILLE, ANGELICA *and* HARRIET

ANGELICA: Nay, madam, you will spoil all, if you give way to this tenderness—instead of tears, you should rejoice at his distraction.

HARRIET: Aye, pray madam, keep up your spirits: do not let them sink in the very last stage.

LADY BELVILLE: I beg your pardon: I am ashamed of my weakness; but indeed I cannot help it. Pray, give me leave one moment—I am ashamed of these foolish tears—they will soon be over, and I shall recover.

ANGELICA: Madam, we have betrayed him into the very condition we could wish—mad with shame and jealousy, which we must heighten, and play upon, till we have made him as much afraid to look at a cap or a pettycoat, excepting your ladyship's, as a beaten coward is to look at the point of a naked sword—and face him you must; we will take no denial.

LADY BELVILLE: But in what manner shall I approach him?

ANGELICA: O, as flying into the arms of your lover, by all means—totally abandoned to gallantry and conjugal revenge.

Enter TOWNLY

HARRIET: Well, Mr. Townly, what is he about?

TOWNLY: I could hear nothing but a confused rage, and a violent exclamation now and then.

LADY BELVILLE: Pray, sir, is he among the recruits again?

TOWNLY: No, madam: Lucy met him on the stairs, and prevailed upon him to go into the little room at the end of the gallery; do you intend an interview with him, madam?

ANGELICA: O by all means—see him with spirit, madam; draw your resentment; exert your pride; and dart a virtuous indignation on him. Ah! I wish I had the handling of him—I would make him as humble in half an hour as a disgraced minister in the hands of public justice.

Enter LUCY

HARRIET: Well, Mrs. Engine,[1] how is my lover, your criminal? have you tortured him? is he on the rack?

LUCY: O madam, I had such a piece of work with him at first: I thought he would have ran mad, or have jumped out of the window to come at the lady.

LADY BELVILLE: And pray, Mrs. Lucy, in what temper is he now?

LUCY: You shall hear, madam.   When I found he was in such a rage to see the lady, in order to quiet him I told him it was impossible, for that the lady was gone out of the house—And the captain with her? says he, ha, ha, ha! staring like a madman—No, no, no, sir, says I, the captain is in the house still—that appeased him a little; so to make his poor tender heart quite easy, I let him know that the captain stayed behind by the lady's particular orders, till matters were prepared by her that she might return to him with more safety—Return to him! cried he. What, does she return to him?—O yes, sir, says I, yes, yes, she returns indeed; he, he, he, he! and I understand they are to spend the evening together at a certain apartment of his in Leicester fields[2]—ha, ha, ha!

OMNES: Ha, ha, ha!

ANGELICA: Excellent.

LUCY: At which, I thought verily he would have expired with rage— he tore off his grenadier's cap, dashed it into the fire; and after fretting, bursting crying, and raving, he flounced into a great chair, leaned his head on one hand, and with the other, both legs, and every part of him, shook and beat the devil's tattoo—as if he and the old gentleman were to set out that instant.

OMNES: Ha, ha, ha!

ANGELICA: Excellent symptoms, madam, excellent—now is the very crisis of his disease, and the very moment to effect his cure.

LUCY: I asked him if he would steal out with me through the private door of the laundry, into the garden.   He snapt me up—No; I will stay till that lady returns—then earnestly begged, when she came back, that he might see her before the captain.

ANGELICA: To our wish—Lucy, go bring him into this room; we shall be ready for him.

[1] i.e. Mrs. Artful: engine (with accent on the second syllable) meant artfulness.
[2] Now Leicester Square.

LUCY: Yes, madam—O, I forgot to tell you, madam, your brother is come.

ANGELICA: How do you know?

LUCY: Sam is below, madam: the captain was set down a little while ago at Arthur's; he is but just stepped home with the general, and will be here in five minutes.

ANGELICA: Very well; go you to Mr. Jackson. (*Exit* LUCY) Now, madam, we have got another accomplice—a dying swain of that lady's, and a brother of mine; a real captain, as wild as myself, who will be ready to come into any mischief for your ladyship's service.

LADY BELVILLE: I am obliged to you, my dear; but I hope my interview with my lord will render all farther expedients unnecessary.

ANGELICA: I hope so too. Come, then, madam; let us remove to make way for our hero—and be sure you act the scene with spirits; keep it up, keep it up, madam; give him no quarter: should the gentleman be violent, we will be near to second you, and my life we manage him amongst us. Your ladyship's hand if you please: I think it will be very strange if so many women have not mischief enough in their heads to tame one man. (*Hands her out*)

HARRIET: Ha, ha, ha! fine spirits, Mr. Townly—are you not afraid to venture on them?

TOWNLY: Just as much as you are, madam, to venture on the spirits of her brother: I love her for them.

LUCY: (*Without*) Don't go in there: this way; this way, sir.

TOWNLY: Here they come: we must begone.

HARRIET: Quick! quick, quick! (*They run off*)

Enter LORD BELVILLE *and* LUCY

LUCY: Lord, sir! you were going into the very room where that cursed captain is.

LORD BELVILLE: Was I? I know not what I do—I am distracted.

LUCY: But, sir, I cannot imagine why you are so eager to see this lady—of what service can she be to you?

LORD BELVILLE: Prithee, ask no questions. I tell thee, it will save us all; it will save my life—I cannot live without seeing her.

LUCY: Bless us! sure she has bewitched you.

LORD BELVILLE: She has, she has—I feel the charm gnawing at my heart—go, fly, attend her coming: and, dear Lucy, as you would save my life and be rewarded with gratitude and affluence, let not the captain see her; be careful, dear girl.

LUCY: I will; I will, sir.

LORD BELVILLE: Go; go.

LUCY: I am gone, sir. (*Exit*)

LORD BELVILLE: Is it possible a woman of her prudence, of her pride, of her virtue could fall so suddenly? I thought her heart the mansion of fidelity, and virtuous affection—it cannot be—there must be some delusion in it—and yet jealousy—aye, that fiend—what rage, what vengeance will it not work in a woman's heart? I feel its poison in my own. Perhaps they are together now—now—now, while I am on the rack—my conduct, my neglect of her—I deserve it; but my vice, my profligacy is no plea for hers—no mitigation. Should the world know of my disgrace, how their malice would exult—the women would applaud their conduct; call it spirit, justice. O, how their tongues would ring with slander, and their invention teem with complicated falsehoods—aye, but truth, truth would be a sharper poignard in my heart, than all their malice could invent.

Enter LUCY

LUCY: The lady is come, sir.

LORD BELVILLE: Where is she?

LUCY: Below, waiting to see the captain.

LORD BELVILLE: To see the captain—Zounds! why did you not shew her up here?

LUCY: She asked for the captain, sir.

LORD BELVILLE: 'Sdeath! run down before he sees her. Quick; fly.

LUCY: But sir—the captain——

LORD BELVILLE: Distraction! I tell you he must not see her—I shall run mad if he does.

LUCY: Well—but, sir—

LORD BELVILLE: Not a word. (*Pushes her out*) Should they meet before I see her, she were irrecoverably lost. This perverseness of of our nature is incredible—but now I am in danger of losing her, she is dearer to my heart than all the lewd variety that ever swayed it: I tremble with shame and apprehension. She comes—'tis a dreadful interview, but I must bear it.

Enter LADY BELVILLE

184

LADY BELVILLE: Where is my life, my love, my other self? let me fly into his arms—Ah! bless me! who—what—what are you? heavens, what monster is this?

LORD BELVILLE: What your infidelity has made him, madam—

LADY BELVILLE: My eyes deceive me sure! that face and voice methinks I know—but the dress, the mien—I cannot believe my senses.

LORD BELVILLE: Madam, you may—why I am in this unseemly garb, I shall explain hereafter: a more tender, dreadful subject must engross the present moment. I see, madam, you are disappointed and alarmed; I know your rapture was not meant for a vulgar husband's, but a youthful lover's arms.

LADY BELVILLE: I understand you not.

LORD BELVILLE: Nay, madam, assume not strangeness or disguise—hide your shame you cannot, for I know each particular of your conduct in this house.

LADY BELVILLE: I am glad of it, my lord—for then you know each particular of your own deserts.

LORD BELVILLE: How, madam! do you justify yourself?

LADY BELVILLE: I need not—your example does that, my lord; for it hath taught me that laws of wedlock are made only for vulgar souls, but to the great they are mere cobwebs gallantry may break through at will—and since in these our polished days, this nice modish reasoning extends it to the polite in either sex, I am determined it shall be the great ruler of my conduct and affections.

LORD BELVILLE: This is amazing! is this a doctrine fit for modest tongues, or for a husband's ears? does it suit your sex, your rank, or the noble house you sprung from?

LADY BELVILLE: That reasoning with tenfold force let me retort on you —on you, my lord, whose knowledge sways in a nation's council, and oft suggests its wisest measures—on you, I say, whose blood has run for ages in noblest veins, in fields and senates distinguished by applauding millions for dignity and rarest worth—yet you, with these proud monitors in your heart, can set a base example to your wife, your children, and the world; and suffer your illustrious roll of recorded greatness to be defaced and stained by the vile indulgence of a distempered appetite.

LORD BELVILLE: I own my follies, and can urge no defence—but you, madam, pray reflect; as yet your honour is safe.

LADY BELVILLE: I can but be miserable: and when the business of my life was to please an ungrateful man, what was my recompence? a menaced separation!

LORD BELVILLE: Forget it.

LADY BELVILLE: Never.

LORD BELVILLE: I will make any atonement.

LADY BELVILLE: You can make none.

LORD BELVILLE: The threat was not real—only the peevish policy of angry vice, impatient of detection and reproach; not the dictates of my heart, which in the height of all its wanderings ever loved you: then let my avowed contrition and amendment, and my faithful tears, solicit the return of your affection. The business of this night has awakened and roused me from a dream of vice, which fills my mind with terror and self-disgrace—my own shame —the strangeness of your revenge with a giddy thoughtless youth —think what your rashness leads to; and let me beg by the love you once made me believe your heart had treasured up for mine, that you will suspend your purpose, and all resentment, but till to-morrow.

LADY BELVILLE: Well, my lord—so far you shall prevail.

LORD BELVILLE: Madam, neither the time, the place, nor my present circumstances will admit of longer expostulation—by my dress you may imagine I am in a most ridiculous situation; it flashes shame into my face, and will not let me describe what I have suffered. I own I have merited my disgrace—but my life is in danger, and only your influence can save me.

LADY BELVILLE: My lord, I understand you not—my influence on whom?

LORD BELVILLE: Since you must know it, madam—your lover, your gallant, your captain is the very man that has thus equipped me, and even menaces my life.

LADY BELVILLE: O, my presaging heart! I heard him mention an impostor, a villain, who by a feigned name and false contract had seduced his sister, and driven her to distraction.

LORD BELVILLE: I am that villain.

LADY BELVILLE: You, my lord! impossible! you cannot be so black, so deep in vice.

186

LORD BELVILLE: Do not wound me with farther questions—I am that wretch.

LADY BELVILLE: Unhappy ruined man!

LORD BELVILLE: Pray—no more—it shocks, it wounds my tenderest nature.

LADY BELVILLE: If your vicious spirits cannot bear reflecting on the deed, what must the wretched lady feel whom your perfidy has undone? What must her brother, parents, kindred, and what must my resentment feel?

LORD BELVILLE: I will make any reparation.

LADY BELVILLE: Your crime is beyond atonement, past the scope of mercy—justice forbids my interposition, or farther intercourse with such a man. Farewell for ever—tears are all the comfort pity or justice can afford you.

LORD BELVILLE: You shall not go.

LADY BELVILLE: I will.

LORD BELVILLE: Death shall not part us.

LADY BELVILLE: You strive in vain—I can call assistance.

LORD BELVILLE: You will not be so cruel?

LADY BELVILLE: I will. Help! help!

LORD BELVILLE: Inhuman, relentless woman.

Enter ANGELICA *and* SERJEANT, CORPORAL *and* RECRUITS

ANGELICA: Seize him! Villain, let go the lady.

LORD BELVILLE: Never.

ANGELICA: Force him; cut off his hold—so—secure, bind and take him aboard immediately. Come, madam, we will protect you—as for that vile man, you shall never see or hear of him more. Madam you have behaved like a heroine—the day is our own, madam—victory! victory!

CORPORAL: Why my dear comrade, you are a damned obstropulous fellow, I find. What the devil—was you going about to ravish the captain's wife before his face—hah?

Enter CAPTAIN MANWARING *and* SERVANT

CAPTAIN: Who are these, Sam?

SERVANT: Some of your honour's recruits.

CAPTAIN: What are the fellows doing here? hark'ee corporal, what business have you in this room?

CORPORAL: Why, sir, and please your honour, we are commanded to take this man, our comrade here, into an arrest.

CAPTAIN: What is his crime?

RECRUIT: No crime at all, sir—he was only going to ravish a lady, that's all.

CAPTAIN: What do you mean, you rascal?

RECRUIT: Indeed, I have told you all I mean.

CAPTAIN: Let him go.   Fall back.   Who are you, fellow?

LORD BELVILLE: A man.

CAPTAIN: A man, sir—speak to be understood, or I shall break your head.

LORD BELVILLE: Sir, you have the appearance of a gentleman—I put myself under your protection, and beg your assistance.

CAPTAIN: Explain!

LORD BELVILLE: I have got into a kind of enchantment here—am confined by lawless power: an incensed wife, and a captain—an enraged military stripling—have conspired to wrong my honour: nay, to destroy my life.

CAPTAIN: What the devil is this? how the fellow stares and chafes!   Be cool and explain, friend—what do you mean by a captain and a wife?

LORD BELVILLE: Sir, the truth must be my apology: you shall know the whole.   In short, sir, I came here to the lady of the house, upon an affair of gallantry.

CAPTAIN: Gallantry! with the lady of this house!

LORD BELVILLE: I beg, sir, you will hear me.

CAPTAIN: Do you know, scoundrel, that the lady of this house is my sister?

LORD BELVILLE: Your sister, sir?

CAPTAIN: Yes, rascal, my sister.

LORD BELVILLE: Soh! here is another of the family—there is no end of my perplexity.

CAPTAIN: This is some impostor—go, call my sister, or Harriet, and order the serjeant hither.   Take down your men, corporal, and be ready below.   (*Exeunt* CORPORAL, RECRUITS, *and* SERVANT)

LORD BELVILLE: If you will hear me patiently, sir, however criminal I may be, you will find I am no impostor.

CAPTAIN: Quick: speak; who are you?

LORD BELVILLE: A lord.

CAPTAIN: A lord?

LORD BELVILLE: Patience, pray sir: though I blush to own it, that is my rank—Lord Belville.

CAPTAIN: Impossible—how came you in that disguise?

LORD BELVILLE: Your brother, sir, imposed it on me.

CAPTAIN: The fellow is certainly mad—my brother—I have no brother.

LORD BELVILLE: Your sister's brother then, or one to whom she gives that appellation—who like me I find was here upon intrigue.

CAPTAIN: Sir, I really do not understand your story: it seems to me most improbable; all I can say to it at present is, that if you are Lord Belville—for I have not the honour of knowing your person—you shall have redress. Let us go in and see this brother, and try to clear up this affair. O, here comes one of the ladies.

Enter HARRIET

CAPTAIN: My dearest Harriet.

HARRIET: Welcome from France, sir; in health I hope—not wounded, we have heard.

CAPTAIN: Your kind wishes, madam, and auspicious love protected me.

HARRIET: By your letter, we expected you in town yesterday.

CAPTAIN: When I wrote, madam, that was my hope—but soldiers and lovers you know are never at their own command: but here is a gentleman tells me I have got a brother, an officer, since I have been abroad.

HARRIET: O, sir, your humble servant—pray, Captain Manwaring, let me have the honour of introducing you to my friend—one Mr Jackson, a Staffordshire gentleman, a person of strict honour, and a gallant of mine, sir—ha, ha, ha!

CAPTAIN: Prithee, Harriet, what is the meaning of all this? you are all at cross purposes—this is not Mr. Jackson; this is Lord Belville.

HARRIET: Aye, aye, that may be: but a nobleman may have a travelling name too—occasionally—ha, ha, ha! when he goes upon an amorous expedition, you know—ha, ha, ha! and would draw a lady's honour into an ambuscade by false intelligence. Ha, ha, ha!

LORD BELVILLE: So, so—recovered, I see.

HARRIET: But be his name and title what it will, he is to be my wedded spouse, sir—as soon as his grandpapa dies—ha, ha, ha! are you not, Mr. Jackson? ha, ha, ha! nay, nay, do not look so strange upon me, and so angry, my dear—what, do you turn away from me, false man? I hope you will not be so base as to deny it, sir—captain, I have a contract under his hand.

LORD BELVILLE: So, madam, you have found your wits, I see.

HARRIET: I have, sir—ha, ha, ha! just where you lost yours.

LORD BELVILLE: Your West Country dialect, and dowdy rusticity?

HARRIET: All gone, sir—I wore them only to oblige a couple of loving turtles, who are now billing and cooing—an officer, a brother of mine, and a female friend of yours, one Lady Belville.

LORD BELVILLE: Damnation!

HARRIET: You may fume and fret, sir; but it is very true.

ANGELICA (*Without*) Why is he not aboard? send up a file of men, and take him away this instant.

HARRIET: Here the captain comes—and one of the gallantest officers in the service, I assure you.

Enter ANGELICA

ANGELICA: Why are you not on board, sir? how dare you loiter here?

LORD BELVILLE: Villain, let this answer you. (*Snatches the* CAPTAIN's *sword and thrusts at* ANGELICA)

ANGELICA and HARRIET: Ah!

CAPTAIN: Hold, sir: are you mad?

HARRIET: O, heavens! have a care what you do, sir—she is a woman—she is a woman.

LORD BELVILLE: Let me go: he shall not live.

ANGELICA: Pray, sir, forgive me: on my knees I beg your pardon; indeed there is no wrong done you—for I am but a woman, a foolish frighted woman.

LORD BELVILLE: What means the villain?

CAPTAIN: She tells you the truth, sir: patience one moment—she is a woman, sir, upon my honour; and my sister.

LORD BELVILLE: A woman!

HARRIET: She is indeed, sir; as errant a woman as I am.

LORD BELVILLE: I will not be imposed on so. Let me go, sir.

CAPTAIN: You shall not stir—nay, no struggling: I insist upon my sword.

LORD BELVILLE: You have it, sir—but it shall not end so.

HARRIET: Stand up, Angelica.

ANGELICA: Dear Harriet, I am frighted out of my wits—I shall never recover my spirits.

CAPTAIN: You wild creature! what in the name of madness have you all been about here? and how came you into these breeches, madam?

ANGELICA: Ask no questions: I am almost dead with fright.

CAPTAIN: Almost dead with fright! you mad creature, you had like to have been quite dead with a sword. Is this your captain, my lord? Why, this is a downright, wild, impertinent, giddy female—and my sister.

LORD BELVILLE: Sir, that shall not pass upon me.

CAPTAIN: Nay, my lord, if you will not believe me—take her into the next room, and convince yourself.

HARRIET: O fye, captain.

CAPTAIN: Nay, upon my honour, I think she deserves some punishment for her frolic.

ANGELICA: Very well, sir! I may see you with your love-sick, complaining face on—fretting, raving, and begging me to be your advocate to this lady—I may.

LORD BELVILLE: And are you really a woman?

ANGELICA: At your service, Mr. Jackson—as sure as you are a ridiculous man.

HARRIET: In short, sir, every person you have seen to-night in this house, except this captain, have been as rank cheats as yourself. We have all been acting a sort of comedy at your expence, the design of which was to shew you to yourself, and the justice of it to revenge your cruelty to the best of women.

LORD BELVILLE: Is this true? do not deceive me, I charge you.

HARRIET: I do not, sir.

LORD BELVILLE: And is this person your sister, sir?

CAPTAIN: Upon my honour.

LORD BELVILLE: And pray, madam, where is Lady Belville now?

ANGELICA: Below with your nephew: bathed in tears for the unkind part we compelled her to assume, lest it should hurt your peace, or raise your indignation.

LORD BELVILLE: Lead me to her: let me throw myself at her feet; implore her pardon for the wrongs I have done her; and with a heart exulting with joy and revived fondness, thank her for the happy change her virtue hath wrought in it.

HARRIET: My lord, I fear that manner of approaching her will be too precipitate—it may overcome her spirits.

LORD BELVILLE: Be you, then, my heart's welcome harbinger: tell her, how it lauds her conduct, admires her virtuous stratagem, and pants to give her amplest, endless proofs of its gratitude and fidelity.

HARRIET: My lord, as willingly as if the happiness of the tidings were all my own.   (*Exit*)

CAPTAIN: Well, Lady Errant, is your fight pretty well over? suppose you had got yourself run through the body by your frolic—

ANGELICA: If I had, I believe few would have pitied me.

CAPTAIN: Pitied you! no, for you richly deserved it—but what could provoke you to such a wild, romantic indiscretion?

ANGELICA: That which provokes most people to indiscretions, brother: whim, giddiness, and the dear desire of doing what we like; but his lordship's sword, and a little reflection, have thoroughly cured me of my folly.

LORD BELVILLE: I ask your pardon, madam, for the terror I put you in —but you really had provoked me beyond human bearing.

ANGELICA: I believe, my lord, we did carry our mirth a little too far; I fear beyond the bounds of decency.   I assure you, my lady was most averse to it: the imprudence and rashness of the business were all mine; and I ask your lordship's pardon—but we had got you into our power, and when women have power, my lord, they seldom know where to stop; the vanity of shewing it will hurry us into indecorums we never intended, which was my case: but I was like to have paid for my frolic with my life.

LORD BELVILLE: It might have been fatal indeed—but we seldom see indiscretion till the ugly monster stares us in the face.   I think, madam, we must e'en do like rash duellists—mutually exchange forgiveness; profit by our errors; and become better friends: for my part I confess I richly deserved all the ignominy and torture your wicked imagination made me suffer.

Enter LADY BELVILLE, HARRIET, *and* TOWNLY

LADY BELVILLE: Prostrate on the earth, let me implore your pardon for my indiscretion this night.

LORD BELVILLE: That penitent posture should be mine: rise, madam— my arms, my heart is the place you must for ever dwell in.

LADY BELVILLE: Did you but know, my lord, what I endured while I assumed that levity which I saw draw tears from your relenting heart, all your resentment would turn to pity and forgiveness.

LORD BELVILLE: My dear, the virtuous simulation I not only pardon, but applaud, for it hath made me think—made me to see your worth, and my own demerit. It was your duty to check, to wound, to kill the vice that was assassinating your peace and my honour—and I thank you all, who have contributed to expose me to myself.

LADY BELVILLE: My lord, this goodness is too much.

LORD BELVILLE: Instead of grieving, I will rejoice at what is past; and proudly tell the world—I am not ashamed to own, nor to forsake my vice.

LADY BELVILLE: My lord, I have a favour to request, which, on this occasion, I am sure you will have a pleasure in granting.

LORD BELVILLE: My dear, command it.

LADY BELVILLE: Mr. Townly loves this lady: their affections are mutual.

LORD BELVILLE: Was he in the plot against me too?

TOWNLY: Not as a principal, my lord, only as a humble accessory—but if your lordship has a mind to be revenged upon me, for my part in it—and upon the wicked contriver of all the mischief—here the culprits kneel and beg your sentence.

CAPTAIN: Pray, my lord, be revenged upon her—let matrimony be her punishment.

LORD BELVILLE: No, it shall be her reward: and every kindness in my power shall wait upon the happy union.

ANGELICA: Generous indeed, my lord, and much kinder than I deserve: but I shall be more careful for the future to merit your lordship's favour, than I have been.

CAPTAIN: Well, Harriet, does not this example give you courage?

ANGELICA: Nay, nay, she shall give you her hand—her heart you have already: I know that. I will not go to church without her, I am resolved—she shall not laugh at me. Here: take her; take her, brother.

HARRIET: Nay, dear Angelica—

ANGELICA: Nay, nay: you shall give him your hand.

HARRIET: Well, well; do not be so violent: sure I can do it without being forced—there.

193

ANGELICA: Why, that is well done.

CAPTAIN: My charmer! now, Madam Angelica, whenever you lead the way, depend upon it, we shall follow you.

ANGELICA: Oh! you are a daring hero—we all know.

HARRIET: I hope your ladyship will prevail upon Mr. Jackson to favour us with his company to-night, if his Staffordshire gravity will permit him to sup abroad so late.

OMNES: Ha, ha, ha!

LORD BELVILLE: Ha, ha! with pleasure, madam. He shall sit in his penitentials as a public example of ridicule and reformation—and with the captain's leave, he will preserve them as relics of his folly, and laughing mementos of this night's vicissitudes.

CAPTAIN: Your lordship has my consent to canonize them; if you please.

ANGELICA: What a deal of bustle, deceit, farce, and folly we have had in our three hours adventures—all of which I shall sum up in an extempore couplet; and then, good folks, to mirth and supper with what appetite you may—

> Our plot has finished just as we intended:
> The wife's redressed, the husband schooled and mended.

FINIS

Epilogue

Silence, ye Gods above, and Critics below—before, behind, all round
    I pray!
We are going fairly to try the Author of the play.
And that no charms of eloquence may influence the Court—with your
    permission
The stile and measure shall be those of honest Frances Harris's peti-
    tion.[1]
Besides, that every person here may thoroughly understand the Cause,
Know that the probable and moral are the true fundamental Parnas-
    sian Laws.
The Judges the judicious few; the Jury, the Ladies; and the rival Poet-
    asters the counsel for the Crown
For those you know are feed of course to hunt all Dullness down
Except their own.   The Court being formed—the Attorney-General,
    no little half-strained, cautious, bashful nibbler,
But a thorough-paced, pilfering, French-farce, sousing scribbler,
With pert Corinthian front, incessant laugh, and the true sheer-wit
    sneer,
He thus opens the Cause—My Lords, hem, hem, the hero of the piece
    being a man of sense, a senator, and a peer,
We, the Bedford wits agree, his punishment is too low, farcical and
    severe;
Nay, illegal—and for this reason, my Lords, hem, hem, because
That peers are privileged in *Vice* by Custom's laws.
We allow that making the husband believe the wife had made reprisals
    was well enough;
But to dress him in a Grenadier's cap was such vile low stuff;
Then making him run after every woman he sees is quite out of Nature;
My Lords, there can be no such man—therefore 'tis *Scandalum Magna-*
    tum—not a general satire:
From which premises, my Lords, just Criticism must conclude

[1] Cf. Jonathan Swift, *The Petition of Mrs. Frances Harris* (1711).

That this honourable Court will damn the piece as low, farcical and
    rude.

My Lords, hem, hem, I am counsel on the other side, and shall cut this
    matter very short,

Having resolved not to take up the time unnecessarily of this honour-
    able Court.

Mr. Attorney's critical conscience has been so extremely nice

To condemn the pains inflicted on our Leviathan of Vice;

To which we answer, that all comic punishment from the Nature of the
    crime should grow,

And just like that, be great, or small, serious, or merry, high or low.

He urges too that there is no such husband as Belville, but that, my
    Lords, we look upon as mere raillery,

Especially as the contrary may be proved this very instant even from
    the middle gallery.

Do but look—observe how close and snug the sly ones sit!

And then, my Lords, below—see how they are scattered up and down
    the pit.

There is one there, I am sure you all know—that grave spark with the
    full wig, and mourning clothes,

My Lords, he sits near that very handsome gentleman with the wide
    mouth, long chin, and crooked nose.

Nay, and could we narrowly inspect the husbands in the boxes,

I fancy, my Lords, we might find there too a few sly, old lurching
    foxes.

So that to Mr. Attorney's whole charge and arguments we plead

That all is common-place, frivolous, and mere Bedford Coffeehouse
    criticism indeed.

But, my Lords, should the reasons we have urged against rigid censure
    all fail,

We have one still left that we are sure will on your Equity prevail.

'Tis this—know that for the future, we at this House, like the other,
    intend

With sheer variety to make the Town our friend.

Spare us but to-night, and we promise that next year

You shall have another new-vamped Earl of Essex here.

The Tears and Trials of Parnassus too, and in martial spirit to send you
    home,

Epilogue

I will strut another Lieutenant-General Honeycombe;[1]
And to shew our Genius and willingness to merit public praise,
If we cannot write new we will swell our old French farces into new
    British plays.
And then that your taste for true Humour may be raised, improved,
    and elegantly fed,
You shall have a whole shopboard of taylors—without one head.
In such ingenious works errors must be, small ones we know you'll
    spare
For lack of wit you have lately borne elsewhere,
And our dullness humbly begs but neighbour's fare.

[1] The references are to Henry Brooke's *Earl of Essex* (first performed in Dublin in 1750), Robert Lloyd's ode for music, *The Tears and Trials of Parnassus,* and George Colman's *Polly Honeycombe*: all these had first performances at Drury Lane in December 1760, and were in the current repertory.

The Man of the World

A COMEDY

In Five Acts

Theatrical Note

The Man of the World was often revived. Among other productions, two months before the author's death Fawcett and Mrs. Mattocks played Sir Pertinax and Lady Rodolpha at Covent Garden, where G. F. Cooke and Mrs. Glover were to appear for the first time in these leads in 1802; at Drury Lane in 1822 there were Edmund Kean and Miss Booth; and in the same year at Bath Charles Young and Mrs. Bunn: Young appeared with Mrs. Chatterley at Covent Garden the following year. Samuel Phelps gave a striking performance at Sadler's Wells on 27 November, 1851, and was very highly praised—indeed John Masson, the Chairman of the Scottish and Hanover Park Club, in writing his congratulations praised Phelp's Scottish accent, and preferred his performance to those of Cooke and Young. More recently, there was an amateur production by the Swansea Little Theatre in 1951, and it had successful professional performances at the Pitlochry Festival Theatre during the 1962 season, when William McAllister played Sir Pertinax and Rosamund Dixon Lady Rodolpha.

The Man of the World

COVENT GARDEN
10 MAY, 1781

SADLERS WELLS
27 NOVEMBER, 1851

Dramatis Personae[1]

	COVENT GARDEN	SADLERS WELLS
Sir Pertinax Macsycophant	Mr. Macklin	Mr. Phelps
Egerton	Mr. Lewis	Mr. F. Robinson
Lord Lumbercourt	Mr. Wilson	Mr. Barrett
Sidney	Mr. Aicken	Mr. Graham
Melville	Mr. Clarke	Mr. H. Mellon
Counsellor Plausible	Mr. Wewitzer	Mr. Wilkins
Serjeant Eitherside	Mr. Booth	Mr. Williams
Sam	Mr. J. Wilson	Mr. Meagreson
John	Mr. Thompson	Mr. C. Fenton
Tomlins	Mr. Sharpe	Mr. C. Mortimer
Lady Macsycophant	Miss Platt	Mrs. H. Marston
Lady Rodolpha Lumbercourt	Miss Younge	Mrs. Fitzpatrick
Constantia	Miss Satchell	Miss Lucy Rafter
Betty	Mrs. Wilson	Miss Eliza Travers
Nanny	Mrs. Daveneth	Mrs. Graham

Time: three hours.

Scene: Sir Pertinax Macsycophant's Library, in his
House ten miles from London.

[1] In the 1770 MS., while the other characters are the same, there are Sir Hector and Lady Mackcrafty and their son Montgomery.

The Man of the World

ACT I

A Library. Enter BETTY *and* SAM

BETTY: The postman is at the gate, Sam; pray step and take in the letters.

SAM: John the gardener is gone for them, Mrs. Betty.

BETTY: Bid John bring them to me, Sam: tell him I am here in the library.

SAM: I'll send him to your ladyship in a crack, madam.   (*Exit*)

Enter NANNY

NANNY: Miss Constantia desires to speak to you, Mrs. Betty.

BETTY: How is she now? any better, Nanny?

NANNY: Something; but very low spirited still.   I verily believe it is as you say.

BETTY: O, I would take my book oath of it.   I can not be deceived in that point, Nanny—aye, aye, her business is done, she is certainly breeding, depend upon it.

NANNY: Why, so the housekeeper thinks too.

BETTY: Nay, I know the father—the man that ruined her.

NANNY: The deuce you do?

BETTY: As sure as you are alive, Nanny, or I am greatly deceived— and yet—I can't be deceived neither.   Was not that the cook that came galloping so hard over the common just now?

NANNY: The same: how very hard he galloped—he has been but three quarters of an hour, he says, coming from Hyde Park Corner.

BETTY: And what time will the family be down?

NANNY: He has orders to have dinner ready by five; there are to be lawyers and a great deal of company here—he fancies there is to be a private wedding to-night between our young Master Charles and Lord Lumbercourt's daughter, the Scotch lady, who he says is just come post from Bath in order to be married to him.

203

BETTY: Aye, aye, Lady Rodolpha—nay, like enough, for I know it
has been talked of a good while—well, go tell Miss Constantia that
I will be with her immediately.

NANNY: I shall, Mrs. Betty. (*Exit*)

BETTY: Soh! I find they all think the impertinent creature is breeding—that's pure! it will soon reach my lady's ears, I warrant.

Enter JOHN

BETTY: Well, John, ever a letter for me?

JOHN: No, Mrs. Betty, but here is one for Miss Constantia.

BETTY: Give it me—Hum! my lady's hand.

JOHN: And here is one which the postman says is for my young master
—but it's a strange direction. (*Reads*) 'To Charles Egerton,
Esquire'—

BETTY: O, yes, yes—that is for Master Charles, John; for he has
dropped his father's name of Macsycophant, and has taken up
that of Egerton—the parliament has ordered it.

JOHN: The parliament? prithee, why so, Mrs. Betty?

BETTY: Why you must know, John, that my lady, his mother, was an
Egerton by her father—she stole a match with our old master, for
which all her family on both sides have hated Sir Pertinax and the
whole crew of the Macsycophants ever since.

JOHN: Except Master Charles, Mrs. Betty.

BETTY: O, they doat upon him, though he is a Macsycophant; he is the
pride of all my lady's family: and so, John, my lady's uncle, Sir
Stanley Egerton dying an old bachelor, and as said before, mor-
tally hating our old master—and all the crew of the Macsycophants—left his whole estate to Master Charles, who was his
godson—but on condition that he should drop his father's name
of Macsycophant, and take up that of Egerton—and that is
the reason, John, why the parliament has made him change his
name.

JOHN: I am glad that Master Charles has got the estate, however, for he
is a sweet tempered gentleman.

BETTY: As ever lived—but come John, as I know you love Miss Constantia, and are fond of being where she is, I will make you happy
—you shall carry her letter to her.

JOHN: Shall I, Mrs. Betty? I am very much obliged to you—where is
she?

BETTY: In the housekeeper's room, settling the dessert—give me Mr. Egerton's letter, and I'll leave it on the table in his dressing room. I see it's from his brother Sandy. So—now go and deliver your letter to your sweetheart, John.

JOHN: That I will—and I am much beholden to you for the favour of letting me carry it to her: for though she should never have me, yet I shall always love her, and wish to be near her—she is so sweet a creature. Your servant, Mrs. Betty. (*Exit*)

BETTY: Your servant, John. Ha, ha, ha! poor fellow—he perfectly doats on her, and daily follows her about with nosegays and fruit and the first of every thing in the season. Aye, and my young master Charles too is in as bad a way as the gardener—in short, every body loves her—and that's one reason why I hate her! For my part, I wonder what the deuce the men see in her—a creature that was taken in for charity—I am sure she's not so handsome. I wish she was out of the family once—if she was, I might then stand a chance of being my lady's favourite myself— aye, and perhaps of getting one of my young masters for a sweetheart—or at least the chaplain; but as to him, there would be no such great catch if I could get him. I will try for him, however —and my first step shall be to tell the doctor all I have discovered about Constantia's intrigues with her spark at Hadley—yes—that will do—for the doctor loves to talk with me—loves to hear me talk too—and I verily believe, he, he, he! that he has a sneaking kindness for me; and this story will make him have a good opinion of my honesty—and that, I am sure, will be one step towards— Oh! bless me! here he comes—and my young master with him. I'll watch an opportunity to speak to him as soon as he is alone— for I will blow her up, I am resolved—as great a favourite and as cunning as she is. (*Exit*)

Enter EGERTON *in great warmth and emotion;* SIDNEY *following, as in conversation*

SIDNEY: Nay, dear Charles, but why are you so impetuous?—why do you break from me so abruptly?

EGERTON: (*With great warmth*) I have done, sir—you have refused—I have nothing more to say upon the subject. I am satisfied.

SIDNEY: (*With a glow of tender friendship*) Come, come—correct this warmth; it is the only weak ingredient in your nature, and you ought to watch it carefully. If I am wrong, I will submit without reserve; but consider the nature of your request—and how it would affect me. From your earliest youth, your father has honoured me with the care of your education, and the general conduct of your mind—and however singular and morose his temper may be to others, to me he has ever been respectful and liberal. I am now under his roof too—and because I will not abet an unwarrantable passion by an abuse of my sacred character, in marrying you beneath your rank, and in direct opposition to your father's hopes and happiness—you blame me—you angrily break from me—and call me unkind.

EGERTON: (*With tenderness and conviction*) Dear Sidney—for my warmth I stand condemned: but for my marriage with Constantia, I think I can justify it upon every principle of filial duty, honour—and worldly prudence.

SIDNEY: Only make that appear, Charles, and you know you may command me.

EGERTON: (*With great filial regret*) I am sensible how unseemly it appears in a son to descant on the unamiable passions of a parent; but—as we are alone, and friends—I cannot help observing in my own defence, that when a father will not allow the use of reason to any of his family—when his pursuit of greatness makes him a slave abroad, only to be a tyrant at home—when a narrow partiality to Scotland, on every trivial occasion, provokes him to enmity even with his wife and children, only because they dare give a national preference where they think it most justly due—and when, merely to gratify his own ambitions, he would marry his son into a family he detests, (*With great warmth*) sure, Sidney, a son thus circumstanced—from the dignity of human reason and the feelings of a loving heart—has a right—not only to protest against the blindness of a parent, but to pursue those measures that virtue and happiness point out.

SIDNEY: The violent temper of Sir Pertinax, I own, cannot be defended on many occasions, but still—your intended alliance with Lord Lumbercourt—

EGERTON: (*With great impatience*) O, contemptible! a trifling, quaint, haughty, voluptuous, servile tool—the mere lackey of party and corruption; who, for the prostitution of nearly thirty years and the ruin of a noble fortune, has had the despicable satisfaction, and the infamous honour of being kicked up and kicked down—kicked in and kicked out—just as the insolence, compassion, or convenience of leaders predominated: and now, being forsaken by all parties, his whole political consequence amounts to the power of franking a letter[1]—and the right honourable privilege of not paying a tradesman's bill.

SIDNEY: But, my dear Charles, you are not to wed my lord—but his daughter.

EGERTON: Who is as disagreeable to me for a companion, as her father for a friend, or an ally.

SIDNEY: What—her Scotch accent, I suppose, offends you?

EGERTON: No, upon my honour, not in the least; I think it entertaining in her—but were it otherwise—in decency—and indeed in national affection, being a Scotchman myself—I can have no objection to her on that account: besides, she is my near relation.

SIDNEY: So I understand. But, pray, Charles, how came Lady Rodolpha, who, I find, was born in England, to be bred in Scotland?

EGERTON: From the dotage of an old, formal, obstinate, stiff, rich, Scotch grandmother; who, upon a promise of leaving this grandchild all her fortune, would have the girl sent to her in Scotland, when she was but a year old—and there she has been ever since, bred up with this old lady in all the vanity and unlimited indulgence that fondness and admiration could bestow on a spoiled child —a fancied beauty and a pretended wit.

SIDNEY: Oh! you are too severe upon her.

EGERTON: I do not think so, Sidney, for she seems a being expressly fashioned by nature to figure in these days of levity and dissipation: her spirits are inexhaustible; her parts strong and lively, with a sagacity that discerns, and a talent not unhappy in pointing out the weak side of whatever comes before her—but what raises her merit to the highest pitch in the laughing world is her boundless vanity and spirits in the exertion of those talents which often render her much more ridiculous than the most whimsical of the characters she exposes. (*In a tone of friendly affection*) And is

---

[1] The former privilege of members of either House of Parliament to have letters bearing their signature sent free of charge.

this a woman fit to make my happiness—this the partner that Sidney would recommend to me for life?—to you, who best know me, I appeal.

SIDNEY: Why Charles, it is a delicate point, unfit for me to determine—besides, your father has set his heart upon the match.

EGERTON: (*Impatiently*) All that I know; but I still ask, and insist upon your candid judgment—is she the kind of woman that you think could possibly contribute to my happiness? I beg you will give me an explicit answer.

SIDNEY: The subject is disagreeable—but, since I must speak—I do not think she is.

EGERTON: (*In a sort of friendly rapture*) I know you do not; and I am sure you will never advise the match.

SIDNEY: I never did. I never will.

EGERTON: (*With a start of joy*) You make me happy—which I assure you I could never be with your judgment against me on this point.

SIDNEY: And yet, Charles, give me leave to observe, that Lady Rodolpha, with all her ridiculous and laughing vanity, has a goodness of heart, and a kind of vivacity that not only entertains, but, upon seeing her two or three times, improves upon you; and, when her torrent of spirits abates, and she condescends to converse gravely —you really like her.

EGERTON: Why, aye! she is sprightly, good humoured, and though whimsical, and often too high in her colouring of characters and in the trifling business of the idle world—yet I think she has principles and a good heart. (*With a glow of conjugal tenderness*) But in a partner for life, Sidney—you know your own precept and your own judgment—affection, capricious in its nature, must have something even in the external manners—nay, in the very mode, not only of beauty, but of virtue itself—which both heart and judgment must approve, or our happiness in that delicate point cannot be lasting.

SIDNEY: I grant it.

EGERTON: And that mode, that amiable essential I never can meet—but in Constantia. You sigh.

SIDNEY: No. I only wish that Constantia had a fortune equal to yours. But pray, Charles, suppose I had been so indiscreet as to have agreed to marry you to Constantia—would she have consented, think you?

EGERTON: That I cannot say positively—but I suppose so.

SIDNEY: Did you never speak to her upon that subject then?

EGERTON: In general terms only—never directly requested her consent in form: (*He starts into a warmth of amorous resolution*) but I will this very moment—for I have no asylum from my father's arbitrary design, but my Constantia's arms. Pray do not stir from hence—I will return instantly. I know she will submit to your advice—and I am sure you will persuade her to my wish, as my life, my peace, my earthly happiness, depend on my Constantia. (*Exit*)

SIDNEY: Poor Charles! he little dreams that I love Constantia too, but to what degree I knew not myself, till he importuned me to join their hands—yes, I love—but must not be a rival; for he is dear to me as fraternal affinity—my benefactor, my friend! and that name is sacred: it is our better self, and ever ought to be preferred—for the man who gratifies his passions at the expence of his friend's happiness wants but a head to contrive—for he has a heart capable of the blackest vice.

Enter BETTY, *running up to* SIDNEY

BETTY: I beg pardon for my intrusion, sir. I hope, sir, I do not disturb your reverence.

SIDNEY: Not in the least, Mrs. Betty.

BETTY: I humbly beg you will excuse me, sir—but—I wanted to break my mind to your honour—about a scruple that lies upon my conscience: and indeed I should not have presumed to trouble you, sir—but that I know you are my young master's friend—and my old master's friend, and my lady's friend—and indeed a friend to the whole family: (*Runs up to him and curtsies very low*) for to give you your due, sir, you are as good a preacher as ever went into a pulpit.

SIDNEY: Ha, ha, ha! do you think so, Mrs. Betty?

BETTY: Aye in truth do I; and as good a gentleman as ever came into a family, and one that never gives a servant a bad word, nor that does any one an ill turn—neither behind their back, nor before their face.

SIDNEY: Ha, ha, ha! why you are a mighty well spoken woman, Mrs.

Betty, and I am mightily beholden to you for your good character of me.

BETTY: Indeed, it is no more than you deserve, and what all the world and all the servants say of you.

SIDNEY: I am much obliged to them, Mrs. Betty.   But pray what are your commands with me?

BETTY: Why, I'll tell you, sir—to be sure I am but a servant, as a body may say; and every tub should stand upon its own bottom—but— (*She takes hold of him familiarly, looks first about cautiously, and speaks in a low familiar tone of great secrecy*) my young master is now in the china room in close conference with Miss Constantia: I know what they are about—but that is no business of mine— and therefore I made bold to listen a little—because, you know, one would be sure—before one took away any body's reputation.

SIDNEY: Very true, Mrs. Betty—very true indeed.

BETTY: O, heavens forbid that I should take away any young woman's good name—unless I had a good reason for it—but, sir, (*With great solemnity*) if I am in this place alive—as I listened, with my ear close to the door, I heard my young master ask Miss Constantia the plain marriage question—upon which I started—and trembled: nay, my very conscience stirred within me so—that I could not help peeping through the keyhole.

SIDNEY: Ha, ha, ha! and so your conscience made you peep through the keyhole, Mrs. Betty?

BETTY: It did indeed, sir: and there I saw my young master upon his knees—lord bless us—kissing her hand as if he would eat it! and protesting—and assuring her, he knew that you, sir, would consent to the match—and then the tears ran down her cheeks so fast—

SIDNEY: Aye!

BETTY: They did indeed—I would not tell your reverence a lie for the world.

SIDNEY: I believe it, Mrs. Betty—and what did Constantia say to all this?

BETTY: Oh! O, she is sly enough; she looks as if butter would not melt in her mouth; but all is not gold that glitters; smooth water, you know, runs deepest—I am sorry my young master makes such a fool of himself; but—um!—take my word for it, he is not the man;

for though she looks as modest as a maid at a christening, (*Hesitating*) yet—ah! when sweethearts meet—in the dusk of the evening—and stay together a whole hour, in the dark grove—and embrace—and kiss—and weep at parting: why then you know, sir, it is easy to guess all the rest.

SIDNEY: Why, did Constantia meet anybody in this manner?

BETTY: (*Starting with surprise*) Oh! heavens! I beg, sir, you will not misapprehend me; for I assure you I do not believe they did any harm—that is, not in the grove—at least, not when I was there—and she may be honestly married for aught I know. O, lud! sir, I would not say an ill thing of Miss Constantia for the world—for to be sure she is a good creature: 'tis true, my lady took her in for charity, and indeed has bred her up to the music and figures—aye, and reading all the books about Homer, and Paradise—and Gods, and Devils, and everything in the world—as if she had been a dutchess: but some people are born with luck in their mouths, and then—as the saying is—you may throw them into the sea: but (*Deports herself most affectedly*) if I had had dancing masters—and music masters—and French mounseers to teach me—I believe I might have read the globes, and the maps—and have danced, and have been as clever as other folks.

SIDNEY: Ha, ha, ha! no doubt on it, Mrs. Betty. But you mentioned something of a dark walk—kissing a—sweetheart—and Constantia.

BETTY: (*Starts into a cautious hypocrisy*) O, lud, sir! I don't know anything of the matter—she may be very honest for aught I know: I only say, that they did meet in the dark walk—and all the servants observe that Miss Constantia wears her stays very loose—looks very pale—is sick in a morning, and after dinner: and, as sure as my name is Betty Hint, something has happened that I won't name—but—nine months hence—a certain person in this family may ask me to stand godmother; for I think I know what's what, when I see it, as well as another.

SIDNEY: No doubt you do, Mrs. Betty.

BETTY: (*Cries, turns up her eyes, and acts a most friendly hypocrisy*) I do, indeed, sir. I am very sorry for Miss Constantia. I never thought she would have taken such courses—for in truth I love her as if she was my own sister; and though all the servants say

that she is breeding—yet, for my part, I don't believe it—but—
one must speak according to one's conscience, you know, sir.

SIDNEY: Oh! I see you do.

BETTY: (*Going and returning*) I do indeed, sir: and so your servant, sir
—but—I hope you won't mention my name in this business, or
that you had any item from me.

SIDNEY: I shall not, Mrs. Betty.

BETTY: For, indeed, sir, I am no busy body, nor do I love fending or
proving;[1] and, I assure you, sir, I hate all tittling and tattling, and
gossipping and backbiting, and taking away a person's good name.

SIDNEY: I observe you do, Mrs. Betty.

BETTY: I do indeed.   I am the farthest from it in the world.

SIDNEY: I dare say you are.

BETTY: I am indeed, sir, and so your humble servant.

SIDNEY: Your servant, Mrs. Betty:

BETTY: (*Aside, in great exultation*) Soh!   I see he believes every word I
say: that's charming—I'll do her business for her, I am resolved.
(*Exit*)

SIDNEY: What can this ridiculous creature mean by her dark walk—
her private spark, her kissing, and all her slanderous insinuations
against Constantia, whose conduct is as unblameable as innocence
itself?   I see envy is as malignant in a paltry waiting wench, as in
the vainest or most ambitious lady of the court.   It is always an
infallible mark of the basest nature; and merit in the lowest, as
well as in the highest station, must feel the shaft of envy's constant
agents—falsehood and slander.

Enter SAM

SAM: Sir, Mr. Egerton and Miss Constantia desire to speak with you in
the china room.

SIDNEY: Very well, Sam.   (*Exit* SAM) I will not see them—what is to
be done? inform his father of his intended marriage? no, that
must not be—for the overbearing nature and ambitious policy of
Sir Pertinax would exceed all bounds of moderation—for he is of
a sharp, shrewd, unforgiving nature.   He has banished one son
already, only for daring to differ from his judgment concerning
the merits of a Scotch and an English historian.[2]   But this young

---

[1] Arguing and discussing.
[2] Cf. Boswell, *ed. cit.*, II, pp. 236–8.

MACKLIN AS SIR PERTINAX MACSYCOPHANT
PORTRAIT by DE WILDE

(By courtesy of the Garrick Club)

man must not marry Constantia—would his mother were here! She, I suppose, knows nothing of his indiscretion—but she shall, the moment she comes hither. I know it will offend him—no matter: it is our duty to offend, when that offence saves the man we love from a precipitate action, which the world must condemn, and his own heart, perhaps, upon reflection, for ever repent. Yes, I must discharge the duty of my function, and of a friend—though I am sure to lose the man, whom I intend to serve. (*Exit*)

END OF THE FIRST ACT

ACT II

Enter CONSTANTIA *and* EGERTON

CONSTANTIA: Mr. Sidney is not here, sir.

EGERTON: I assure you I left him here, and begged he would stay till I returned.

CONSTANTIA: His prudence, you see, sir, has made him retire; therefore we had better defer the subject till he is present—in the mean time, sir, I hope you will permit me to mention an affair that has greatly alarmed and perplexed me: I suppose you guess what it is.

EGERTON: I do not, upon my word.

CONSTANTIA: That is a little strange—you know, sir, that you and Mr. Sidney did me the honour of breakfasting with me this morning in my little study.

EGERTON: We had that happiness, madam.

CONSTANTIA: Just after you left me, upon opening my book of accompts, which lay in the drawer of my reading desk—to my great surprise, I there found this case of jewels, containing a most elegant pair of ear-rings, a necklace of great value, and two bank bills in this pocket book—the mystery of which, sir, I presume you can explain.

EGERTON: I can.

CONSTANTIA: They were of your conveying, then?

EGERTON: They were, madam.

CONSTANTIA: I assure you they startled and alarmed me.

EGERTON: I hope it was a kind alarm—such as blushing virtue feels, when, with her hand, she gives her heart and last consent.

CONSTANTIA: It was not, indeed, sir.

EGERTON: Do not say so, Constantia: come, be kind at once—my peace and worldly bliss depend upon this moment.

CONSTANTIA: What would you have me do?

EGERTON: What love and virtue dictate.

CONSTANTIA: O, sir, experience but too severely proves that such unequal matches as ours never produce aught but contempt and

214

anger in parents, censure from the world, and a long train of sorrow and repentance in the wretched parties—which is but too often entailed upon their hapless issue.

EGERTON: But that, Constantia, cannot be our case: my fortune is independent and ample—equal to luxury and splendid folly. I have a right to choose the partner of my heart.

CONSTANTIA: But I have not, sir—I am a dependant on my lady—a poor, forsaken, helpless orphan. Your benevolent mother found me, took me to her bosom, and there supplied my parental loss with every tender care—indulgent dalliance—and with all the sweet persuasion that maternal fondness, religious precept, polished manners, and hourly example could administer. She fostered me—(*Weeps*) and shall I now turn viper, and with black ingratitude sting the tender heart that thus hath cherished me? shall I seduce her house's heir, and kill her peace? No—though I loved to the mad extreme of female fondness; though every worldly bliss that woman's vanity or man's ambition could desire, followed the indulgence of my love—and all the contempt and misery of this life, the denial of that indulgence—I would discharge my duty to my benefactress—my earthly guardian, my more than parent.

EGERTON: My dear Constantia, your prudence, your gratitude, and the cruel virtue of your self-denial, do but increase my love, my admiration—and my misery.

CONSTANTIA: Sir, I must beg you will give me leave to return these bills and jewels.

EGERTON: Pray do not mention them: sure my kindness and esteem may be indulged so far without suspicion or reproach. I beg you will accept of them—nay—I insist.

CONSTANTIA: I have done, sir: my station here is to obey. I know, sir, they are gifts of a virtuous mind—and mine shall convert to the tenderest and most grateful use.

EGERTON: Hark! I hear a coach—it is my father. Dear girl, retire and compose yourself. I will send Sidney and my lady to you, and by their judgment we will be directed—will that satisfy you?

CONSTANTIA: I can have no will but my lady's. With your leave I will retire—I would not see her in this confusion.

EGERTON: Dear girl, adieu! and think of love, of happiness, and the man who can never be blest without you.

Exit CONSTANTIA: *enter* SAM

SAM: Sir Pertinax and my lady are come, sir, and my lady desires to speak with you in her own room—oh! here she is, sir.   (*Exit*)

Enter LADY MACSYCOPHANT

LADY MACSYCOPHANT: (*In great confusion and distress*) Dear child, I am glad to see you: why did you not come to town yesterday to attend the levee? Your father is incensed to the uttermost at your not being there.

EGERTON: (*With great warmth*) Madam, it is with extreme regret I tell you, that I can no longer be a slave to his temper, his politics, and his scheme of marrying me to this woman—therefore you had better consent at once to my going out of the kingdom, and my taking Constantia with me, for without her I never can be happy.

LADY MACSYCOPHANT: As you regard my peace, or your own character, I beg you will not be guilty of so rash a step—you promised me you never would marry her without my consent.   I will open it to your father: pray, dear Charles, be ruled—let me prevail.

SIR PERTINAX: (*Without, in great anger*) Sir, wull ye do as ye are bid, and haud yeer gab, ye rascal—ye are so full of gab, ye scoondrel. Tak the chesnut gelding, I say, and return till town directly, and see what is become of my Lord Lumbercourt.

LADY MACSYCOPHANT: Here he comes—I will get out of his way.   But I beg, Charles, while he is in this ill humour, that you will not oppose him, let him say what he will—when his passion is a little cool, I will return, and try to bring him to reason: but do not thwart him.

EGERTON: Madam, I will not.   (*Exit* LADY MACSYCOPHANT)

SIR PERTINAX: (*Without*) Here, ye, Tomlins, where is my son Egerton?

TOMLINS: (*Without*) In the library, sir.

SIR PERTINAX: (*Without*) As soon as the lawyers come, be sure bring me word.

Enter SIR PERTINAX *with great haughtiness, and in anger:* EGERTON *bows two or three times most submissively low.*

SIR PERTINAX: Weel, sir—vary weel—vary weel! are na ye a fine spark? are na ye a fine spark, I say?   Ah! ye are a—so ye would na come up till the levee?

216

EGERTON: Sir, I beg your pardon—but—I was not very well; besides, I did not think my presence there was necessary.

SIR PERTINAX: (*Snapping him up*) Sir, it was necessary—I tauld ye it was necessary—and, sir, I mun noo tell ye, that the whole tenor of yeer conduct is maist offensive.

EGERTON: I am sorry you think so, sir; I am sure I do not intend to offend you.

SIR PERTINAX: I care na what ye intend—sir, I tell ye, ye do offend. What is the meaning of this conduct, sir? neglact the levee! 'Sdeath, sir, ye—what is yeer reason, I say, for thus neglacting the levee, and disobeying my commands?

EGERTON: (*With a stifled filial resentment*) Sir, I am not used to levees: nor do I know how to dispose of myself—or what to say, or do, in such a situation.

SIR PERTINAX: (*With a proud, angry resentment*) Zoons! sir, do ye na see what aithers do? gentle and simple—temporal and speeretual —lords, members, judges, generals, and bishops—aw crooding, bustling, and pushing foremost intill the middle of the circle, and there waiting, watching, and striving till catch a leuk or a smile frai the great mon; which they meet wi' an amicable reesebeelety of aspect, a modest cadence of body, and a conceeliating co-opera-tion of the whole mon—which axpresses an offeecious prompti-tude for his service, and indicates that they leuk upon themsels as the suppliant appendages of his power, and the enlisted Swiss of his poleetecal fortune—this, sir, is what ye ought till do—and this, sir, is what I never aince omitted for these five and thratty years— lat wha would be meenister.

EGERTON: (*Aside*) Contemptible!

SIR PERTINAX: What is that ye mutter, sir?

EGERTON: Only a slight reflection, sir, not relative to you.

SIR PERTINAX: Sir, yeer absenting yeersel frai the levee at this juncture is suspeecious; it is leuked on as a kind of disaffaction; and aw yeer country men are heeghly offended at yeer conduct—for, sir, they donna leuk upon ye as a freend or a weel-wisher aither till Scotland or Scotchmen.

EGERTON: (*With a quick warmth*) Then, sir, they wrong me, I assure you—but pray, sir, in what particular can I be charged either with coldness or offence to my country?

SIR PERTINAX: Why, sir, ever sin yeer maither's uncle, Sir Stanley Egerton, left ye this three thoosand pounds a year, and that ye hai, in compleeance wi' his wull, taken up the name of Egerton, they think ye are grown prood: that ye hai estranged yeersel frai the Macsycophants—hai associated wi' yeer maither's family—wi' the opposeetion, and wi' those wha do na wish weel till Scotland—besides, sir, the aither day, in a conversation at dinner at yeer cousin Campbell Mackenzie's, before a whole table full of yeer ain relations, did na ye publicly wish a total extinguishment of aw party, and of aw national distinctions whatever, relative to the three kingdoms? (*With great anger*) And, ye blockheed—was that a prudent wish before so many of yeer ain countrymen? or was it a filial language till haud before me?

EGERTON: Sir, with your pardon, I cannot think it unfilial or imprudent. (*With a most patriotic warmth*) I own I do wish—most ardently wish for a total extinction of all party—particularly that those of English, Irish, and Scotch might never more be brought into contest or competition; unless, like loving brothers, in generous emulation for one common cause.

SIR PERTINAX: Hoo, sir! do ye persist? what! would ye banish aw party, and aw distinction between English, Irish, and yeer ain countrymen?

EGERTON: (*With great dignity of spirit*) I would, sir.

SIR PERTINAX: Then damn ye, sir—ye are nai true Scot. Aye, sir, ye may leuk as angry as ye wull; but again I say—ye are nai true Scot.

EGERTON: Your pardon, sir, I think he is the true Scot, and the true citizen, who wishes equal justice to the merit and demerit of every subject of Great Britain—amongst whom I know but of two distinctions.

SIR PERTINAX: Weel, sir, and what are those? what are those?

EGERTON: The knave—and the honest man.

SIR PERTINAX: Pshaw! redeeculous.

EGERTON: And he, who makes any other—let him be of the North, or of the South—of the East, or of the West—in place, or out of place—is an enemy to the whole, and to the virtues of humanity.

SIR PERTINAX: Aye, sir, this is yeer braither's impudent doctrine—for the which I hai banished him for ever frai my presence, my heart, and my fortune. Sir, I wull hai nai son of mine, because truly he has been educated in an English seminary, presume, under the mask of candour, till speak against his native land, or against my preenciples. [Sir, Scotchmen—Scotchmen, sir—wherever they meet throughoot the globe—should unite and stick together, as it were in a poleetecal phalanx. Sir, the whole world hates us, and therefore we should loove yean anaither.[1]]

EGERTON: I never did—nor do I intend it.

SIR PERTINAX: Sir, I do na believe ye—I do na believe ye. But, sir, I ken yeer connactions and associates; and I ken too ye hai a saucy, lurking prejudice against yeer country—ye hate it—yas, yeer mother, her faimily, and yeer braither, sir, hai aw the same dark, disaffected rankling—and, by that and their politics together, they will be the ruin of ye, themsels, and of aw wha connact wi' them. Hooever, nai mair of that noo—I wull talk at large till ye aboot that anon. In the mean while, sir—notwithstanding yeer contempt of my advice, and yeer disobedience till my commands, I wull convince ye of my paternal attention till yeer welfare, by my management of this voluptuary—this Lord Lumbercourt—whose daughter ye are till marry. Ye ken, sir, that the fallow has been my patron above these five and thratty years.

EGERTON: True, sir.

SIR PERTINAX: Vary weel—and now, sir, ye see, by his prodigality, he is become my dependant; and accordingly I hai made my bargain wi' him—the deevil a baubee he has in the world but what comes through these clutches; for his whole estate, which has three impleecit boroughs[2] upon it—mark—is noo in my custody at nurse; the which estate, on my paying off his debts, and allowing him a life rent of five thoosand pounds per annum, is till be made over till me for my life, and at my death is till descend till ye and yeer issue—the peerage of Lumbercourt, ye ken, wull follow of course—so, sir, ye see there are three impleecit boroughs, the whole patrimony of Lumbercourt, and a peerage at yean slap: why, it is a stroke—a hit—a hit—Zoons! sir, a mon may live a century, and na mak siccan a hit again.

---

[1] This passage is in the 1770 MS., not in the others. It was printed in play-collections and is quoted by Appleton.

[2] Three boroughs returning members to Parliament went with the estate; a valuable property because of bribery and corruption.

EGERTON: It is a very advantageous bargain indeed, sir—but what will my lord's family say to it?

SIR PERTINAX: Why, mon, he cares na guin his faimily were aw at the deevil so his luxury is but gratified—ainly lat him hai his race-horse till feed his vanity—his harridan till drink drams wi' him, scrat his face, and burn his periwig, when she is in her maudlin hysterics—and three or four discontented patriotic dependants till abuse the meenistry, and settle the affairs of the nation, when they are aw intoxicated; and then, sir, the fallow has aw his wishes, and aw his wants—in this world—and the naxt.

Enter TOMLINS

TOMLINS: Lady Rodolpha is come, sir.

SIR PERTINAX: And my lord?

TOMLINS: Not yet, sir—he is about a mile behind, the servants say.

SIR PERTINAX: Lat me ken the instant he arrives.

TOMLINS: I shall, sir. (*Exit*)

SIR PERTINAX: Step ye oot, Charles, and receive Lady Rodolpha: and I desire ye wull treat her wi' as muckle respect and gallantry as possible; for my lord has hinted that ye hai been vary remiss as a loover—so gang, gang and receive her.

EGERTON: I shall, sir.

SIR PERTINAX: Vary weel—vary weel—a guid lad: gang—gang and receive her as a loover should. (*Exit* EGERTON) Hah! I mun keep a deevelish tight hond upon this fallow, I see, or he wull be touched wi' the patriotic frenzy of the times, and run coonter till aw my deseegns—I find he has a strong inclination till hai a judgment of his ain, independent of mine, in aw poleetecal maiters: but as soon as I hai finally settled the marriage wreetings wi' my lord, I wull hai a thorough expostulation wi' my gentleman, I am resolved, and fix him unalterably in his poleetecal conduct. Ah! I am freeghted oot of my wits, lest his maither's faimily should seduce him till desert till their party, which would totally ruin my scheme, and break my heart. A fine time of day for a blockheed till turn patriot—when the character is exploded—marked—proscribed—why, the common people, the vary vulgar, hai foond oot the jest, and laugh at a patriot noo a days—just as they do at a conjuror, a magician, or ainy aither impostor in society.

Enter TOMLINS *and* LORD LUMBERCOURT

TOMLINS: Lord Lumbercourt. (*Exit*)

LORD LUMBERCOURT: Sir Pertinax, I kiss your hand.

SIR PERTINAX: Yeer lordship's maist devoted.

LORD LUMBERCOURT: Why, you stole a march upon me this morning—gave me the slip, Mac; though I never wanted your assistance more in my life—I thought you would have called on me.

SIR PERTINAX: My dear lord, I bag tan millions of pardons for leaving town before ye, but ye ken that yeer lordship at dinner yesterday settled it that we should meet this morning at the levee.

LORD LUMBERCOURT: That I acknowledge, Mac—I did promise to be there, I own.

SIR PERTINAX: Ye did, indeed—and accordingly I was at the levee and waited there till every soul was gone, and, seeing ye did na come, I concluded that yeer lordship was gone before.

LORD LUMBERCOURT: Why, to confess the truth, my dear Mac, those old sinners, Lord Freakish, General Jolley, Sir Anthony Soaker, and two or three more of that set, laid hold of me last night at the opera—and, as the General says, 'from the intelligence of my head this morning', I believe we drank pretty deep ere we departed—ha, ha, ha!

SIR PERTINAX: Ha, ha, ha! nay, guin ye were wi' that party, my lord, I donna wonder at nai seeing yeer lordship at the levee.

LORD LUMBERCOURT: The truth is, Sir Pertinax, my fellow let me sleep too long for the levee. But I wish I had seen you before I left town—I wanted you dreadfully.

SIR PERTINAX: I am heartily sorry that I was na in the way—but on what accoont did ye want me?

LORD LUMBERCOURT: Ha, ha, ha! a cursed awkward affair—and—ha, ha, ha! yet I can't help laughing at it neither—though it vexed me confoundedly.

SIR PERTINAX: Vexed ye, my lord! Zoons, I wish I had been wi' ye —but for heaven's sake, my lord, what was it that could possibly vex yeer lordship?

LORD LUMBERCOURT: Why, that impudent, teasing, dunning rascal, Mahogany, my upholsterer—you know the fellow?

SIR PERTINAX: Perfactly, my lord.

LORD LUMBERCOURT: The impudent scoundrel has sued me up to some damned kind of a—something or other in the law, that I think they call an execution.

SIR PERTINAX: The rascal!

LORD LUMBERCOURT: Upon which, sir, the fellow, by way of asking pardon—ha, ha, ha! had the modesty to wait on me two or three days ago, to inform my honour—ha, ha, ha! as he was pleased to dignify me—that the execution was now ready to be put in force against my honour—but that out of respect to my honour—as he had taken a great deal of my honour's money—he would not suffer his lawyer to serve it, till he had first informed my honour, because he was not willing to affront my honour—ha, ha, ha! a son of a whore!

SIR PERTINAX: I never heard of so impudent a dog.

LORD LUMBERCOURT: Now, my dear Mac—ha, ha, ha! as the scoundrel's apology was so very satisfactory, and his information so very agreeable to my honour—I told him that, in honour, I thought that my honour could not do less than to order his honour to be paid immediately.

SIR PERTINAX: Vary weel, vary weel—ye were as complaisant as the scoondrel till the full, I think, my lord.

LORD LUMBERCOURT: You shall hear; you shall hear, Mac—so, sir, with composure, seeing a smart oaken cudgel that stood very handily in a corner of my dressing room, I ordered two of my fellows to hold the rascal, and another to take the cudgel and return the scoundrel's civility with a good drubbing as long as the stick lasted.

SIR PERTINAX: Ha, ha, ha! admirable—as guid a stroke of humour as ever I heard of—and did they drub him, my lord?

LORD LUMBERCOURT: Most liberally—most liberally, sir. And there I thought the affair would have rested, till I should think it proper to pay the scoundrel—but this morning, just as I was stepping into my chaise, my servants all about me—a fellow, called a tipstaff,[1] stepped up and begged the favour of my footman who threshed the upholsterer, and of the two that held him, to go along with him upon a little business to my Lord Chief Justice.

SIR PERTINAX: The deevil!

LORD LUMBERCOURT: And at the same instant, I, in my turn, was accosted by two other very civil scoundrels, who, with a most

A bailiff or sheriff's officer, whose sign of office was a metal-tipped staff.

insolent politeness, begged my pardon, and informed me that I must not go into my own chaise.

SIR PERTINAX: Hoo, my lord? nai intill yeer ain carriage?

LORD LUMBERCOURT: No, sir—for that they, by the order of the sheriff, must seize it, at the suit of a gentleman—one Mr. Mahogany, an upholsterer.

SIR PERTINAX: An impudent villain!

LORD LUMBERCOURT: It is all true, I assure you; so you see, my dear Mac, what a damned country this is to live in, where noblemen are obliged to pay their debts, just like merchants, cobblers, peasants, or mechanics—is not that a scandal, dear Mac, to the nation?

SIR PERTINAX: My lord, it is na ainly a scandal, but a national grievance.

LORD LUMBERCOURT: Sir, there is not another nation in the world has such a grievance to complain of.   Now in other countries were a mechanic to dun, and tease, and behave as this Mahogany has done, a noble might extinguish the reptile in an instant—and that only at the expence of a few sequins, florins, or louis d'ors, according to the country where the affair happened.

SIR PERTINAX: Vary true, my lord, vary true—and it is monstrous that a mon of yeer lordship's condeetion is na entitled till run yean of these mechanics through the body, when he is impertinent aboot his money: but oor laws shamefully, on these occasions, mak nai distinction of persons amongst us.

LORD LUMBERCOURT: A vile policy indeed, Sir Pertinax—but, sir, the scoundrel has seized upon the house too, that I furnished for the girl I took from the opera.

SIR PERTINAX: I never heard of siccan a scoondrel.

LORD LUMBERCOURT: Aye, but what concerns me most—I am afraid, my dear Mac, that the villain will send down to Newmarket, and seize my string of horses.

SIR PERTINAX: Yeer string of horses? zoos! we mun prevent that at aw events—that would be siccan a disgrace.   I wull dispatch an axpress till town directly, till put a stop till the rascal's proceedings.

LORD LUMBERCOURT: Prithee do, my dear Sir Pertinax.

SIR PERTINAX: Oh! it shall be done, my lord.[1]

LORD LUMBERCOURT: Thou art an honest fellow, Sir Pertinax, upon honour.

SIR PERTINAX: O, my lord, it is my duty till oblige yeer lordship till the utmaist stretch of my abeelety.

Enter TOMLINS

TOMLINS: Colonel Toper presents his compliments to you, sir, and having no family with him down in the country, he and Captain Hardbottle, if not inconvenient, will do themselves the honour of taking a family dinner with you.

SIR PERTINAX: They are twa of oor meeletia officers—does yeer lordship ken them?

LORD LUMBERCOURT: By sight only.

SIR PERTINAX: I am afraid, my lord, they wull interrupt oor business.

LORD LUMBERCOURT: Not at all: I should be glad to be acquainted with Toper; they say he's a damned jolly fellow.

SIR PERTINAX: Oh! deevelish jolly—deevelish jolly: he and the captain are the twa hardest drinkers in the coonty.

LORD LUMBERCOURT: So I have heard: let us have them by all means, Mac; they will enliven the scene.   How far are they from you?

SIR PERTINAX: Just across the meadows—nai half a mile, my lord: a step, a step.

LORD LUMBERCOURT: O, let us have the jolly dogs, by all means.

SIR PERTINAX: My compliments—I shall be prood of their company. (*Exit* TOMLINS)   Guin ye please, my lord, we wull gang and chat a bit wi' the women: I hai na seen Lady Rodolpha sin she returned frai the Bath.   I long till hai a leetle news frai her aboot the company there.

LORD LUMBERCOURT: Oh! she'll give you an account of them, I warrant you.

LADY RODOLPHA: (*Laughing very loudly, without*)   Ha, ha, ha! weel I vow, cousin Egerton, ye hai a vast deal of shrewd humour—but, Lady Macsycophant, which way is Sir Pertinax?

LADY MACSYCOPHANT: (*Without*) Strait forward, madam.

---

[1] Instead of this speech, the 1770 MS. has about thirty lines of dialogue stressing Lord Lumbercourt's concern to pay his gambling debts of honour, and his indifference about what he owes to tradesmen.

LORD LUMBERCOURT: Here the hairbrain comes: it must be her, by the noise.

LADY RODOLPHA: (*Without*) *Allons*—guid folks—follow me—*sans cérémonie*.

Enter LADY RODOLPHA, LADY MACSYCOPHANT, EGERTON, *and* SIDNEY

LADY RODOLPHA: (*Running up to* SIR PERTINAX) Sir Pertinax, yeer maist devoted, maist obsequious, and maist obedient vassal.

SIR PERTINAX: (*Bowing ridiculously low*) Lady Rodolpha, down till the ground, my congratulations and duty attend ye, and I should rejoice till kiss yeer ladyship's footsteps.

LADY RODOLPHA: (*Curtesying very low*) O, Sir Pertinax, yeer humeelety is maist sublimely complaisant—at present, unanswerable; but I shall intensely study till return it, fifty fald.

SIR PERTINAX: Yeer ladyship does me singular honour—weel, madam—ha! ye leuk gaily—weel, and hoo—hoo is yeer ladyship, after yeer jaunt till the Bath?

LADY RODOLPHA: Never better, Sir Pertinax—as weel as youth, health, riotous speerets, and a careless happy heart can mak me.

SIR PERTINAX: I am meeghty glad till hear it, my lady.

LORD LUMBERCOURT: Aye, aye—Rodolpha is always in spirits, Sir Pertinax: *vive la bagatelle* is the philosophy of our family—ha? Rodolpha—ha?

LADY RODOLPHA: Traith it is, my lord; and upon honour I am determined it shall never be changed wi' my consent. Weel, I vow—ha, ha, ha! *vive la bagatelle* would be a maist brilliant motto for the chariot of a belle of fashion. What say ye till my fancy, Lady Macsycophant?

LADY MACSYCOPHANT: It would have novelty at least to recommend it, madam.

LADY RODOLPHA: Which of aw charms is the maist delightful that can accompany wit, taste, loove, or freendship—for novelty I tak till be the true *je ne sçais quoi* of aw worldly bliss. Cousin Egerton, should na ye like to hai a wife wi' *vive la bagatelle* upon her wedding chariot?

EGERTON: Oh! certainly, madam.

LADY RODOLPHA: Yas, I think it would be quite oot of the common, and singularly ailegant.

EGERTON: Indisputably, madam—for as a motto is a word to the wise, or rather a broad hint to the whole world of a person's taste and principles—*vive la bagatelle* would be most expressive at first sight of your ladyship's characteristic.

LADY RODOLPHA: O, Maister Egerton, ye touch my vary heart wi' yeer approbation—ha, ha, ha! that is the vary spirit of my intention, the instant I commence bride. Weel! I am immensely prood that my fancy has the approbation of so sound an understanding, and so polished a taste as that of the aw-accomplished Mr. Egerton.

SIR PERTINAX: Weel—but, Lady Rodolpha, I wanted till ask yeer ladyship some questions aboot the company at the Bath—they say ye had aw the world there.

LADY RODOLPHA: O, yas! there was a vary great mob there indeed—but vary leetle company. Aw *canaille*—except oor ain party. The place was crooded wi' yeer leetle purse-prood mechanics—an odd kind of queer leuking animals that have started intill fortune frai lottery tickets, rich prizes at sea, gambling in a 'Change-Alley, and sic like caprices of fortune; and awa they aw crood till the Bath till learn genteelety, and the names, titles, intrigues and bon-mots of us people of fashion—ha, ha, ha!

LORD LUMBERCOURT: Ha, ha, ha! I know them—I know the things you mean, my dear, extremely well. I have observed them a thousand times, and wondered where the devil they all came from—ha, ha, ha!

LADY MACSYCOPHANT: Pray, Lady Rodolpha, what were your diversions at Bath?

LADY RODOLPHA: Guid traith, my lady, the company were my diversion—and better nai human follies ever afforded; ha, ha, ha! sic a mixture—and sic oddities—ha, ha, ha! a perfact gallimaufry—Lady Kunegunda Mackenzie and I used till gang aboot till every part of this human chaos, on purpose till reconnoitre the monsters and pick up their freevoleties; ha, ha, ha!

SIR PERTINAX: Ha, ha, ha! why that mun hai been a heegh entertainment till yeer ladyship.

LADY RODOLPHA: Superlative and inexhaustible, Sir Pertinax—ha, ha, ha! Madam, we had in yean group a peer and a sharper—a dutchess and a pinmaker's wife—a boarding school miss and her grandmaither—a fat parson, a lean general, and a yellow admiral —ha, ha, ha! aw speaking together—and bawling and wrangling in fierce contention, as if the fame and fortune of aw the parties were till be the issue of the conflict.

SIR PERTINAX: Ha, ha, ha! pray, madam, what was the object of their contention?

LADY RODOLPHA: O, a very important yean, I assure ye—of nai less consequence, madam, than hoo an odd trick at whist was lost, or meeght hai been saved.

OMNES: Ha, ha, ha!

LADY MACSYCOPHANT: Ridiculous!

LORD LUMBERCOURT: Ha, ha, ha! my dear Rodolpha, I have seen that very conflict a thousand times.

SIR PERTINAX: And so hai I, upon honour, my lord.

LADY RODOLPHA: In anaither party, Sir Pertinax—ha, ha, ha! we had what was called the cabinet cooncil, which was composed of a duke and a haberdasher; a red hot patriot and a sneering courtier; a discarded statesman and his scribbling chaplain, wi' a busy, bawling, muckleheeded prerogative lawyer[1]—aw of whom were every meenute ready till gang together by the lugs, aboot the in and the oot meenistry—ha, ha, ha!

SIR PERTINAX: Ha, ha, ha! weel, that is a droll motley cabinet, I vow— vary whimsical upon honour; but they are aw great poleteecians at Bath, and settle a meenistry there wi' as muckle ease as they do the tune of a country dance.

LADY RODOLPHA: Then, Sir Pertinax, in a retired part of the room— in a bye corner—snug—we had a Jew and a bishop—

SIR PERTINAX: A Jew and a bishop! ha, ha! a deevelish guid connaction that—and pray, my lady, what were they aboot?

LADY RODOLPHA: Why, sir, the bishop was striving till convert the Jew —while the Jew, by intervals, was slily picking up intelligence frai the bishop aboot the change in the meenistry, in hopes of making a stroke in the stock.

OMNES: Ha, ha, ha!

SIR PERTINAX: Ha, ha, ha! admirable! admirable!   I honour the

---

[1] One retained on behalf of the royal prerogative, or one practising in an archbishop's prerogative court concerned with testamentary matters.

smouse[1]—hah! it was deevelish clever of him, my lord—deevelish clever.

LORD LUMBERCOURT: Yes, yes—the fellow kept a sharp look out; I think it was a fair trial of skill on both sides, Mr. Egerton.

EGERTON: True, my lord—but the Jew seems to have been in the fairer way to succeed.

LORD LUMBERCOURT: Oh! all to nothing, sir, ha, ha, ha! Well, child, I like your Jew and your bishop much—it's devilish clever: let us have the rest of the history, pray, my dear.

LADY RODOLPHA: Guid traith, my lord, the sum total is—that there we aw danced, and wrangled, and flattered, and slandered, and gambled, and cheated, and mingled, and jumbled, and wolloped[2] together—clean and unclean—even like the animal assembly in Noah's ark.

OMNES: Ha, ha, ha!

LORD LUMBERCOURT: Ha, ha, ha! well, you are a droll girl, Rodolpha, and—upon my honour—ha, ha, ha! you have given us as whimsical a sketch as ever was hit off.

SIR PERTINAX: Ah! yas, my lord, especially the animal assembly in Noah's ark—it is an axcellent picture of the oddities that yean meets wi' at the Bath.

LORD LUMBERCOURT: Why yes, there is some fancy in it, I think, Egerton?

EGERTON: Very characteristic indeed, my lord.

LORD LUMBERCOURT: What say you, Mr. Sidney?

SIDNEY: Upon my word, my lord, the lady has made me see the whole assembly in distinct colours.

LADY RODOLPHA: O, Maister Sidney, yeer approbation maks me as vain as a reigning toast before her leuking-glass. But, Lady Macsycophant, I canna help observing that ye hai yean uncka, unsalutary fashion here in the Sooth, at yeer routs,[3] yeer assemblies, and aw yeer dancing bouts—the which I am astonished ye do na relegate frai amongst ye.

LADY MACSYCOPHANT: Pray, madam, what may that be?

[1] Jew, in contemporary slang.
[2] Scottish dialect: to make noisy and heavy movements.
[3] Large fashionable assemblies, especially evening parties.

LADY RODOLPHA: Why, yeer orgeats, capillaires,[1] lemonades, and aw yeer slips and slops, wi' which ye drench yeer weimbs, when ye are dancing—upon honour, they awways mak a swish-swash in my boowels, and gi' me the wooly-wambles.[2]

OMNES: Ha, ha, ha!

LORD LUMBERCOURT: Ho, ho, ho! you indelicate creature—why, my dear Rodolpha—ha, ha, ha! what are you talking about?

LADY RODOLPHA: Weel, weel, my lord, guin ye laugh till ye brust—the fact is still true. Noo in Edinburgh—in Edinburgh, my lady—we hai nai sic pinch-gut doings—for there, guid traith, we awways hai a guid comfortable dish of cutlets or collops, or a nice warm, savory haggiss,[3] wi' a guid swig of whiskey punch till recruit oor spirits, after oor dancing and sweating.

OMNES: Ha, ha, ha!

SIR PERTINAX: Aye, and that is muckle wholesomer, Lady Rodolpha, than aw their slips and slops here in the Sooth.

LORD LUMBERCOURT: Ha, ha, ha! Well, my dear Rodolpha, you are a droll girl, upon honour—and very entertaining, I vow—(*He whispers*) but, my dear child—a little too much of the dancing, and sweating, and the wooly-wambles.[4]

OMNES: Ha, ha, ha!

Enter TOMLINS

TOMLINS: Colonel Toper and Captain Hardbottle are come, sir.

SIR PERTINAX: Oh! vary weel. Dinner directly.

TOMLINS: It is ready, sir. (*Exit*)

SIR PERTINAX: My lord, we attend yeer lordship.

LORD LUMBERCOURT: Lady Mac, your ladyship's hand, if you please.

(*Exit with* LADY MACSYCOPHANT)

SIR PERTINAX: And here, Lady Rodolpha, is an Arcadian swain that has a hond at yeer ladyship's devotion.

LADY RODOLPHA: (*Giving her hand to* EGERTON) And I, sir, hai yean at his—there, sir—as till hearts, ye ken, cousin, they are na brought intill the accoont of human dealings noo a days.

---

[1] Cooling drinks, flavoured with orange-flower water and made from almonds or syrup of maidenhair fern.

[2] Stomach qualms, collywobbles.

[3] Thick slices of fried or grilled meat: the 'chieftain o' the pudding race', a sheep's stomach stuffed with minced sheep's offal and oatmeal.

[4] Coarse and unrefined speech was regarded as a Scottish characteristic. Cf. *TSS*, pp. 153, 157–8, 233.

EGERTON: O, madam, they are mere temporary baubles, especially in courtship; and no more to be depended upon than the weather, or a lottery ticket.

LADY RODOLPHA: Ha, ha, ha! twa axcellent seemelies, I vow, Mr. Egerton—axcellent! for they illustrate the vagaries and inconstancy of my dissipated heart as axactly as if ye had meant till describe it. (*Exit with* EGERTON)

SIR PERTINAX: Ha, ha, ha! what a vast fund of spirits and guid humour she has, Maister Sidney.

SIDNEY: A great fund indeed, Sir Pertinax.

SIR PERTINAX: Come, lat us till dinner. Hah! by this time to-morrow, Maister Sidney, I hope we shall hai every thing ready for ye till put the last hond till the happiness of your freend and pupil—and then, sir, my cares will be over for this life: for, as till my aither son, I axpect nai guid of him, nor should I grieve, were I till see him in his coffin. But this match—O, it wull mak me the happiest of aw human beings. (*Exeunt*)

END OF THE SECOND ACT

ACT III

Enter SIR PERTINAX *and* EGERTON

SIR PERTINAX: (*In warm resentment*) Zoons! sir, I wull na hear a word aboot it; I insist upon it ye are wrong—ye should hai paid yeer court till my lord, and nai hai scrupled swallowing a bumper or twa, or twanty, till oblige him.

EGERTON: Sir, I did drink his toast in a bumper.

SIR PERTINAX: Yas—ye did; but hoo? hoo?—just as a bairn taks physic —wi' aversions and wry faces, which my lord observed: then, till mend the maiter, the moment that he and the colonel got intill a drunken dispute ye slily slunged[1] awa.

EGERTON: I thought, sir, it was time to go, when my lord insisted upon half-pint bumpers.

SIR PERTINAX: Sir, that was na levelled at ye, but at the colonel, in order till try his bottom; but they aw agreed that ye and I should drink oot of smaw glasses.

EGERTON: But, sir, I beg pardon—I did not choose to drink any more.

SIR PERTINAX: But zoons! sir, I tell ye there was a necessity for yeer drinking mair.

EGERTON: A necessity! in what respect, sir?

SIR PERTINAX: Why, sir, I hai a certain point till carry, independent of the lawyers, wi' my lord, in this agreement of yeer marriage— aboot which I am afraid we shall hai a warm squabble—and there- fore I wanted yeer assistance in it.

EGERTON: But how, sir, could my drinking contribute to assist you in your squabble?

SIR PERTINAX: Yas, sir, it would hai contreebuted—and greatly hai contreebuted till assist me.

EGERTON: How so, sir?

SIR PERTINAX: Nay, sir, it meeght hai prevented the squabble entirely; for as my lord is prood of ye for a son-in-law, and is fond of yeer leetle French songs, yeer stories, and yeer bon-mots, when ye are

[1] Dialect past tense of slink.

231

in the humour—and guin ye had but stayed, and been a leetle jolly—and drank half a score bumpers wi' him, till he got a leetle tipsy—I am sure, when we had him in that mood, we meeght hai settled the point as I could wish it, among oorsels, before the lawyers came; but noo, sir, I do na ken what wull be the consequence.

EGERTON: But when a man is intoxicated, would that have been a seasonable time to settle business, sir?

SIR PERTINAX: The maist seasonable, sir—for, sir, when my lord is in his cups, his suspeecion is asleep—and his heart is aw jollity, fun, and guid fallowship; and, sir, can there be a happier moment than that for a bargain, or till settle a dispute wi' a freend? What is it ye shrug up yeer shoulders at, sir?

EGERTON: At my own ignorance, sir—for I understand neither the philosophy nor the morality of your doctrine.

SIR PERTINAX: I ken ye do na, sir—and, what is worse—ye never wull understand it, as ye proceed:[1] in yean word, Charles, I hai often tauld ye, and noo again I tell ye, aince for aw, that the manœuvres of pleeabeelety are as necessary till rise in the world, as wrangling and logical subtlety are till rise at the bar: why ye see, sir, I hai acquired a noble fortune, a princely fortune—and hoo do ye think I raised it?

EGERTON: Doubtless, sir, by your abilities.

SIR PERTINAX: Doubtless, sir, ye are a blockheed—nai, sir, I'll tell ye hoo I raised it. Sir, I raised it by boowing—by boowing, sir; I never could stand straight in the presence of a great mon, but awways boowed, and boowed, and boowed—as it were by instinct.

EGERTON: How do you mean by instinct, sir?

SIR PERTINAX: Hoo do I mean by instinct? why, sir, I mean by—by—by the instinct of interest, sir, which is the universal interest of monkind. Sir, it is wonderful till think, what a cordial, what an amicable—nay, what an infallible influence, boowing has upon the pride and vanity of human nature. Charles, answer me sin-

---

[1] At this point the 1770 MS. includes a substantial scene, not in the other MSS., in which Sir Hector Mackcrafty attacks such persons as Bolingbroke, Plato, Cicero and Swift for envious hostility to those in power. Much is made of the letter (cf. p. 249 below) reporting the second son's political activities. Sir Hector also viciously abuses his wife and her family for supporting her sons' politics and being hostile to Scotland.

cerely, hai ye a mind till be convinced of the force of my doctrine, by example and demonstration?

EGERTON: Certainly, sir.

SIR PERTINAX: Then, sir, as the greatest favour I can confer upon ye, I'll gi' ye a short sketch of the stages of my boowing—as an excitement, and a landmark for ye till boow by—and as an infallible nostrum for a mon of the world till thrive in the world.

EGERTON: Sir, I shall be proud to profit by your experience.

SIR PERTINAX: Vary weel, sir: sit ye down then, sit ye down here: (*They sit down*) and noo, sir, ye mun recall till yeer thoughts, that yeer grandfather was a mon, whose penurious income of half pay was the sum total of his fortune—and, sir, aw my proveesion frai him was a modicum of Latin, an axpertness in areethmetic, and a short system of worldly coonsel, the principal ingredients of which were, a persevering industry, a rigid œconomy,[1] a smooth tongue, a pleeabeelety of temper, and a constant attention till mak every mon weel pleased wi' himsel.

EGERTON: Very prudent advice, sir.

SIR PERTINAX: Therefore, sir, I lay it before ye—noo, sir, wi' these materials I set oot a raw-boned stripling frai the North, till try my fortune wi' them here in the Sooth; and my first step intill the world was a baggarly clerkship in Sawney Gordon's coonting hoose, here in the city of London, which ye'll say afforded but a barren sort of a prospect.

EGERTON: It was not a very fertile one indeed, sir.

SIR PERTINAX: The reverse, the reverse: weel, sir, seeing mysel in this unprofitable situation, I reflacted deeply: I cast aboot my thoughts morning, noon, and neeght, and marked every mon and every mode of prosperity—at last I concluded that a matrimonial adventure, prudently conducted, would be the readiest gait I could gang for the bettering of my condeetion, and accordingly I set aboot it: noo, sir, in this pursuit, beauty! beauty!—ah! beauty often struck mine een, and played aboot my heart, and fluttered, and beat, and knocked, and knocked, but the deevil an entrance I ever lat it gat—for I observed, sir, that beauty is generally a prood, vain, saucy, axpensive, impertinent sort of a commodity.

EGERTON: Very justly observed, sir.

[1] Cf. p. 52, n. 1, above.

233

SIR PERTINAX: And therefore, sir, I left it till prodigals and coxcombs, that could afford till pay for it; and in its stead, sir—mark—I leuked oot for an auncient, weel-jointured, superannuated dowager—a consumptive, toothless, phthisicky, wealthy widow—or a shreevelled, cadaverous piece of deformity in the shape of an izzard, or an appersiand—or, in short, ainy thing, ainy thing that had the siller, the siller; for that, sir, was the north star of my affactions.   Do ye tak me, sir? was na that reeght?

EGERTON: O, doubtless—doubtless, sir.

SIR PERTINAX: Noo, sor, where do ye think I ganged till leuk for this woman wi' the siller?—na till court, na till playhooses or assemblies—nai, sir, I ganged till the kirk, till the anabaptist, independent, Bradlonian, and Muggletonian meetings;[1] till the morning and evening service of churches and chapels of ease, and till the midnight, melting, conceeliating loove-feasts of the methodists; and there, sir, at last, I fell upon an auld, rich, sour, sleeghted, musty maiden, that leuked—ha, ha, ha! she leuked just like a skeleton in a surgeon's glass case.   Noo, sir, this meeserable object was releegiously angry wi' hersel and aw the world, had nai comfort but in metapheesecal veesions and supernatural deleeriums; ha, ha, ha! sir she was as mad—as mad as a bedlamite.

EGERTON: Not improbable, sir, there are numbers of poor creatures in the same condition.

SIR PERTINAX: O, numbers—numbers.   Noo, sir, this cracked creature used till pray, and sing, and seegh, and groan, and weep, and wail, and gnash her teeth constantly, morning and evening, at the Tabernacle in Moorfields:[2] and as soon as I found she had the siller, aha! guid traith, I plumped me down upon my knees, close by her—cheek by jowl—and prayed, and seeghed, and sung, and groaned, and gnashed my teeth as vehemently as she could do for the life of her; aye, and turned up the whites of mine een, till the strings awmaist cracked again—I watched her motions, handed her till the chair, waited on her home, got maist releegiously intimate wi' her in a week—married her in a fortnight—buried her in a month—touched the siller: and, wi' a deep suit of mourning, a melancholy port, a sorrowful veesage, and a joyful heart, I

---

[1] Extravagant and enthusiastic dissenting sects.
[2] The chief meeting-house (erected 1757) of Whitfield's Calvinistic Methodists.

234

began the world again—and this, sir, was the first boow, that is, the first effactual boow, I ever made till the vanity of human nature—noo, sir, do ye understand this doctrine?

EGERTON: Perfectly well, sir.

SIR PERTINAX: Aye, but was it na reeght? was it na ingenious, and weel hit off?

EGERTON: Certainly, sir, extremely well.

SIR PERTINAX: My next boow, sir, was till yeer ain maither, whom I ran awa wi' frai the boarding school; by the interest of whose faimily I got a guid smart place in the Treasury—and, sir, my vary next step was intill Parliament, the which I entered wi' as ardent and as determined an ambeetion as ever agitated the heart of Caesar himsel. Sir, I boowed, and watched, and hearkened, and ran aboot, backwards and forwards; and attended, and dangled upon the then great mon, till I got intill the vary boowels of his confidence—and then, sir, I wriggled, and wrought, and wriggled, till I wriggled mysel among the vary thick of them: hah! I got my snack of the clothing, the foraging, the contracts, the lottery tickets, and aw the poleetecal bonuses—till at length, sir, I became a much wealthier mon than yean half of the golden calves I had been so long a boowing till; (SIR PERTINAX *rises, and* EGERTON *rises too*) and was na that boowing till some purpose?

EGERTON: It was indeed, sir.

SIR PERTINAX: But are ye convinced of the guid affacts, and of the utility of boowing?

EGERTON: Thoroughly, sir.

SIR PERTINAX: Sir, it is infallible—but, Charles, ah! while I was thus boowing, and wriggling, and raising this princely fortune—ah! I met wi' many heart-sores and disappointments frai the want of leeterature, ailoquence, and aither popular abeeleties. Sir, guin I could but hai spoken in the hoose, I should hai done the deed in half the time; but the instant I opened my mooth there, they aw fell a laughing at me—aw which defeeciencies, sir, I determined, at ainy axpence, till hai supplied by the polished education of a son, wha, I hoped, would yean day raise the hoose of Macsycophant till the heeghest pitch of meenisterial ambeetion. This, sir, is my plan: I hai done my part of it. Nature has done hers: ye are popular, ye are ailoquent; aw parties like and respact ye; and noo, sir, it ainly remains for ye till be diracted—completion follows.

EGERTON: Your liberality, sir, in my education, and the judicious choice you made of the worthy gentleman, to whose virtue and abilities you entrusted me, are obligations I shall ever remember with the deepest gratitude.

SIR PERTINAX: Vary weel, sir: but, Charles, hai ye had ainy conversation yat wi' Lady Rodolpha, aboot the day of yeer marriage—yeer equipage—or yeer domestic establishment?

EGERTON: Not yet, sir.

SIR PERTINAX: Pah! why there again ye are wrong—vary wrong.

EGERTON: Sir, we have not had an opportunity.

SIR PERTINAX: Why, Charles, ye are vary tardy in this business.

LORD LUMBERCOURT: (*Sings without, flushed with wine*) 'What have we with day to do?'

SIR PERTINAX: Oh! here comes my lord.

LORD LUMBERCOURT: (*Sings without*) 'Sons of care, 'twas made for you.'
Enter LORD LUMBERCOURT, *drinking a dish of coffee;* TOMLINS
waiting, with a salver in his hands

LORD LUMBERCOURT: 'Sons of care, 'twas made for you.'—very good coffee indeed, Mr. Tomlins. 'Sons of care, 'twas made for you.' Here, Mr. Tomlins.

TOMLINS: Will your lordship please to have another dish?

LORD LUMBERCOURT: No more, Mr. Tomlins. (*Exit* TOMLINS) Ha, ha, ha! my host of the Scotch pints, we have had warm work.

SIR PERTINAX: Yas; ye pushed the bottle aboot, my lord, wi' the joy and veegour of a Bacchanal.

LORD LUMBERCOURT: That I did, my dear Mac; no loss of time with me: I have but three motions, old boy—charge—toast—fire—and off we go; ha, ha, ha! that's my exercise.

SIR PERTINAX: And fine warm axercise it is, my lord, especially wi' the half-pint glasses.

LORD LUMBERCOURT: Zounds! it does execution point blanc—aye, aye, none of your pimping acorn glasses for me, but your manly, old English, half-pint bumpers, my dear—they try a fellow's stamina at once. But, where's Egerton?

SIR PERTINAX: Just at hond, my lord: there he stands, leuking at yeer lordship's picture.

LORD LUMBERCOURT: My dear Egerton.

EGERTON: Your lordship's most obedient.

LORD LUMBERCOURT: I beg pardon: I did not see you—I am sorry you left us so soon after dinner: had you stayed, you would have been highly entertained. I have made such examples of the commissioner, the captain, and the colonel.

EGERTON: So I understand, my lord.

LORD LUMBERCOURT: But, Egerton, I have slipped from the company for a few moments, on purpose to have a little chat with you. Rodolpha tells me she fancies there is a kind of demur on your side, about your marriage with her.

SIR PERTINAX: A demur! hoo so, my lord?

LORD LUMBERCOURT: Why, as I was drinking my coffee with the women just now, I desired they would fix the wedding night, and the etiquette of the ceremony; upon which the girl burst into a loud laugh, telling me she supposed I was joking, for that Mr. Egerton had never yet given her a single glance or hint upon the subject.

SIR PERTINAX: My lord, I hai been just noo talking till him aboot his shyness till the lady.

Enter TOMLINS

TOMLINS: Counsellor Plausible is come, sir, and Serjeant Eitherside.

SIR PERTINAX: Why then, we can settle the business this vary evening, my lord.

LORD LUMBERCOURT: As well as in seven years—and, to make the way as short as possible, pray, Mr. Tomlins, present your master's compliments and mine to Lady Rodolpha, and let her ladyship know we wish to speak with her directly: (*Exit* TOMLINS) he shall attack her this instant, Sir Pertinax.

SIR PERTINAX: Aye! this is doing business effactually, my lord.

LORD LUMBERCOURT: O, I will pit them in a moment, Sir Pertinax— that will bring them into the heat of the action at once, and save a great deal of awkwardness on both sides. Oh! here your Dulcinea comes, sir.

Enter LADY RODOLPHA, *singing, a music paper in her hand*

LADY RODOLPHA: I hai been learning this air of Constantia: I protest, her touch on the harpsichord is quite brilliant, and really her voice nai amiss. Weel, Sir Pertinax, I attend yeer commands, and yeers, my paternal lord. (LADY RODOLPHA *curtsies very low;*

LORD LUMBERCOURT *bows very low, and answers in the same tone and manner*)

LORD LUMBERCOURT: Why then, my filial lady, we are to inform you that the commission for your ladyship and this enamoured cavalier, commanding you to serve your country, jointly and inseparably, in the honourable and forlorn hope of matrimony, is to be signed this very evening.

LADY RODOLPHA: This evening, my lord!

LORD LUMBERCOURT: This evening, my lady. Come Sir Pertinax, let us leave them to settle their liveries, wedding suits, carriages, and all their amorous equipage, for the nuptial campaign.

SIR PERTINAX: Ha, ha, ha! axcellent! axcellent! weel, I vow, my lord, ye are a great officer—this is as guid a manœuvre till bring on a rapid engagement as the ablest general of them aw could hai started.

LORD LUMBERCOURT: Aye, aye! leave them together; they'll soon come to a right understanding, I warrant you, or the needle and load-stone have lost their sympathy. (*Exit* LORD LUMBERCOURT *and* SIR PERTINAX)

LADY RODOLPHA *stands at that side of the stage, where they went off, in amazement:* EGERTON *is at the opposite side, and, after some anxious emotion, settles into a deep reflection—this part of the scene must be managed by a nice whispering tone of self-conversation mutually observed by the lovers*

LADY RODOLPHA: (*Aside*) Why, this is downreeght tyranny! it has quite damped my spirits—and my betrothed yonder seems planet-struck, too, I think.

EGERTON: (*Aside*) A whimsical situation, mine!

LADY RODOLPHA: (*Aside*) Ha, ha, ha! methinks we leuk like a couple of cautious generals, that are obliged till tak the field, but neither of us seems wulling till come till action.

EGERTON: (*Aside*) I protest, I know not how to address her.

LADY RODOLPHA: (*Aside*) He wull na advance, I see: what am I till do in this affair? guid traith, I wull even do as I suppose many brave heroes hai done before me—clap a guid face upon the maiter, and so conceal an aching heart under a swaggering coontenance. (*As she advances, she points at him, and smothers a laugh; but when she speaks to him, the tone must be loud, and rude on the word 'Sir'*) Sir!

as we hai, by the commands of oor guid fathers, a business of some leetle consequence till transact—I hope ye wull excuse my taking the leeberty of recommending a chair till ye, for the repose of yeer body—in the embarrassed deleeberation of yeer perturbed spirits.

EGERTON: (*Greatly embarrassed*) Madam, I beg your pardon. (*Hands her a chair, then one for himself*) Please to sit, madam. (*They sit down with great ceremony: she sits down first. He sits at a distance from her. They are silent for some time. He coughs, hems, and adjusts himself. She mimics him*)

LADY RODOLPHA: (*Aside*) Aha! he's resolved nai till come too near till me, I think.

EGERTON: (*Aside*) A pleasant interview, this—hem, hem!

LADY RODOLPHA: (*Aside, mimics him to herself*) Hem! he wull na open the congress, I see—then I wull. (*Very loud*) Come! sir! when wull ye begin?

EGERTON: (*Greatly surprised*) Begin! what, madam?

LADY RODOLPHA: Till mak loove till me.

EGERTON: Love, madam?

LADY RODOLPHA: Aye, loove, sir—why, ye hai never said a word till me on the subject; nor cast a single glance at me; nor heaved yean tender seegh; nor even secretly squeezed my loof[1]—noo, sir, though oor fathers are so tyrannical as till dispose of us wi'oot the consent of oor hearts; yat ye, sir, I hope, hai mair humanity than till think of marrying me wi'oot admeenestering some of the preleemenaries usual on those occasions—if nai till my understanding and sentiments, yat till the vanity of my sex, at least, I hope ye wull pay some leetle treebute of ceremony and adulation: that, I think, I have a reeght till axpact.

EGERTON: Madam, I own the reproach is just—I shall therefore no longer disguise my sentiments, but fairly let you know my heart.

LADY RODOLPHA: (*Starts up, and runs to him*) That's reeght—that is reeght, cousin; honourably and affectionately reeght—that is what I like of aw things in my swain. Aye, aye, cousin—open yeer mind frankly till me as a true loover should. But sit ye down, sit ye down again: I shall return yeer frankness and yeer passion, cousin, wi' a melting tenderness, equal till the amorous enthusiasm of an auncient heroine.

[1] Cf. p. 49, n. 3, above.

EGERTON: Madam, if you will hear me—

LADY RODOLPHA: But, remember, ye mun begin wi' fervency—and a maist rapturous vehemency: for ye are till conseeder, cousin, that oor match is na to arise frai the union of hearts, and a long decorum of ceremonious courtship; but is instantly till start at aince—oot of necessity, or mere accident, ha, ha, ha!—like a match in an auncient romance, where, ye ken, cousin, the knight and the damsel are mutually smitten and dying for each aither at first seeght—or by an amorous sympathy before they axchange a single glance.

EGERTON: Dear madam, you entirely mistake—

LADY RODOLPHA: And oor fathers—ha, ha, ha! oor fathers are till be the dark magicians that are till fascinate oor hearts and conjure us together, whether we wull or na.

EGERTON: Ridiculous!

LADY RODOLPHA: So noo, cousin, wi' the true romantic enthusiasm—ye are till suppose me the lady of the enchanted castle, and ye—ha, ha, ha! ye are till be the knight of the sorrowful coontenance—ha, ha, ha! and, upon honour, ye leuk the character admirably—ha, ha, ha!

EGERTON: Rude, trifling creature!

LADY RODOLPHA: Come, sir—why do ye na begin till ravish me wi' yeer valour, yeer vows, yeer knight errantry, and yeer amorous phrenzy. Nay, nay, nay! guin ye do na begin at aince, the lady of the enchanted castle wull vanish in a twankling.

EGERTON: Lady Rodolpha, I know your talent for raillery well—but at present, in my case, there is a kind of cruelty in it.

LADY RODOLPHA: Raillery! upon honour, cousin, ye mistak me quite and clean—I am serious—very serious—aye, and I hai cause till be serious: nay, I wull submit my case even till yeersel. (*Whines*) Can ainy poor lassy be in a mair lamentable condeetion than till be sent four hundred miles, by the command of a positive grandmaither, to marry a mon, wha I find has nai mair affaction for me, than guin I had been his wife these seven years.

EGERTON: Madam, I am extremely sorry—

LADY RODOLPHA: (*Cries and sobs*) But it is vary weel, cousin—I see yeer unkindness and aversion plain enough—and, sir, I mun tell ye fairly, ye are the ainly mon that ever sleeghted my person, or that drew tears frai these een. But—it is vary weel—it's vary weel—I wull return till Scotland to-morrow morning, and lat my grandmaither ken hoo I hai been affronted by yeer sleeghts, yeer contempts, and yeer aversions.

EGERTON: If you are serious, madam, your distress gives me a deep concern—but affection is not in our power; and when you know that my heart is irrecoverably given to another woman, I think your understanding and good nature will not only pardon my past coldness and neglect of you—but forgive me when I tell you, I never can have that honour which is intended me, by a connection with your ladyship.

LADY RODOLPHA: (*Starting up*) Hoo, sir!—are you serious?

EGERTON: (*Rises*) Madam, I am too deeply interested, both as a man of honour and a lover, to act otherwise with you on so tender a subject.

LADY RODOLPHA: And so ye persist in sleeghting me?

EGERTON: I beg your pardon, madam; but I must be explicit—and at once declare, that I can never give my hand where I cannot give my heart.

LADY RODOLPHA: (*In great anger*) Why then, sir, I mun tell ye, that yeer declaration is sic an affront as nai woman of speeret can, or ought till bear—and here I mak a solemn vow never till pardon it, but on yean condeetion.

EGERTON: If that condition be in my power, madam—

LADY RODOLPHA: (*Snaps him up*) Sir, it is in yeer power.

EGERTON: Then, madam, you may command me.

LADY RODOLPHA: (*With a firm peremptory command*) Why then, sir, the condeetion is this: ye mun here gi' me yeer honour, that nai importunity—command—or menace of yeer father—in fine, that nai conseederation whatever—shall induce ye till tak me, Rodolpha Lumbercourt, till be yeer wedded wife.

EGERTON: Madam, I most solemnly promise, I never will.

LADY RODOLPHA: And I, sir, maist solemnly, and sincerely, (*Curtsies*) thank ye—for (*Curtsies*) yeer resolution, and yeer agreeable aversion—ha, ha, ha! for ye hai made me as happy as a poor wretch, reprieved in the vary instant of intended axecution.

EGERTON: Pray, madam, how am I to understand all this?

LADY RODOLPHA: (*With frankness, and a reverse of manners*) Why, sir, yeer frankness and sincerity demand the same behaviour on my side—therefore, withoot farther disguise or ambiguity, ken, sir, that I mysel (*With a deep sigh*) am as deeply smitten wi' a certain swain, as I understand ye are wi' yeer Constantia.

EGERTON: Indeed, madam!

LADY RODOLPHA: (*With an amiable, soft, tender sincerity*) O, sir, notwithstanding aw my shew of courage and mirth, here I stand—as errant a trembling Thisbe as ever seeghed or mourned for her Pyramus—and, sir, aw my axtravagant levity and redeeculous behaviour in yeer presence noo, and ever sin yeer father prevailed on mine till consent till this match, has been a premeditated scheme till provoke yeer gravity and guid sense intill a cordial disgust, and a positive refusal.

EGERTON: Madam, you have contrived and executed your scheme most happily.

LADY RODOLPHA: Then, sin Cupid has thus luckily disposed of ye till yeer Constantia, and me till my swain, we hai naithing till think of noo sir, but till contrive hoo till reduce the inordinate passions of oor parents intill a temper of prudence and humanity.

EGERTON: Most willingly I consent to your proposal.   But, with your leave, madam, if I may presume so far—pray, who is your lover?

LADY RODOLPHA: Why, in that too I shall surprise ye perhaps mair than ever.   In the first place—he is a baggar, and in disgrace wi' an unforgiving father—and in the naxt place, he is— (*Curtsies*) yeer ain braither.

EGERTON: Is it possible?

LADY RODOLPHA: A maist amorous truth, sir—that is, as far as a woman can answer for her ain heart.   (*In a laughing gaiety*)   So ye see, cousin Charles, though I could na mingle affactions wi' ye—I hai na ganged oot of the faimily.

EGERTON: (*A polite rapture; frank*) Madam, give me leave to congratulate myself upon your affection—you could not have placed it upon a worthier object; and whatever is to be our chance in this lottery of our parents, be assured that my fortune shall be devoted to your happiness and his.

LADY RODOLPHA: Generous, indeed, cousin—but nai a whit nobler, I assure ye, than yeer braither Sandy believes of ye—and be assured, sir, that we shall baith remember it, while the heart feels, or the memory retains a sense of gratitude.   But, noo sir, lat me ask yean question—pray, hoo is yeer maither affacted in this business?

EGERTON: She knows of my passion, and will, I am sure, be a friend to the common cause.

LADY RODOLPHA: Ah! that's lucky. Oor first step then mun be till tak her advice upon oor conduct, so as till keep the fathers in the dark till we can hit off some measure that wull wind them aboot till oor ain purpose, and the common interest of oor ain passion.

EGERTON: You are very right, madam, for, should my father suspect my brother's affection for your ladyship, or mine for Constantia, there is no guessing what would be the consequence. His whole happiness depends upon this bargain with my lord; for it gives him the possession of three boroughs, and those, madam, are much dearer to him than the happiness of his children. I am sorry to say it, but, to gratify his political rage, he would sacrifice every social tie that is dear to friend or family. (*Exeunt*)

END OF THE THIRD ACT

ACT IV

Enter SIR PERTINAX *and* COUNSELLOR[1] PLAUSIBLE

SIR PERTINAX: Nai, nai; come awa, Coonsellor Plausible, come awa, I say—lat them chew upon it. Why, Coonsellor, did ye ever see so impertinent, so meddling, and so obstinate a blockheed, as that Serjeant[2] Eitherside? Confoond the fallow—he has put me oot of aw temper.

PLAUSIBLE: He is very positive, indeed, Sir Pertinax—and no doubt was intemperate and rude. But, Sir Pertinax, I would not break off the match notwithstanding; for certainly, even without the boroughs, it is an advantageous bargain both to you and your son.

SIR PERTINAX: But—Zoons! Plausible, do ye think I wull gi' up the nomination till three boroughs? why, I would rather gi' him twanty—nay thratty thoosand pounds in ainy aither part of the bargain—especially at this juncture, when votes are likely till become so valuable. Why, mon, if a certain affair comes on, they wull rise above five hundred per cent.

PLAUSIBLE: You judge very rightly, Sir Pertinax—but what shall we do in this case? for Mr. Serjeant insists that you positively agreed to my lord's having the nomination to the three boroughs during his own life.

SIR PERTINAX: Why yas; in the first sketch of the agreement, I believe I did consent—but at that time, mon, my lord's affairs did na appear till be half so desperate, as I noo find they turn oot. Sir, he mun acquiesce in whatever I demand, for I hai got him intill sic a hobble that he canna exist wi'oot me.

PLAUSIBLE: No doubt, Sir Pertinax, you have him absolutely in your power.

SIR PERTINAX: Vary weel—and ought na a mon till mak his vantage of it?

PLAUSIBLE: No doubt you ought—no manner of doubt. But, Sir

---

[1] Cf. p. 84, n. 2, above.
[2] A member of a superior order of barristers abolished in 1880.

Pertinax, there is a secret spring in this business, that you do not seem to perceive—and which, I am afraid, governs the matter respecting these boroughs.

SIR PERTINAX: What spring do ye mean, Coonsellor?

PLAUSIBLE: Why, this Serjeant Eitherside—I have some reason to think that my lord is tied down by some means or other to bring the serjeant in, the very first vacancy, for one of these boroughs: now that, I believe, is the sole motive why the serjeant is so strenuous that my lord should keep the boroughs in his own power—fearing that you might reject him for some man of your own.

SIR PERTINAX: Odzwuns and death! Plausible, ye are clever—deevelish clever. By the blood, ye hai hit upon the vary string that has made aw this discord—Oh! I see it—I see it noo; but haud, haud —bide a wee bit—a wee bit, mon—I hai a thought come intill my heed—yas—I think, Plausible, wi' a leetle twist in our negociation, this vary string, properly tuned, may be still made till produce the vary harmony we wish for. Yas, yas! I hai it: this serjeant, I see, understands business—and, if I am na mistaken, kens hoo till tak a hint.

PLAUSIBLE: O, nobody better, Sir Pertinax.

SIR PERTINAX: Why then, Plausible, the short road is awways the best wi' sic a mon—ye mun even come up till his mark at aince, and assure him frai me, that I wull secure him a seat for yean of these vary boroughs.

PLAUSIBLE: Oh! that will do, Sir Pertinax—that will do, I'll answer for't.

SIR PERTINAX: And further—I bag ye wull lat him ken that I think mysel obliged till conseeder him in this affair, as acting for me as weel as for my lord—as a common friend till baith—and for the services he has awready done us, mak my special compliments till him: and pray lat this amicable bit of paper be my faithful advocate till convince him of what my gratitude further intends for his great (*Gives him a bank bill*) equity in adjusting this agreement betwixt my lord and me.

PLAUSIBLE: Ha, ha, ha! upon my word, Sir Pertinax, this is noble—aye, aye! this is an eloquent bit of paper indeed.

SIR PERTINAX: Maister Plausible, in aw human dealings the maist effactual method is that of ganging at aince till the vary bottom of a mon's heart—for if we axpact that men should serve us, we mun first win their affactions by serving them. Oh! here they baith come.

Enter LORD LUMBERCOURT *and* SERJEANT EITHERSIDE

LORD LUMBERCOURT: My dear Sir Pertinax, what could provoke you to break off this business so abruptly? you are really wrong in the point—and if you will give yourself time to recollect, you will find that my having the nomination to the boroughs for my life was a preliminary article: I appeal to Mr. Serjeant Eitherside here, whether I did not always understand it so.

EITHERSIDE: I assure you, Sir Pertinax, that in all his lordship's conversation with me upon this business, and in his positive instructions, both he and I always understood the nomination to be in my lord, *durante vita*.

SIR PERTINAX: Why, then, my lord, till shorten the dispute, aw that I can say in answer till yeer lordship is, that there has been a total mistak between us in that point—and therefore the treaty mun end here. I gi' it up—O, I wash my honds of it for ever.

PLAUSIBLE: Well—but gentlemen; gentlemen, a little patience—sure this mistake, some how or other, may be rectified. Prithee, Mr. Serjeant, let you and I step into the next room by ourselves, and reconsider the clause relative to the boroughs, and try if we cannot hit upon a medium that will be agreeable to both parties.

EITHERSIDE: (*With great warmth*) Mr. Plausible, I have considered the clause fully—am entirely master of the question—my lord cannot give up the point. It is unkind and unreasonable to expect it.

PLAUSIBLE: Nay, Mr. Serjeant, I beg you will not misunderstand me. Do not think I want his lordship to give up any point without an equivalent—Sir Pertinax, will you permit Mr. Serjeant and me to retire a few moments to reconsider this point?

SIR PERTINAX: Wi' aw my heart, Maister Plausible; ainy thing till oblige his lordship—ainy thing till accommodate his lordship— ainy thing.

PLAUSIBLE: What say you, my lord?

LORD LUMBERCOURT: Nay, I submit it entirely to you and Mr. Serjeant.

PLAUSIBLE: Come, Mr. Serjeant, let us retire.

LORD LUMBERCOURT: Aye, aye—go, Mr. Serjeant, and hear what Mr. Plausible has to say.

EITHERSIDE: Nay, I'll wait on Mr. Plausible, my lord, with all my heart, but I am sure I cannot suggest the shadow of a reason for altering my present opinion: impossible—impossible.

PLAUSIBLE: Well, well, Mr. Serjeant, do not be positive. I am sure reason, and your client's conveniency, will always make you alter your opinion.

EITHERSIDE: Aye, aye—reason, and my client's conveniency, Mr. Plausible, will always controul my opinion, depend upon it: aye, aye! there you are in the right. Sir, I attend you. (*Exeunt* LAWYERS)

SIR PERTINAX: I am sorry, my lord, axtremely sorry indeed, that this mistak has happened.

LORD LUMBERCOURT: Upon my honour, and so am I, Sir Pertinax.

SIR PERTINAX: But come noo, after aw, yeer lordship mun allow ye hai been in the wrong: come, my dear lord, ye mun allow me that noo.

LORD LUMBERCOURT: How, so, my dear Sir Pertinax?

SIR PERTINAX: Nai aboot the boroughs, my lord, for those I do na mind of a baubee—but aboot yeer distrust of my freendship. Why, do ye think noo—I appeal till yeer ain breast, my lord—do ye think, I say, that I should ever hai sleeghted yeer lordship's nomination till these boroughs?

LORD LUMBERCOURT: Why, really, I do not think you would, Sir Pertinax, but one must be directed by one's lawyer, you know.

SIR PERTINAX: Hah! my lord, lawyers are a dangerous species of animals till hai ainy dependance upon: They are awways starting punctilios and deeffeculties among freends. Why, my dear lord, it is their interest that aw mankind should be at variance: for disagreement is the vary manure wi' which they enrich and fatten the land of leetegation; and as they find that it constantly produces the best crop, depend upon it, they wull awways be sure till lay it on as thick as they can.

LORD LUMBERCOURT: Come, come, my dear Sir Pertinax, you must not be angry with the serjeant for his insisting so warmly on this point —for those boroughs, you know, are my sheet anchor.

SIR PERTINAX: I ken it, my lord—and, as an instance of my promptness to study, and of my acquiescence till yeer lordship's inclination, as I see that this Serjeant Eitherside wishes ye weel, and ye him, I think noo he would be as guid a mon till be returned for yean of those boroughs as could be pitched upon—and as such, I humbly recommend him till yeer lordship's conseederation.

LORD LUMBERCOURT: Why, my dear Sir Pertinax, to tell you the truth, I have already promised him. He must be in for one of them, and that is one reason why I have insisted so strenuously—he must be in.

SIR PERTINAX: And why na? Odzwuns! why na? is na yeer word a fiat? and wull it na be awways so till me? are ye na my freend—my patron—and are we na, by this match of oor cheeldren, to be united intill yean interest?

LORD LUMBERCOURT: So I understand it, Sir Pertinax.

SIR PERTINAX: My lord, it can na be aitherwise: then, for heaven's sake, as yeer lordship and I can hai but yean interest for the future, lat us hai nai mair words aboot these paltry boroughs, but conclude the agreement just as it stands; aitherwise there mun be new wreetings drawn, new consultations of lawyers, new objactions and delays wull arise—creditors wull be impatient and impertinent, so that we shall na finish the Lord kens when.

LORD LUMBERCOURT: You are right, you are right: say no more, Mac, say no more. Split the lawyers—you shall judge the point better than all Westminster-hall could. It shall stand as it is: yes, you shall settle it your own way, for your interest and mine are the same, I see plainly.

SIR PERTINAX: Nai doubt of it, my lord.

LORD LUMBERCOURT: Oh! here the lawyers come.

Enter COUNSELLOR PLAUSIBLE *and* SERJEANT EITHERSIDE

LORD LUMBERCOURT: So, gentlemen—well, what have you done? How are your opinions now?

EITHERSIDE: My lord, Mr. Plausible has convinced me—fully convinced me.

PLAUSIBLE: Yes, my lord, I have convinced him; I have laid such arguments before Mr. Serjeant as were irresistible.

EITHERSIDE: He has indeed, my lord: besides, as Sir Pertinax gives his honour that your lordship's nomination shall be sacredly observed —why, upon a nearer review of the whole matter, I think it will be the wiser measure to conclude the agreement just as it is drawn.

LORD LUMBERCOURT: I am very glad you think so, Mr. Serjeant, because that is my opinion too: so, my dear Eitherside, do you and Plausible dispatch the business now as soon as possible.

EITHERSIDE: My lord, every thing will be ready in less than an hour. Come, Mr. Plausible, let us go and fill up the blanks, and put the last hand to the writings on our part.

PLAUSIBLE: I attend you, Mr. Sarjeant. (*Exeunt* LAWYERS)

LORD LUMBERCOURT: And while the lawyers are preparing the writings, Sir Pertinax, I will go and saunter with the women.

SIR PERTINAX: Do, do, my lord; and I wull come till ye presently.

LORD LUMBERCOURT: Very well, my dear Mac, I shall expect you. (*Exit, singing 'Sons of care'*)

SIR PERTINAX: So! a leetle flattery mixed wi' the finesse of a gilded promise on the yean side, and a *quantum sufficit* of the *aurum palpabile* on the aither, hai at last made me the happiest father in Great Britain. Hah! my heart axpands itself, as it were through every part of my whole body, at the completion of this business, and feels naithing but dignity and elevation—haud, haud! bide a wee, bide a wee! I hai but yean leetle maiter mair in this affair till adjust, and then, Sir Pertinax, ye may dictate till Fortune hersel, and send her till govern feuls, while ye shew and convince the world that wise men awways govern her. Wha's there?

Enter SAM

SIR PERTINAX: Tell my son Egerton, I would speak wi' him here in the library. (*Exit* SAM) Noo I hai settled the grand point wi' my lord, this, I think, is the proper juncture till feel the poleetecal pulse of my spark, and, aince for aw, till set it till the exact measure that I would hai it constantly beat.[1]

Enter EGERTON

SIR PERTINAX: Come hither, Charles.

EGERTON: Your pleasure, sir?

SIR PERTINAX: Aboot twa 'oors sin, I tauld ye, Charles, that I received this latter axpress,[2] complaining of yeer brother's acteevety at an elaction in Scotland against a parteecular freend of mine, which has gi'en great offence; and sir, ye are mentioned in the letter as weel as he: to be plain, I mun roondly tell ye, that on this inter-

---

[1] In the 1770 MS. this speech has a few more lines stressing the son's politics further.
[2] Cf. p. 232, n. 1, above.

view depends my happiness as a father and as a mon; and my affaction till ye, sir, as a son for the remainder of oor days.

EGERTON: I hope, sir, I shall never do any thing either to forfeit your affection, or disturb your happiness.

SIR PERTINAX: I hope so too—but till the point.   The fact is this: there has been a motion made this vary day till bring on the grand affair, which is settled for Friday seven-night—noo, sir, as ye are popular, hai talents, and are weel heard—it is axpected, and I insist upon it, that ye endeavour till atone, sir, for yeer late misconduct, by preparing, and taking a large share in that question, and supporting it wi' aw yeer power.

EGERTON: Sir, I have always divided as you directed, except on one occasion—never voted against your friends, only in that affair—but, sir, I hope you will not so exert your influence as to insist upon my supporting a measure by an obvious, prostituted sophistry, in direct opposition to my character and my conscience.

SIR PERTINAX: Conscience! why, ye are mad! did ye ever hear ainy mon talk of conscience in poleetecal maiters?   Conscience, quotha?   I hai been in Parliament these three and thratty years, and never heard the tarm made use of before—sir, it is an unparliamentary word, and ye wull be laughed at for it—therefore I desire ye wull na offer till impose upon me wi' sic phantoms, but lat me ken yeer reason for thus sleeghting my freends and disobeying my commands.   Sir, gi' me an immediate and an axpleecit answer.

EGERTON: Then, sir, I must frankly tell you, that you work against my nature; you would connect me with men I despise, and press me into measures I abhor; would make me a devoted slave to selfish leaders, who have no friendship but in faction—no merit but in corruption—nor interest in any measure, but their own—and to such men I cannot submit; for know, sir, that the malignant ferment[1] which the venal ambition of the times provokes in the heads and hearts of other men, I detest.

SIR PERTINAX: What are ye aboot, sir? malignant ferment! and venal ambition!   Sir, every mon should be ambeetious till serve his country—and every mon should be rewarded for it: and pray, sir,

---

[1] This passage differs from the versions in the MSS., themselves different: but all attack political venality.

would na ye wish till serve yeer country?   Answer me that—I say, would na ye wish till serve yeer country?

EGERTON: Only shew me how I can serve my country, and my life is hers.   Were I qualified to lead her armies, to steer her fleets, and deal her honest vengeance on her insulting foes—or could my eloquence pull down a state leviathan, mighty by the plunder of his country—black with the treasons of her disgrace, and send his infamy down to a free posterity, as a monumental terror to corrupt ambition, I would be foremost in such service, and act it with the unremitting ardour of a Roman spirit.

SIR PERTINAX: Vary weel, sir! vary weel! the fallow is beside himsel.

EGERTON: But to be a common barker at envied power—to beat the drum of faction, and sound the trumpet of insidious patriotism, only to displace a rival—or to be a servile voter in proud corruption's filthy train—to market out my reason, and my trust, to the party-broker, who best can promise, or pay for prostitution; these, sir, are services my nature abhors—for they are such a malady to every kind of virtue, as must in time destroy the fairest constitution that ever wisdom framed, or virtuous liberty fought for.

SIR PERTINAX: Why, are ye mad, sir? ye have certainly been bit by some mad whig or aither:[1] but noo, sir, after aw this foul-mouthed phrenzy, and patriotic vulgar intemperance, suppose we were till ask ye a plain question or twa: pray, what single instance can ye, or ainy mon, gi' of the poleetecal vice or corruption of these days, that has na been practised in the greatest states, and in the maist virtuous times?   I challenge ye till gi' me a single instance.

EGERTON: Your pardon, sir—it is a subject I wish to decline: you know, sir, we never can agree about it.

SIR PERTINAX: Sir, I insist upon an answer.

EGERTON: I beg you will excuse me, sir.

SIR PERTINAX: I wull na excuse ye, sir.   I insist.

EGERTON: Then, sir, in obedience, and with your patience, I will answer your question.

SIR PERTINAX: Aye! aye! I wull be patient, never fear: come, lat us hai it, lat us hai it.

---

[1] The 1779 MS., instead of this sentence, which is struck out, has a few lines mentioning the Robin Hood and Westminster Forum debating societies.

EGERTON: You shall; and now, sir, let prejudice, the rage of party, and the habitual insolence of successful vice pause but for one moment —and let religion, laws, power herself, the policy of a nation's virtue, and Britain's guardian genius, take a short impartial retrospect but of one transaction, notorious in this land—then must they behold yeomen, freemen, citizens, artizans, divines, courtiers, patriots, merchants, soldiers, sailors, and the whole plebian tribe, in septennial procession, urged and seduced by the contending great ones of the land to the altar of perjury—with the bribe in one hand, and the evangelist in the other—impiously and audaciously affront the Majesty of Heaven, by calling Him to witness that they have not received, nor ever will receive, reward or consideration for their suffrage. Is not this a fact, sir? Can it be denied? Can it be believed by those who know not Britain? Or can it be matched in the records of human policy? Who then, sir, that reflects one moment, as a Briton or a Christian, on this picture, would be conducive to a people's infamy and a nation's ruin?

SIR PERTINAX: Sir, I hai heard yeer rhapsody wi' a great deal of patience—and great astonishment—and ye are certainly beside yeersel. What the deevil business hai ye till trouble yeer head aboot the sins or the souls of aither men? Ye should leave these maiters till the clergy, wha are paid for leuking after them; and lat every mon gang till the deevil his ain way: besides, it is na decent till find fault wi' what is winked at by the whole nation— nay, and practised by aw parties.

EGERTON: That sir, is the very shame, the ruin I complain of.

SIR PERTINAX: Oh! ye are vary young, vary young in these maiters, but axperience wull convince ye, sir, that every mon in public business has twa consciences—a releegious, and a poleetecal conscience. Why, ye see a merchant noo, or a shop-keeper, that kens the science of the world, awways leuks upon an oath at a custom-hoose, or behind a coonter, ainly as an oath in business, a thing of course, a mere thing of course, that has naithing till do wi' releegion—and just so it is at an election: for instance noo—I am a candidate, pray observe, and I gang till a periwig maker, a hatter, or a hosier, and I gi' tan, twanty, or thratty guineas for a periwig, a hat, or a pair of hose; and so on, through a majority of voters—vary weel—what is the consequence? Why, this commercial intercourse, ye see, begats a freendship betwixt us, a commercial freendship—and, in a day or twa these men gang and gi' me their suffrages; weel, what is the inference? Pray, sir, can ye or ainy lawyer, divine, or casuist, caw this a bribe? Nai, sir, in fair poleetecal reasoning, it is ainly generosity on the yean side, and gratitude on the aither—so, sir, lat me hai nai mair of yeer releegious or philosophical refinements, but prepare, attend, and speak till the question; or ye are nai son of mine. Sir, I insist upon it.

Enter SAM

SAM: Sir, my lord says the writings are now ready, and his lordship and the lawyers are now waiting for you and Mr. Egerton.

SIR PERTINAX: Vary weel: we'll attend his lordship. (*Exit* SAM) I tell ye, Charles, aw this conscientious refinement in politics is downright ignorance, and impracticable romance; and, sir, I desire I may hear nai mair of it. Come, sir, lat us gang down and finish this business.

EGERTON: (*Stopping* SIR PERTINAX *as he is going off*) Sir, with your permission, I beg you will first hear a word or two upon this subject.

SIR PERTINAX: Weel, sir, what would ye say?

EGERTON: I have often resolved to let you know my aversion to this match—

SIR PERTINAX: Hoo, sir?

EGERTON: But my respect, and fear of disobliging you, have hitherto kept me silent—

SIR PERTINAX: Yeer aversion! yeer aversion, sir! hoo dare ye use sic language till me? Yeer aversion! leuk ye, sir, I shall cut the maiter vary short—conseeder, my fortune is nai inheritance; aw mine ain acquiseetion: I can mak ducks and drakes of it—so do na provoke me, but sign the articles directly.

EGERTON: I beg your pardon, sir, but I must be free on this occasion, and tell you at once, that I can no longer dissemble the honest passion that fills my heart for another woman.

SIR PERTINAX: Hoo? anaither woman! and, ye villain, hoo dare ye loove anaither woman wi'oot my leave? But what aither woman—wha is she? Speak, sir, speak.

EGERTON: Constantia.

SIR PERTINAX: Constantia! O, ye profligate! what, a creature taken in for charity?

EGERTON: Her poverty is not her crime, sir, but her misfortune: her birth is equal to the noblest—and virtue, though covered with a village garb, is virtue still; and of more worth to me than all the splendour of ermined pride or redundant wealth. Therefore, sir—

SIR PERTINAX: Haud yeer jabbering, ye villain, haud yeer jabbering; none of yeer romance or refinement till me.[1] I hai but yean question till ask ye—but yean question—and then I hai done wi' ye for ever, for ever; therefore think before ye answer. Wull ye marry the lady, or wull ye break my heart?

EGERTON: Sir, my presence shall not offend you any longer: but when reason and reflection take their turn, I am sure you will not be pleased with yourself for this unpaternal passion. (*Going*)

SIR PERTINAX: Tarry, I command ye; and I command ye likewise nai till stir till ye hai gi'en me an answer, a defeenetive answer—wull ye marry the lady, or wull ye na?

EGERTON: Since you command me, sir, know then, that I cannot, will not marry her. (*Exit*)

SIR PERTINAX: Oh! the villain has shot me through the heed! he has cut my vitals! I shall run distracted—the fallow destroys aw my measures, aw my schemes—there never was sic a bargain as I hai made wi' this feulish lord—possession of his whole estate, wi' three boroughs upon it—sax members—why, what an acquiseetion! what consequence! what dignity! what weight till the hoose of Macsycophant! O, damn the fallow—three boroughs, only for sending down sax broomsticks—Oh! meeserable! meeserable! ruined! undone! For these five and twenty years, ever sin this fallow came intill the world, hai I been secretly preparing him for meenisterial dignity—and wi' the fallow's ailoquence, abeeleties, popularity, these boroughs, and proper connactions, he might certainly, in a leetle time, hai done the deed—and sure never were times so favourable; every thing conspires; for aw the auld poleetecal post-horses are broken-winded, and foondered, and canna get on—and as till the rising generation, the vanity of surpassing ain anaither in what they feulishly caw taste and

---

[1] The De Wilde portrait, reproduced opposite p. 212, illustrates this moment in the action.

ailegance, binds them hond and foot in the chains of luxury, which wull awways set them up till the best bidder; so that if they can but get wherewithal till supply their dissipation,[1] a meenister may convert the poleetecal morals of aw sic voluptuaries intill a vote that would sell the nation till Prester John, and their boasted leeberties till the great Mogul[2]—and this opportunity I shall lose by my son's marrying a vartuous baggar for loove! Oh! confoond her vartue! it wull drive me distracted.

END OF THE FOURTH ACT

[1] The 1770 MS. gives some details of their dissipations.
[2] Cf. p. 171, n. 1, above.

ACT V

Enter SIR PERTINAX *and* BETTY HINT

SIR PERTINAX: Come this way, Betty—come this way—ye are a guid girl, and I wull reward ye for this discovery. O, the villain! offer her marriage!

BETTY: It is true, indeed, sir—I would not tell your honour a lie for the world—but in troth it lay upon my conscience—and I thought it my duty to tell your worship.

SIR PERTINAX: Ye are reeght—ye are reeght—it was yeer duty till tell me, and I'll reward ye for it. But ye say Maister Sidney is in loove wi' her too—pray hoo came ye by that intelligence?

BETTY: O, sir, I know when folks are in love, let them strive to hide it as much as they will—I know it by Mr. Sidney's eyes, when I see him stealing a sly side look at her—by his trembling—his breathing short—his sighing when they are reading together—besides, sir, he has made love verses upon her, in praise of her virtue—and her playing upon the music. Aye! and I suspect another thing, sir—she has a sweetheart, if not a husband, not far from hence.

SIR PERTINAX: Wha? Constantia?

BETTY: Aye, Constantia, sir—Lord, I can know the whole affair, sir, only for sending over to Hadley, to farmer Hilford's youngest daughter, Sukey Hilford.

SIR PERTINAX: Then send this instant and get me a parteecular accoont of it.

BETTY: That I will, sir.

SIR PERTINAX: In the mean time, keep a strict watch upon Constantia —and be sure ye bring me word of whatever new maiter ye can pick up aboot her, my son, or this Hadley husband or sweetheart.

BETTY: Never fear, sir. (*Exit*)

SIR PERTINAX: This loove of Sidney's for Constantia is na unlikely— there is something promising in it—yas! I think it is na impossible till convert it intill a special and immediate advantage. It is but trying. Wha's there?—if it misses, I am but where I was.

Act V

SIR PERTINAX: Where is Maister Sidney?

TOMLINS: In the dining room, Sir Pertinax.

SIR PERTINAX: Tell him I would speak wi' him. (*Exit* TOMLINS) 'Tis mair than probable. Spare till speak and spare till speed. Try —try—awways try the human heart: try is as guid a maxim in politics as in war. Why, suppose this Sidney noo should be preevy till his freend Charles's loove for Constantia—what then? guid traith, it is natural till think that his ain loove wull demand the preference—aye, and obtain it too—yas, self—self is an ailo-quent advocate on these occasions, and seldom loses his cause. I hai the general preenciple of human nature at least till encourage me in the axperiment—for ainly mak it a mon's interest till be a rascal, and I think we may safely depend upon his integrity—in serving himsel.

Enter SIDNEY

SIDNEY: Sir Pertinax, your servant—Mr. Tomlins told me you desired to speak with me.

SIR PERTINAX: Yas, I wanted till speak wi' ye upon a vary singular business. Maister Sidney, gi' me yeer hand—guin it did na leuk like flattery, which I detest, I would tell ye, Maister Sidney, that ye are an honour till yeer cloth, yeer country, and till human nature.

SIDNEY: Sir, you are very obliging.

SIR PERTINAX: Sit ye down, Maister Sidney—sit ye down here by me. (*They sit*) My freend, I am under the greatest obligations till ye for the care ye hai taken of Charles. The preenciples—releegious, moral, and poleetecal—that ye hai infused intill him, demand the warmest return of gratitude both frai him and frai me.

SIDNEY: Your approbation, sir, next to that of my own conscience, is the best test of my endeavours, and the highest applause they can receive.

SIR PERTINAX: Sir, ye deserve it; richly deserve it—and noo, sir, the same care that ye hai had of Charles, the same my wife has taken of her favourite Constantia—and sure, never were accomplish-ments, knowledge, or preenciples, social and releegious, infused intill a better nature.

SIDNEY: In truth, sir, I think so too.

SIR PERTINAX: She is besides a gentlewoman, and of as guid a faimily as ainy in this coonty.

SIDNEY: So I understand, sir.

SIR PERTINAX: Sir, her father had a vast estate—the which he dissipated and melted in feastings, and freendships, and charities, hospitalities, and sic kind of nonsense. But to the business—Maister Sidney, I loove ye—yas—I loove ye—and I hai been leuking oot and contriving hoo till settle ye in the world. Sir, I want till see ye comfortably and honourably fixed at the heed of a respectable faimily—and guin ye were mine ain son, a thoosand times—I could na mak a mair valuable present till ye for that purpose, as a partner for life, than this same Constantia—wi' sic a fortune down wi' her as ye yeerself shall deem till be competent—and an assurance of every canonical contingency in my power till confer or promote.

SIDNEY: Sir, your offer is noble and friendly—but though the highest station would derive lustre from Constantia's charms and worth, yet, were she more amiable than love could paint her in the lover's fancy—and wealthy beyond the thirst of the miser's appetite—I could not—would not wed her. (*Rises*)

SIR PERTINAX: Nai wed her! Odzwuns, mon! ye surprise me! why so?—what hinders? (*Rises*)

SIDNEY: I beg you will not ask a reason for my refusal, but—briefly and finally—it cannot be: nor is it a subject I can longer converse upon.

SIR PERTINAX: Weel, weel, weel, sir, I hai done—I hai done—sit down, mon; sit down again—sit ye down. (*They sit*) I shall mention it nai mair—na but I mun honestly confess till ye, freend Sidney, that the match, had ye approved of my proposal, besides profiting ye, would hai been of singular service till me likewise—hooever, ye may still serve me as effactually as guin ye had married her.

SIDNEY: Then, sir, I am sure I will most heartily.

SIR PERTINAX: I believe it, freend Sidney—and I thank ye—I hai nai freend till depend on, but yeersel. My heart is awmaist broke—I canna help these tears—and, till tell ye the fact at aince, yeer freend Charles is struck wi' a maist dangerous malady—a kind of insanity—ye see I canna help weeping when I think of it—in short, this Constantia, I am afraid, has cast an evil eye upon him. Do ye understand me?

SIDNEY: Not very well, sir.

SIR PERTINAX: Why, he is grievously smitten wi' the loove of her—and, I am afraid, wull never be cured wi'oot a leetle of yeer assistance.

SIDNEY: Of my assistance! pray, sir, in what manner?

SIR PERTINAX: In what manner? Lord, Maister Sidney, hoo can ye be so dull? Why, hoo is ainy mon cured of his loove till a wench, but by ganging till bed till her? Noo do ye understand me?

SIDNEY: Perfectly, sir, perfectly.

SIR PERTINAX: Vary weel—noo then, guin ye would but gi' him that hint, and tak an opportunity till speak a guid word for him till the wench—and guin ye would likewise cast aboot a leetle noo, and contrive till bring them together aince—why, in a few days after he would na care a pinch of snuff for her. (SIDNEY *starts up*) What is the maiter wi' ye, mon? What the deevil gars ye start and leuk so astoonded?

SIDNEY: Sir, you amaze me!—In what part of my mind or conduct have you found that baseness, which entitles you to treat me with this indignity?

SIR PERTINAX: Indignity—what indignity do ye mean, sir? Is asking ye till serve a freend wi' a wench an indignity? Sir, am I nai yeer patron and benefactor? Ha?

SIDNEY: You are, sir, and I feel your bounty at my heart—but the virtuous gratitude, that sowed the deep sense of it there, does not inform me that, in return, the tutor's sacred function, or the social virtue of the man must be debased into the pupil's pander, or the patron's prostitute.

SIR PERTINAX: Hoo! what, sir! do ye dispute? are ye na my dependant, ha? and do ye hesitate aboot an ordinary civeelety, which is prac-tised every day by men and women of the first fashion? Sir, lat me tell ye—hooever nice ye may be—there is na a client aboot the court that would na jump at sic an opportunity till oblige his patron.

SIDNEY: Indeed, sir, I believe the doctrine of pimping for patrons, as well as that of prostituting eloquence and public trust for private lucre, may be learned in your party schools—for where faction and public venality are taught as measures necessary to good government and general prosperity—there every vice is to be expected.

SIR PERTINAX: Oho! oho! vary weel! vary weel! fine slander upon meenisters! fine sedeetion against government! O, ye villain! ye —ye—ye are a black sheep—and I'll mark ye—I am glad ye shew yeersel. Yas, yas—ye hai taken off the mask at last—ye hai been in my service for many years, and I never kenned yeer preenciples before.

SIDNEY: Sir, you never affronted them before—if you had, you should have known them sooner.

SIR PERTINAX: It is vary weel—I hai done wi' ye. Aye, aye; noo I can accoont for my son's conduct—his aversion till courts, till meenisters, levees, public business, and his disobedience till my commands. Ah! ye are a Judas—a perfeedious fallow—ye hai ruined the morals of my son, ye villain—but I hai done wi' ye. Hooover, this I wull prophecy at oor parting, for yeer comfort—that guin ye are so vary squeamish aboot bringing a lad and a lass together, or aboot doing sic a harmless innocent job for yeer patron, ye wull never rise in the church.

SIDNEY: Though my conduct, sir, should not make me rise in her power, I am sure it will in her favour, in the favour of my own conscience too, and in the esteem of all worthy men—and that, sir, is a power and a dignity beyond what patrons, or any minister can bestow. (*Exit*)

SIR PERTINAX: What a reegorous, saucy, stiff-necked rascal it is! I see my folly noo—I am undone by my ain policy—this Sidney is the last mon that should hai been aboot my son. The fallow, indeed, has gi'en him preenciples that meeght hai done vary weel among the auncient Romans, but are damned unfit for the modern Britons —weel! guin I had a thoosand sons, I never would suffer ain of these English, university-bred fallows till be aboot a son of mine again—for they hai sic a pride of leeterature and character, and sic saucy, English notions of leeberty continually fermenting in their thoughts, that a mon is never sure of them. Noo, guin I had had a Frenchman, or a foreigner of ainy kind, aboot my son, I could hai pressed him at aince intill my purpose—or hai kicked the rascal oot of my hoose in a twankling. But what am I till do? Zoons! he mun na marry this baggar—I canna sit down tamely under that—stay—haud a wee—by the blood, I hai it— yas—I hai hit upon it. I'll hai the wench smuggled till the heegh-lands of Scotland to-morrow morning—yas—yas—I'll hai her smuggled—

Enter BETTY HINT

BETTY: O, sir—I have got the whole secret out.

SIR PERTINAX: Aboot what?

BETTY: About Miss Constantia. I have just got all the particulars from farmer Hilford's youngest daughter, Sukey Hilford.

SIR PERTINAX: Weel, weel, but what is the story? quick, quick, what is it?

BETTY: Why, sir, it is certain that Miss Constantia has a sweetheart—or a husband—a sort of a gentleman—or a gentleman's gentleman, they don't know which—that lodges at Gaffer Hodges's—and it is whispered about the village that she is with child by him; for Sukey says she saw them together last night in the dark walk—and Miss Constantia was all in tears.

SIR PERTINAX: Zoons! I am afraid this is too guid news till be true.

BETTY: O, sir, 'tis certainly true, for I myself have observed that she has looked very pale for some time past—and could not eat—and has qualms every hour of the day. Yes, yes, sir—depend upon it, she is breeding, as sure as my name is Betty Hint—besides, sir, she has just written a letter to her gallant, and I have sent John Gardener to her, who is to carry it to him in Hadley. Now, sir, if your worship would seize it—see—see, sir—here John comes with the letter in his hand.

SIR PERTINAX: Step ye oot, Betty, and leave the fallow till me.

BETTY: I will, sir. (*Exit*)

Enter JOHN, *with a packet and a letter*

JOHN: (*Putting the packet into his pocket*) There—go you into my pocket. There's nobody in the library, so I'll e'en go through the short way. Let me see—what is the name?—Mel—Meltil—O, no!—Melville, at Gaffer Hodges's.

SIR PERTINAX: What latter is that, sir?

JOHN: Letter, sir?

SIR PERTINAX: Gi' it to me, sir.

JOHN: An't please you, sir, it is not mine.

SIR PERTINAX: Deliver it this instant, sir, or I'll break yeer heed.

JOHN: (*Giving the letter*) There, there, your honour.

SIR PERTINAX: Begone, rascal—this, I suppose, wull lat us intill the whole business.

JOHN: (*Aside*) You have got the letter, old surly, but the packet is safe in my pocket. I'll go and deliver that, however, for I will be true to poor Mrs. Constantia in spite of you.

SIR PERTINAX: (*Reading the letter*) Um—um—'and bless my eyes with the sight of you'—um—um—'throw myself into your dear arms'. Zoons! this latter is invaluable. Aha! madam—yas—this wull do —this wull do, I think. Lat me see, hoo is it diracted—'To Mr. Melville'. Vary weel.

Enter BETTY

SIR PERTINAX: O, Betty, ye are an axcellent wench—this letter is worth a million.

BETTY: Is it as I suspected—to her gallant?

SIR PERTINAX: It is—it is. Bid Constantia pack oot of the hoose this instant—and lat them get a chaise ready till carry her wherever she pleases. But first send my wife and son heether.

BETTY: I shall, sir.

SIR PERTINAX: Do so—begone. (*Exit* BETTY) Aha! Master Charles —I believe I shall cure ye of yeer passion for a baggar noo—I think he canna be so infatuated as till be a dupe till a strumpet. Let me see—hoo am I till act noo?—why, like a true poleeteecian, I mun pretend maist sincerity where I intend maist deceit.

Enter EGERTON *and* LADY MACSYCOPHANT

SIR PERTINAX: Weel, Charles, notwithstanding the misery ye hai brought upon me, I hai sent for ye and yeer maither in order till convince ye baith of my affaction and my readiness till forgi'e— nay, and even till indulge yeer perverse passion—for, sin I find this Constantia has got haud of yeer heart, and that yeer maither and ye think that ye can never be happy wi'oot her, why, I'll nai longer oppose yeer inclinations.

EGERTON: Dear sir, you snatch me from sharpest misery—on my knees let me thank you for this goodness.

LADY MACSYCOPHANT: Let me express my thanks too—and my joy— for had you not consented to his marrying her, we all should have been miserable.

SIR PERTINAX: Weel; I am glad I hai foond a way till please ye baith at last—but, my dear Charles, suppose noo that this spotless vestal— this wonder of vartue—this idol of yeer heart—should be a concealed wanton after aw—or should hai an engagement of marriage or an intrigue wi' anaither mon—I say, ainly suppose it, Charles what would ye think of her?

EGERTON: I should think her the most deceitful, and the most subtle of her sex, and, if possible, would never think of her again.

SIR PERTINAX: Wull ye gi' me yeer honour of that?

EGERTON: Most solemnly, sir.

SIR PERTINAX: Enough! I am satisfied—ye mak me young again—yeer prudence has brought tears of joy frai my vary vitals—I was afraid ye were fascinated by the charms of a crack.[1] Do ye ken this hond?

EGERTON: Mighty well, sir.

SIR PERTINAX: And ye, madam?

LADY MACSYCOPHANT: As well as I do my own, sir—it is Constantia's.

SIR PERTINAX: It is so; and a better evidence it is than ainy that can be gi'en by the human tongue. Here is a warm, rapturous, lascivious latter under the hypocreetical siren's ain hond—her ain hond sir.

EGERTON: Pray, sir, let us hear it.

SIR PERTINAX: Aye, aye—here—tak it and read it yeersel—Eloisa never writ a warmer nor a ranker till her Abelard—but judge yeersels.

EGERTON: (*Reads*) 'I have only time to tell you, that the family came down sooner than I expected, and that I cannot bless my eyes with the sight of you till the evening. The notes and jewels which the bearer of this will deliver to you, were presented to me, since I saw you, by the son of my benefactor'—

SIR PERTINAX: (*Interrupting*) Noo mark!

EGERTON: (*Reads*) 'all which I beg you will convert to your immediate use'—

SIR PERTINAX: Mark, I say.

EGERTON: (*Reads*) 'for my heart has no room for any wish or fortune, but what contributes to your relief and happiness'—

SIR PERTINAX: O Charles, Charles, do ye see, sir, what a dupe she makes of ye?—but mark what follows—

EGERTON: (*Reads*) 'Oh! how I long to throw myself into your dear, dear, arms; to sooth your fears, your apprehensions, and your sorrows'—

SIR PERTINAX: I suppose the spark has heard of yeer offering till marry her, and is jealous of ye.

[1] Prostitute, in contemporary slang.

EGERTON: Sir, I can only say that I am astonished.

LADY MACSYCOPHANT: It is incredible.

SIR PERTINAX: Stay, stay, read it oot—read it oot, pray: ah! she is a subtle deevil.

EGERTON: (*Reads*) 'I have something to tell you of the utmost moment, but will reserve it till we meet this evening in the dark walk'—

SIR PERTINAX: In the dark walk—in the dark walk—ah! an evil-eyed curse upon her! yas, yas! she has been often in the dark walk, I believe—but read on.

EGERTON: (*Reads*) 'In the mean time banish all fears, and hope the best from fortune, and your ever dutiful, Constantia Harrington.'

SIR PERTINAX: There—there's a warm epestle for ye! in short, the hussy, ye mun ken, is married till the fallow.

EGERTON: Not unlikely, sir.

LADY MACSYCOPHANT: Indeed, by her letter, I believe she is.

SIR PERTINAX: Nay, I ken she is: but leuk at the hond—peruse it—convince yeersels.

EGERTON: Yes, yes, it is her hand; I know it well, sir.

SIR PERTINAX: Madam, wull ye leuk at it? perhaps it may be forged.

LADY MACSYCOPHANT: No, sir, it is no forgery—well, after this, I think I shall never trust human nature.

SIR PERTINAX: Noo, madam, what amends can ye mak me for coontenancing yeer son's passion for sic a strumpet? and ye, sir, what hai ye till say for yeer disobedience and yeer phrenzy?   Oh! Charles, Charles—

EGERTON: Pray, sir, be patient; compose yourself a moment: I will make you any compensation in my power.

SIR PERTINAX: Then instantly seegn the articles of marriage.

EGERTON: The lady, sir, has never been consulted; and I have some reason to believe that her heart is engaged to another man.

SIR PERTINAX: Sir, that is nai business of yeers—I ken she wull consent, and that's aw we are till conseeder.   O, here comes my lord.

Enter LORD LUMBERCOURT

LORD LUMBERCOURT: Sir Pertinax, every thing is ready, and the lawyers wait for us.

SIR PERTINAX: We attend yeer lordship.   Where is Lady Rodolpha?

LORD LUMBERCOURT: Giving some female consolation to poor Constantia—why, my lady, ha, ha, ha! I hear your vestal has been flirting.

SIR PERTINAX: Yas, yas, my lord, she is in vary guid order for ainy mon that wants a wife and an heir till his estate intill the bargain.

Enter SAM

SAM: Sir, there is a man below that wants to speak to your honour upon particular business.

SIR PERTINAX: Sir, I canna speak till ainy body noo—he mun come anaither time; haud—stay—what, is he a gentleman?

SAM: He looks something like one, sir—a sort of a gentleman—but he seems to be in a kind of a passion, for when I asked his name, he answered hastily, 'it is no matter, friend—go, tell your master there is a gentleman here that must speak to him directly'.

SIR PERTINAX: Must! ha? vary peremptory indeed; prithee, lat's see him for curiosity's sake.   (*Exit* SAM)

Enter LADY RODOLPHA

LADY RODOLPHA: O, my Lady Macsycophant, I am come an humble advocate for a weeping piece of female frailty, wha bags she may be permitted till speak till yeer ladyship, before ye finally reprobate her.

SIR PERTINAX: I bag yeer pardon, Lady Rodolpha, but it mun na be: see her she shall na.

LADY MACSYCOPHANT: Nay, there can be no harm, my dear, in hearing what she has to say for herself.

SIR PERTINAX: I tell ye, it shall na be.

LADY MACSYCOPHANT: Well, my dear, I have done.

Enter SAM *and* MELVILLE

SAM: Sir, that is my master.

SIR PERTINAX: Weel, sir, what is yeer urgent business wi' me?

MELVILLE: To shun disgrace, and punish baseness.

SIR PERTINAX: Punish baseness! what does the fallow mean?   Wha are ye, sir?

MELVILLE: A man, sir—and one, whose fortune once bore as proud a sway as any within this county's limits.

LORD LUMBERCOURT: You seem to be a soldier, sir.

MELVILLE: I was, sir; and have the soldier's certificate to prove my service—rags and scars. In my heart, for ten long years in India's parching clime, I bore my country's cause, and in noblest dangers sustained it with my sword: at length ungrateful peace has laid me down where welcome war first took me up—in poverty, and the dread of cruel creditors. Paternal affection brought me to my native land, in quest of an only child: I found her, as I thought, amiable as parental fondness could desire; but lust and foul seduction have snatched her from me, and hither am I come, fraught with a father's anger, and a soldier's honour, to seek the seducer and glut revenge.

LADY MACSYCOPHANT: Pray, sir, who is your daughter?

MELVILLE: I blush to own her—but—Constantia.

EGERTON: Is Constantia your daughter, sir?

MELVILLE: She is; and the only comfort that nature, fortune, or my own extravagance had left me.

SIR PERTINAX: Guid traith, then, I fancy ye wull find but vary leetle comfort frai her, for she is nai better than she should be. She has had nai damage in this mansion. I am tauld she is wi' bairn, but ye may gang till Hadley, till yean farmer Hodges's, and there ye may learn the whole story, and wha the father of the bairn is, frai a cheeld they caw Melville.

MELVILLE: Melville!

SIR PERTINAX: Yas, sir, Melville.

MELVILLE: Oh! would to heaven she had no crime to answer, but her commerce with Melville!—no, sir, he is not the man; it is your son, your Egerton, that has seduced her; and here, sir, are the evidence of his seduction.

EGERTON: Of my seduction!

MELVILLE: Of yours, if your name be Egerton.

EGERTON: I am that man, sir; but pray what is your evidence?

MELVILLE: These bills, and these gorgeous jewels, not to be had in her menial state, but at the price of chastity—not an hour since, she sent them—impudently sent them—by a servant of this house—contagious infamy started from their touch.

EGERTON: Sir, perhaps you may be mistaken concerning the terms on which she received them: do you but clear her conduct with respect to Melville, and I will instantly satisfy your fears concerning the jewels and her virtue.

MELVILLE: Sir, you give me new life: you are my better angel. I believe in your words—your looks; know then—I am that Melville.

SIR PERTINAX: Hoo, sir! ye that Melville, that was at farmer Hodges's?

MELVILLE: The same, sir: it was he brought Constantia to my arms; lodged and secreted me—once my lowly tenant—now my only friend. The fear of inexorable creditors made me change my name from Harrington to Melville, till I could see and consult some who once called themselves my friends.

EGERTON: Sir, suspend your fears and anger but for a few minutes; I will keep my word with you religiously, and bring your Constantia to your arms, as virtuous, and as happy as you could wish her. (*Exit with* LADY MACSYCOPHANT)

SIR PERTINAX: The clearing up of this wench's vartue is damned unlucky: I am afraid it wull ruin aw oor affairs again—hooever, I hai yean stroke still in my heed that wull secure the bargain wi' my lord, lat maiters gang as they wull. (*Aside*) But I wonder, Maister Melville, that ye did na pick up some leetle maiter of siller in the Indies; ah! there hai been bonny fortunes snapped up there, of late years, by some of the meeletary blades.

MELVILLE: It is very true, sir: but it is an observation among soldiers, that there are some who never meet with any thing in the service but blows and ill fortune—I was one of those, even to a proverb.

SIR PERTINAX: Ah! 'tis peety, sir, a great peety, noo, that ye did na get a Mogul, or some sic an animal, intill yeer clutches. Ah! I should like to hai the strangling of a Nabob, the rummaging of his gold dust, his jewel closet, and aw his magazines of bars and ingots. Ha, ha, ha!—guid traith noo, siccan a fallow would be a bonny cheeld till bring till this town, and till axheebet him riding on an elephant: upon honour, a mon meeght raise a poll-tax by him, that would gang near till pay the debts of the nation.

Enter EGERTON, CONSTANTIA, LADY MACSYCOPHANT, *and* SIDNEY

EGERTON: Sir, I promised to satisfy your fears concerning your daughter's virtue; and my best proof to you, and all the world, that I think her not only the most chaste, but the most deserving of her sex, is, that I have made her the partner of my heart, and the tender guardian of my earthly happiness for life.

SIR PERTINAX: Hoo! married!

EGERTON: I know, sir, at present, we shall meet your anger; but time, reflection, and our dutiful conduct, we hope, will reconcile you to our happiness.

SIR PERTINAX: Never, never—and could I mak ye, her, and aw yeer issue baggars, I would move hell, heaven, and earth till do it.

LORD LUMBERCOURT: Why, Sir Pertinax, this is a total revolution, and entirely ruins my affairs.

SIR PERTINAX: My lord, wi' the consent of yeer lordship, and Lady Rodolpha, I hai an axpedient till offer, that wull na ainly punish that rebellious villain, but answer every end that yeer lordship and the lady proposed by the intended match wi' him.

LORD LUMBERCOURT: I doubt it much, Sir Pertinax—I doubt it much; but what is it, sir?—what is your expedient?

SIR PERTINAX: My lord, I hai anaither son, and, provided the lady and yeer lordship hai nai objection till him, every article of that rebel's intended marriage shall be amply fulfilled upon Lady Rodolpha's union wi' my younger son.

LORD LUMBERCOURT: Why, that is an expedient indeed, Sir Pertinax—but what say you, Rodolpha?

LADY RODOLPHA: Nay, nay, my lord, as I had nai reason till hai the least affaction till my cousin Egerton, and as my intended marriage wi' him was entirely an act of obedience till my grandmaither, provided my cousin Sandy wull be as agreeable till her ladyship as my cousin Charles here would hai been—I hai na the least objaction till the change. Aye, aye! yean braither is as guid till Rodolpha as anaither.

SIR PERTINAX: I'll answer, madam, for yeer grandmaither—noo, my lord, what say ye?

LORD LUMBERCOURT: Nay, Sir Pertinax, so the agreement stands, all is right again. Come, child, let us begone—aye, aye, so my affairs are made easy, it is equal to me whom she marries—I say, Sir Pertinax, let them but be easy, and rat me, if I care if she concorporates with the Cham of Tartary. (*Exit*)

SIR PERTINAX: As till ye, my Lady Macsycophant, I suppose ye concluded, before ye gave yeer consent till this match, that there would be an end of aw intercourse betwixt ye and me. Live wi' yeer Constantia, madam, yeer son, and that black sheep there—

live wi' them; ye shall hai a jointure, but nai a baubee besides, living or dead, shall ye, or ainy of yeer issue, ever see of mine— and so, my vengeance leeght upon ye aw together.   (*Exit*)

LADY RODOLPHA: Weel, cousin Egerton, in spite of the ambeetious frenzy of yeer father, and the thoughtless dissipation of mine, Don[1] Cupid has at last carried his point in favour of his devotees— but I mun noo tak my leave—Lady Macsycophant, yeer maist obedient—Maister Sidney, yeers—permit me, Constantia, till hai the honour of congratulating mysel on oor alliance.

CONSTANTIA: Madam, I shall ever study to deserve and to return this kindness.

LADY RODOLPHA: I am sure ye wull.   But ah! I neglact my poor Sandy aw this while! and, guid traith, mine ain heart begins till tell me what he feels, and chides me for tarrying so long—I wull there- fore fly till him on the wings of loove and guid news; for I am sure the poor lad is pining wi' the pip of axpactation and anxious jeopardy.   And so, guid folks, I wull leave ye wi' the fag end of an auld North Country wish—May mutual love and guid humour be the guests of yeer hearts, the theme of yeer tongues, and the blithsome subjacts of aw yeer tricksey dreams through the rugged road of this deceitful world; and may oor fathers be an axample till oorsels till treat oor bairns better than they hai treated us. (*Exit*)

EGERTON: You seem melancholy, sir.

MELVILLE: These precarious turns of fortune, sir, will press upon the heart—for, notwithstanding my Constantia's happiness, and mine in hers—I own I cannot help feeling some regret, that my mis- fortunes should be the cause of any disagreement between a father, and the man to whom I am under the most endearing obligations.

EGERTON: You have no share in his disagreement; for had you not been born, from my father's nature, some other cause of his resentment must have happened.   But for a time at least, sir, and, I hope, for life, affliction and angry vicissitudes have taken their leaves of us all—if affluence can procure content and ease, they are within our

---

[1] An abbreviation of *dominus* and a title of respect.   Because, using a variant, Spenser has 'Dan Chaucer' and Shakespeare and others 'Dan Cupid', this last is the usual form of the phrase.

reach. My fortune is ample, and shall be dedicated to the happiness of this domestic circle—

> My scheme, though mocked by knave, coquet, and fool,
> To thinking minds will prove this golden rule;
> In all pursuits, but chiefly in a wife,
> Not wealth, but morals, make the happy life.

FINIS